THE AUTHOR

The author of this book, John B. Toews, was born in Coaldale, Alberta, the son of Abram A. and Helena Toews. Both parents participated in the emigration from Russia. Mr. Toews received his public and high school education in Coaldale, Alberta. He has attended the Mennonite Brethren College of Arts, Tabor College (BA), the University of Colorado (MA, PhD), and Fuller Theological Seminary. He is married and the father of two girls.

A historian by profession, the author's research interests lie in the later Middle Ages and twentieth-century Russian Mennonitism. From 1962 to 1966 he was a member of the history department at the University of Alberta, Calgary. During 1966-67 he has been a research fellow at the Institute for Research in the Humanities at the University of Wisconsin.

Toews' articles and reviews have appeared in such periodicals as the *Canadian Journal of History, Medievalia et Humanistica, Church History, Mennonite Quarterly Review,* and the *Catholic Historical Review.* He has also contributed to *His, The Canadian Mennonite,* and the *Mennonite Brethren Herald.*

LOST FATHERLAND

Studies in
Anabaptist and Mennonite History

Edited by

J. C. Wenger, Ernst Correll, Cornelius J. Dyck, Melvin Gingerich,
Guy F. Hershberger, John S. Oyer, and John H. Yoder

°Out of print.

STUDIES IN ANABAPTIST AND MENNONITE HISTORY

No. 12

LOST FATHERLAND

THE STORY OF THE MENNONITE EMIGRATION FROM SOVIET RUSSIA, 1921 - 1927

By John B. Toews

HERALD PRESS
SCOTTDALE, PENNSYLVANIA

LOST FATHER-LAND

The Story of the Mennonite Emigration from Soviet Russia, 1921-1927

By John B. Toews

HERALD PRESS
SCOTTDALE, PENNSYLVANIA

The Herald Press, Scottdale, Pennsylvania, in cooperation with the
Mennonite Historical Society, Goshen College, Goshen, Indiana, is
publishér of the series, Studies in Anabaptist and Mennonite History.
The Mennonite Historical Society is primarily responsible for the
content of the Studies, and the Herald Press for their publication.

LOST FATHERLAND. THE STORY OF THE MENNONITE EMIGRATION
FROM SOVIET RUSSIA, 1921 - 1927

Copyright ©1967 by Herald Press, Scottdale, Pa. 15683
Library of Congress Catalog Card Number: 67-23294
Printed in the United States

Editor's Foreword

Next to the United States, the land in which the Mennonites most happily lived and prospered was the great country of Russia. Opening her doors to the Mennonites in the 1780's, Russia proved to be a most hospitable country in which this religious Protestant minority was able to develop its genius with remarkable freedom, both religious and civil. The story of this unfolding of Mennonite history in the land of the czars has unfortunately not yet been fully told in English. C. Henry Smith (*The Coming of the Russian Mennonites*) and Frank H. Epp (*Mennonite Exodus*) have written substantial monographs on the nineteenth- and twentieth-century migrations of the Mennonites out of Russia. This new study by John B. Toews delineates with clarity and objectivity the emigration of the Mennonites from Russia, especially from the Ukraine, after World War I. The SAMH editors are happy to include this distinguished monograph in their series. The author indicates in his preface the major sources which he utilized in the preparation of this volume. The Mennonite Historical Society is grateful for the financial assistance of the Canadian Mennonite Relief and Immigration Council (CMRIC) in the publication of this book.

I should also like to express appreciation to C. J. Dyck and Melvin Gingerich of the SAMH Editorial Board for reading the manuscript, as well as to Elizabeth Horsch Bender who read it as a copy editor.

We therefore commend the volume not only to all those interested in the recent history of this major sector of world Mennonitism, but also to those concerned with the tragic story of the suppression of those freedoms which the Mennonites had so long enjoyed in Russia, which loss led to the major emigration in the 1920's.

February 22, 1967   J. C. Wenger

Author's Preface

This study attempts to complete the book on the emigration of the Russian Mennonites originally planned by B. B. Janz. As a former emigration leader Janz hoped to preserve his experiences and memories for posterity in the form of memoirs. The Canadian Mennonite Relief and Immigration Council undertook to sponsor the planned book which, however, could not be completed because of Janz's failing health. At the time of his death he had collected a large amount of historical material relative to the emigration and completed several chapters of his memoirs. In view of the available historical material and because of the crucial importance of this period in the life of the Russian Mennonites, the Council decided to ensure the publication of a book dealing specifically with this dramatic episode. Research on the topic began in the late fall of 1964. A. A. Wiens, a member of the Council, was assigned the task of classifying the material left by B. B. Janz. Just after the completion of his work Mr. Wiens passed away. His work proved indispensable to the completion of this volume and the author should like to acknowledge his indebtedness to the efforts of the late A. A. Wiens.

This undertaking in part represents a sequel to the recent book, *Mennonite Exodus*, by Frank H. Epp. The study is a detailed examination of the dramatic Mennonite emigration from Russia between 1923 and 1927. It attempts to reconstruct the events which led to the breakup of the Russian Mennonite settlements and out of which the forces emerged which alienated the colonists from their homeland and motivated many toward a penniless exodus into a foreign land. The book is particularly concerned with the general bankruptcy confronting the Russian Mennonites during this period, the solutions which they sought for their dilemma, and the internal processes related to the emigration itself. The narrative essentially portrays the failure of the Mennonite dialogue with Bolshevism. This dialogue of

9

survival had social, economic, cultural, and spiritual overtones. While these negotiations were still in progress, the preparations for exodus were made in anticipation of their failure. The Mennonite emigration from Russia, as any episode in history, had its tensions, tragedies, and heroes. Its eventual implementation was largely the work of men willing to sacrifice themselves for the welfare of their constituency. The initiative, persistence, and faith of these individuals in the main accounted for the ultimate success of the movement.

The book is based on materials derived from three major archives, and one collection of personal papers. The first is the A. A. Friesen Archive presently in Bethel College Historical Library, North Newton, Kansas, which provided the most important sources for this investigation. A. A. Friesen, in both his capacity as a member of the *Studienkommission* sent out by the Russian Mennonites and also as manager of the Canadian Mennonite Board of Colonization, received most of the original reports sent from Russia. These were usually dispatched via German diplomatic mail from Kharkov to Berlin, then sent to B. H. Unruh in Karlsruhe, Germany. Unruh had these reports duplicated and sent the original documents to Friesen in Rosthern, Saskatchewan. Since in the course of World War II B. H. Unruh's files were lost or destroyed, the Friesen Archive remains the only extensive primary source collection concerned with the internal aspects of the emigration from Russia. Its completeness leaves little to be desired. The letters and reports, often handwritten on poor quality paper and slightly faded, contain a detailed account of the progress of events in Russia and accurately reflect the historical setting out of which they emerged.

The second major archive which undergirds this study is that of the Reverend B. B. Janz, former emigration leader of the Ukrainian Mennonites. It is presently located in the library of the Mennonite Brethren College of Arts, Winnipeg, Manitoba. A large part of the A. A. Friesen Archive in Bethel College Historical Library has now been duplicated and can be found in the Janz files. The collection contains Janz's entire correspondence after he came to Canada in 1926. Janz's unfinished memoirs, clippings of articles from Russian newspapers, as well as articles written by other participants in the emigration movement can also be found in the archive.

The third significant documentary collection is the archive of the Canadian Mennonite Relief and Immigration Council (formerly the Canadian Mennonite Board of Colonization), housed in the Canadian Mennonite Bible College, Winnipeg, Manitoba. Its materials relate mainly to the role of the North American Mennonites in facilitating the exodus from Russia, though some sections of the correspondence shed considerable light upon the conditions prevailing in the Soviet Union. A portion of the files contains material duplicated from the Friesen Archive in Bethel College.

Finally, the private papers of F. F. Isaak, onetime member of the All-Russian Mennonite Agricultural Union, provided considerable information on the activities of the Mennonites in the RSFSR. In some instances this material could not be found elsewhere. The papers also supplemented the correspondence of the Agricultural Union which has been preserved in the previously mentioned archives.

I am obligated to a number of individuals and institutions for their advice and help in the preparation of this work. I should like to express my appreciation to the Canadian Mennonite Relief and Immigration Council, which not only gave me the assignment but manifested a constant interest in the completion of the project. Its chairman, J. J. Thiessen, and Katherine Hooge, secretary, deserve a special word of thanks. I am particularly grateful for the complete freedom the board granted me to use the B. B. Janz and CMBC archives.

Of considerable importance was the service rendered by the Director of the Bethel College Historical Library, Cornelius Krahn, and the Archivist, John F. Schmidt, who were helpful in suggesting possible source materials. The freedom of movement granted me in the utilization of the library's resources, especially the A. A. Friesen Archive, greatly facilitated the progress of my work. Other individuals who were of assistance include Nelson P. Springer, Goshen College Historical Library; Herbert Giesbrecht, Mennonite Brethren College of Arts; Miss Mary Kliewer, Tabor College Library; A. E. Janzen, Mennonite Brethren Historical Library, Tabor College; Paul Schowalter, Christian Neff Library, Weierhof b. Mannheim; Ernst Crous, Mennonitische Forschungsstelle, Krefeld; and H. F. Klassen, editor, *Die Mennonitische Rundschau*.

I wish to acknowledge special debts of gratitude to the official readers of the manuscript whose corrections and suggestions helped to ensure a more precise account: J. J. Thiessen, chairman of the CMRIC; J. A. Toews, faculty member of the Mennonite Brethren College of Arts, Winnipeg; Gerhard Lohrenz, faculty member of the Canadian Mennonite Bible College, Winnipeg; Cornelius Krahn, Director of Bethel College Historical Library; Alvin J. Miller, faculty member of Cleveland State University and MCC relief representative in Soviet Russia during the 1920's.

I must also mention the faithful secretarial services of Mrs. Mary Gortler who typed the manuscript in all of its preparatory stages.

My debt to my wife Lillian cannot easily be described. The text profited from her numerous valuable suggestions and I profited from her constant encouragement and devotion.

February 1, 1967   John B. Toews

Introduction

By Cornelius Krahn

Forty years ago, Mennonites of Canada who had recently come from Russia, while they were hard at work paying back the debts incurred by their travel and essential farm equipment, began to reflect articulately about their past. Some related their experiences in the form of memoirs. Others wrote monographs describing the settlements they had come from, some of which were published in the *Echo Verlag*. These were moving accounts written with deep emotional involvement and love for what they had left behind. World War I and the following Revolution brought great changes to the country of the czars. The Marxist Revolution, in particular, radically changed the political, social, and economic life of the country accompanied by the uprooting of millions of people. The Mennonites, who had come to Russia more than one hundred years previously and had become prosperous, suffered severely with the Russian middle class during the upheaval and the search for a new society and order. Many found a new "fatherland" in North and South America. Some of these narrated their experiences and hardships while leaving the old world and trying to find a new home, encountering apparently insurmountable pioneer hardships, whether in Canada, which was undergoing a severe depression, or under frontier conditions in South America.

That stage of deep emotional involvement in regard to the loss of a beloved home and in the search for a new one belongs to the past. Not only have the refugees of those years established themselves on prosperous farms, in business enterprises, and in numerous other occupations, but their children have by this time grown into their communities, churches, and the larger environment; and

13

what was dear to their parents has become for them only a remote tale.

The account of what happened in the old country and what caused the migration of some 25,000 to Canada can now be presented, with less emotional involvement, on the basis of a thorough study of all available sources. A beginning in this direction was made recently by Frank H. Epp in *Mennonite Exodus* (D. W. Friesen and Sons, Altona, Manitoba, 1962). His assignment was to write the story of the Canadian Board of Colonization which symbolized Canada's hand extended in welcome to those coming from the land of the czars. The outstanding representative of this welcome was David Toews, who was succeeded by J. J. Thiessen.

John B. Toews has continued the research and presents herewith another aspect of the same event in recent Mennonite history. He deals with the effort of the Mennonites of Russia to help themselves in this dire situation with the support of American Mennonite aid centered around the organization known as the *Verband der Bürger holländischer Herkunft* (Association of Citizens of Dutch Extraction) of the Mennonites of the Ukraine and the *All-Russian Mennonite Agricultural Union* with its headquarters in Moscow. It is primarily the former that is treated in this book. The towering figure involved in this effort was B. B. Janz. He, as well as many of those whom he tried to help in their adjustment to the new life in Russia, ultimately migrated to Canada.

Another recent publication which presents a parallel effort among the Mennonites to care for those seeking new homes centers around B. H. Unruh who had been delegated by the Mennonites of the Ukraine to seek help and guidance in Western countries. Unruh's account, *Fügung und Führung im Mennonitischen Welthilfswerk 1920-1933*, was published in 1966 by the Mennonitischer Geschichtsverein (Weierhof).

These books constitute a milestone in historiography in regard to the development of Mennonite migrations and settlements since World War I. Enough time has elapsed to gather presumably all the basic sources and information in order to present the full account of every aspect of the events which have taken place. In addition to this, a new generation of scholars trained in research have been able to present their findings objectively. John B. Toews demonstrates that he has a thorough understanding not only of recent Mennonite history but also of the Russian Revolution, the civil war which followed, and the early years of communist rule which enables

14

him to see this aspect of Mennonite history in its context. **He has** made full use of the sources and files of B. B. Janz, the Canadian Mennonite Board of Colonization, the Bethel College Historical Library, and other pertinent references. Thus John B. Toews' story presents a more detailed portrayal of the background of *Mennonite Exodus* which led to the migration to Canada.

Toews has covered particularly well the knotty question about the Mennonite involvement in a self-defense effort when bandits molested, tortured, and killed the inhabitants of some Mennonite villages of the Ukraine.

The stage in the Mennonite historiography of Russia has now been set for writing the total history of the coming of the Mennonites to Russia, their spread and contribution in that land, and their migrations prior to and after the Revolution of 1917. The availability of primary and secondary sources dealing with both the Mennonite self-understanding and the environment in which they lived should make it possible to write a total, objective history of the Mennonites in Russia. The monograph by John B. Toews dealing with the post-revolutionary years of Mennonitism in Russia furnishes a significant link in this chain of documentation.

North Newton, Kansas

Abbreviations

This list includes some terms commonly reoccurring in the emigration correspondence between 1921 and 1926, but not always mentioned in their Russian form in the text.

ACBN	*Algemeene Commissie voor Buitenlandsche Nooden* (General Committee for Foreign Emergencies)
AMLV	*Allrussischer Mennonitischer Landwirtschaftlicher Verein* (All-Russian Mennonite Agricultural Union)
AMR	American Mennonite Relief
ARA	American Relief Administration
BA	Board Archive (Canadian Mennonite Board of Colonization)
CEC	Central Executive Committee (Russian Communist Party)
Cheka	*Chrezvychainaya Komissiya* (Extraordinary Commission)
CMBC	Canadian Mennonite Board of Colonization
CMRIC	Canadian Mennonite Relief and Immigration Council
CPR	Canadian Pacific Railway
DMH	*Deutsche Mennoniten-Hilfe* (German Mennonite Aid)
FA	A. A. Friesen Archive
GPU	*Gosudarztvennoe Politicheskoe Upravlene* (State Political Administration)
JA	B. B. Janz Archive
KfK	*Kommission für Kirchenangelegenheiten* (Commission for Church Affairs)
Kombedy	*Komitety Bednoty* (Committees of Poor Peasants)
MCC	Mennonite Central Committee
MFF	*Mennonitische Flüchtlingsfürsorge* (Mennonite Refugee Aid)
Narkomfin	*Narodnyi Komissariat Finansov* (People's Commissariat of Finance)
Narkomindel	*Narodnyi Komissariat Inostrannykh Del* (People's Commissariat of Foreign Affairs)
Narkomnats	*Narodnyi Komissariat po Delam Natsional'nostei* (People's Commissariat of Nationalities)
Narkomprod	*Narodnyi Komissariat Prodovol'stviya* (People's Commissariat of Supply)
Narkomzem	*Narodnyi Komissariat Zemledeliya* (People's Commissariat of Agriculture)
NEP	*Novaya Ekonomicheskaya Politika* (New Economic Policy)
RSFSR	Russian Socialist Federal Soviet Republic
RUSCAPA	Russian-Canadian-American-Passenger Agency
Sovnarkom	*Sovet Narodnykh Komissarov* (Council of People's Commissars)

Stdk.	Studienkommission (Study Commission)
STO	*Sovet Truda i Oborony* (Council of Labor and Defence)
Uk. SSR	Ukrainian Socialist Soviet Republic
VBHH	*Verband der Bürger Holländischer Herkunft* (Union of the Citizens of Dutch Lineage)
VMSR	*Verband der Mennoniten Süd-Russlands* (Union of South Russian Mennonites)

Illustrations

Contents

CHAPTER ONE

Revolution and Terror

In the late eighteenth century Russia received its first Mennonite emigrants. Between 1788 and 1796 these colonists settled on the west side of the Dnieper River in the province of Ekaterinoslav.[1] While playing a relatively small role in a more massive German colonization in Russia, the Mennonite settlers nevertheless regarded themselves as quite distinct from the far more numerous Lutheran and Catholic Germans who joined them in their search for a new homeland. For the majority of the Mennonite colonists, the migration to Russia was closely bound up with a quest for religious liberty. As the descendants of the Anabaptist wing of the Reformation their stress on the separation of church and state and their refusal to bear arms had brought frequent conflict with established authority. For over two centuries their movement had been subjected to severe intolerance and unrelenting harassment. Religious persecution in the Lowlands already launched an eastward Mennonite migration to Prussia prior to 1560. During the second half of the century the severity of Spanish rule contributed to a substantial increase in this exodus from the Netherlands. Religious intolerance and economic restrictions in Prussia soon led to a further eastward movement into the Vistula Valley. When the divisions of Poland brought this area back under Prussian administration, the economic and religious pressures returned, and many Mennonites once again looked for a place of refuge.

Meanwhile Russian territorial expansion southward during the course of the eighteenth century had opened up vast fertile lands for settlement north of the Black Sea and the Sea of Azov. Empress Catherine II, anxious to develop the area which later became the breadbasket of Russia, issued two decrees early in her reign inviting foreign colonization. The terms of settlement proved exceedingly generous. Particularly important for the Mennonites were the broad religious and educational freedoms granted the colonists, especially the perpetual exemption from military service. The opportunity to enter Russia emerged at the very moment when Prussian censures of the Mennonites reached their apex. Neither the hazards of the long journey nor the prospects of a rugged frontier life deterred the colonists. Well over 450 families eventually established themselves in the eighteen villages composing Chortitza, which in recognition of its seniority among Mennonite settlements was often called the Old Colony. A second settlement established in the first years of the nineteenth century lay approximately one hundred miles to the southeast. It straddled the Molochnaya River in Taurida province and consequently was simply referred to as the Molotschna. Both colonies had attained considerable economic affluence by the mid-nineteenth century. A shortage of available land led to the establishment of a number of daughter colonies in the Ukraine and elsewhere in Russia by the Chortitza-Molotschna settlements during the second half of the nineteenth century. In addition several settlements were founded by new emigrants arriving from Prussia, where a constitutional revision introduced a universal military conscription allowing no exemptions.

The pioneer years naturally brought with them the hardships of frontier life. Gradually, however, the efficient exploitation of rich agricultural lands as well as the emergence of factories often growing out of cottage industry, brought greater economic affluence to the new settlers. By 1914 the Russian Mennonites boasted comparatively large landholdings, a number of sizable factories usually specializing in the production of agricultural equipment or brick, a modern flour-milling industry, and the facilities for producing such basic necessities as cloth, furniture, and processed foodstuffs. Economic growth brought with it some of the characteristic features of capitalism including hereditary factory and land ownership and the exploitation of a landless proletariat for low cost labor. In general, the Russian Mennonites solved the economic and social tensions emerging within their settlements reasonably well. A gradual religious reawakening after 1860 probably contributed toward a positive change in the prevailing attitudes toward social justice and unfair economic practices. In the field of education the Russian Mennonites privately supported a vast educational complex beginning on the elementary level and culminating in two teachers colleges and an eight-year business college. Hospitals, a mental institution, a school for mutes, an orphanage, and a deaconess home provided impressive evidence of a well-developed social conscience. For a large part of the Russian Mennonite constituency the immediate prewar period was, with some exceptions, a golden age. In 1914 few of the inhabitants of the Mennonite colonies ever imagined that within the next two decades their settlements and way of life would come to a disastrous if protracted end.

The accumulation of unresolved tensions progressed rapidly in czarist Russia during the second half of the nineteenth century and the first years of the twentieth. In most cases the Mennonite colonies, because of their geographic distance from the capital and their overall agricultural character, remained sheltered from the heavy hand of absolutism and the entrenched and inefficient bureaucracy on which it rested. Their remarkable degree of independence in matters of local government, education, religion, and economic development as well as their exemption from military service in part protected them from the tragic fate of economic enslavement to which the Russian peasantry and industrial proletariat had been subjected. The Mennonites had nevertheless experienced sharp pressure in at least two areas prior to 1914. A czarist decree introducing universal military conscription as well as a strong emphasis on Russianization led to the exodus of almost one third of the Mennonite population to the United States and Canada between 1874 and 1880. In view of the widespread Mennonite opposition to direct military involvement the Russian government made provision for alternative service in forestry and industrial work or, in time of war, in a noncombatant medical service *(Sanitätsdienst),* later incorporated into the Red Cross and similar agencies.[2] Russianization affected the Mennonites more directly. Schools were placed under closer state supervision and Russian, with some exceptions, became the official language of instruction. The uncompromising nationality policy of czarist Russia eased somewhat after the Revolution of 1905, which brought to Russia a very limited representative assembly known as the duma.

The threat of war and its actual outbreak brought a revival of Russian nationalism and a renewed demand for conformity. An inevitable hate campaign against the German minority in Russia erupted. A decree published on November 3, 1914, prohibited the use of the German language in either public assembly or press. In February and December of the following year special property liquidation laws were enacted by which all German property owners were compelled to sell their holdings within eight months. Internal unrest and the burden of the war prevented the widespread enactment of the laws. In the face of such outright discrimination the Mennonites, true to their historic commitment to peace, nevertheless endeavored to heal the wounds of war. All men up to the age of forty-five were inducted either into the forestry service or into the noncombatant medical service. The sacrifices made by the Mennonite young men received little official recognition. Their demonstration of loyalty toward Russia went unheeded. Since Germany was Russia's enemy, the Germans in Russia could not expect fair treatment. Government officials as well as the czarist police encouraged a widespread smear campaign designed to incriminate the German colonists as a whole. The Mennonites were not exempt from such proceedings. Regional newspapers frequently carried anti-Mennonite propaganda. Close police supervision was always in evidence. Every act by which the colonists tried to prove their loyalty was misconstrued to make them appear guilty of collaborating with the enemy.[3] The overthrow of Czar Nicholas II in February 1917 and the setting up of a liberal-minded interim government advocating a lenient minority policy momentarily promised some relief to the hard-pressed colonists.

The Ukraine Under the Bolshevik Soviets (November 1917 - April 1918)

As it turned out, the February Revolution of 1917 had little direct influence on the Mennonites since the Provisional Government it brought to power was committed to a continuation of the war. Furthermore, it refused to act decisively and was plagued by internal disunity. Mennonite men in the forestry and medical service began returning to their homes and farms in the Ukraine only after the Bolshevik seizure of power in November 1917 and the signing of the treaty of Brest Litovsk. Most were dramatically introduced to the new political order soon after they had reached their destination. Mennonite local self-government, which had endured for more than a century, suddenly came to an abrupt end. The revolution theoretically gave all authority to local soviets (councils) of workers and peasants. These soviets, composed largely of the poorer and propertyless elements of society, were naturally eager to exploit their newly acquired rights for the betterment of their economic position. Most of the small volosts (administrative subdivisions) in which the Mennonite settlements were located were now under the jurisdiction of a soviet. The new political structure, while initially of brief duration, was costly to the colonists. On one occasion, for instance, the Chortitza Soviet demanded a tribute of

A **Mennonite** court in session in the regional offices at Halbstadt around 1912. The members of the court were elected by the **Volost** Assembly and wore special badges while in session. The existence of such a court illustrated the degree of local self-government enjoyed by the colonists.

two million rubles from the inhabitants of the volost payable in three days. To ensure the payment of the levy several hostages were taken.[4] In the Halbstadt volost the overall losses approached three and one-half million rubles.[5] Almost everywhere lawless elements created a reign of terror characterized by violence, plunder, and murder. Red Guards engaged in a widespread requisitioning of clothing, food, horses, and available currency. Forcible delivery of grain to mills now confiscated and run by the state soon depleted stockpiles. In addition to this a tax of some 2,000 rubles was levied on all large farms. Civil order was not restored until German troops entered the Ukraine in April 1918.

The German Occupation and the Emergence of the Selbstschutz (April 1918 - November 1918)

The peace talks at Brest Litovsk produced an unexpected turn of events for the Ukraine. The Ukrainian Rada, acting on behalf of a newly created autonomous Ukrainian Republic, signed a treaty of peace with the Germans early in 1918. Somewhat later, on March 3, 1918, the Bolsheviks submitted to the treaty of Brest Litovsk; by its terms Lenin's government lost the Ukraine. German troops, assisted by Don-Cossack regiments, moved into the area. The occupation forces were welcomed by the Mennonite colonists, since their presence promised some respite from the prevailing terror.[6] The summer of 1918 passed orderly and quietly. Agricultural and industrial activity gradually revived. Unfortunately the superficial glamour of militarism and Germanism soon captured the fancy of some of the Mennonite youth, and before long some of these were participating in military parades and drills with the occupation troops.

The presence of German troops in the Ukrainian Mennonite settlements had some bearing on the emergence of the loosely knit, semimilitary Mennonite organization known as the *Selbstschutz* (self-protection), whose chief function was protection and self-defense. The precise origins of the movement are somewhat nebulous. In part it reflected a spirit of militarism fostered by the occupation forces; in part it constituted a spontaneous, elemental response to the prevailing civil unrest and lack of public safety. Some units of the *Selbstschutz* seem to have existed prior to the German occupation. Shortly after the Bolshevik seizure of power in the Ukraine, armed robber bands in the area embarked on a reign of terror under the pretext of launching a new political order.

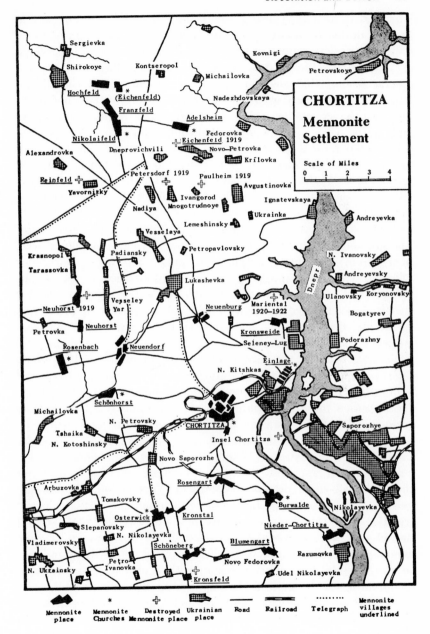

CHORTITZA
Mennonite
Settlement

Scale of Miles
0   1   2   3   4

Sergievka
Shirokoye
Kontseropol
Kovnigi
Michailovka
Petrovskoye
Hochfeld
(Eichenfeld)
Nadezhdovskaya
Franzfeld
Adelsheim
Nikolaifeld
Fedorovka
Eichenfeld 1919
Alexandrovka
Dneprovichvili
Novo–Petrovka
Krílovka
Reinfeld
Petersdorf 1919
Paulheim 1919
Yavornizky
Avgustinovka
Ivangorod
Ignatevskaya
Nadiya
Mnogotrudnoye
Ukrainka
Andreyevka
Lemeshinsky
Vesselaya
Petropavlovsky
Krasnopol
Padiansky
N. Ivanovsky
Tarassovka
Lukashevka
Andreyevsky
Vesseley
Yar
Neuenburg
Mariental
1920–1922
Ulanovsky
Koryonovsky
Neuhorst 1919
Bogatyrev
Petrovka
Neuhorst
Kronsweide
Rosenbach
Neuendorf
Seleney–Lug
Podorazhny
Einlage
N. Kitshkas
Michailovka
Schönhorst
N. Petrovsky
CHORTITZA
Saporozhye
Tshaika
Insel Chortitza
N. Kotoshinsky
Novo Saporozhe
Arbuzovka
Rosengart
Tomakovsky
Burwalde
Nikolayevka
Osterwick
Kronstal
Slepanovsky
Nieder–Chortitza
N. Nikolayevka
Vladimerovsky
Schöneberg
Blumengart
Petro–
Razumovka
Ivanovka
Novo Fedorovka
N. Ukrainsky
Udel Nikolayevka
Kronsfeld

Mennonite place — * Mennonite Churches — ✝ Destroyed Mennonite place — ▦ Ukrainian place — Road — Railroad — Telegraph — Mennonite villages underlined

Unarmed Mennonite villages found themselves under increasing attack. As the Bolshevik position in the area became more unstable, a semimilitary detachment of Mennonite men emerged in the village of Tiegerweide, Molotschna, who occupied the village and arrested several fleeing Red soldiers and locked them up in the village prison. The influence of the Tiegerweide unit spread to neighboring villages. A similar group soon organized in Alexanderkrone, and in the village of Tiege in the volost of Zagradovka eighteen young men formed an armed unit.[7] These patterns were repeated in several other localities. Of particular importance was the formation of the partisan unit in Halbstadt, many of whose adherents were students from the Mennonite College of Commerce in that city.

The spirit of militarism progressively infecting the colonies did not go unchallenged.[8] Pleas for moderation and |repentance were heard from Mennonite pulpits, the press, and even courageous villagers who dared speak up against the formation of the *Selbstschutz*. The warning was disregarded, for public opinion was too strong. A deep-seated unrest assumed such proportions it threatened to divide the colonists. To avert such a catastrophe the constituency leaders convoked an All-Mennonite Conference in Lichtenau, Molotschna, between June 30 and July 2, 1918. Debate on the military question was initiated when the German regional commander in Berdyansk requested the Mennonite settlers to clarify their position toward the formation of an integrated *Selbstschutz* to include all the German colonists in South Russia. A paper by B. H. Unruh on the question reiterated the traditional Mennonite position on nonresistance. When the meeting was opened to discussion it was apparent that the sentiments expressed were not shared by all those present. Nevertheless, debate on the first day was overwhelmingly in favor of upholding the historic peace tradition.[9] An atmosphere of urgency characterized the second day of deliberations when it was learned that the German regional commander in Berdyansk demanded a list of all refusing military service by July 4. Discussion began with a plea for tolerance and compromise on the ground that the matter involved two biblically sanctioned principles—nonresistance and Christian subservience to the state. Some felt the conference must sanction both views. Others thought it was possible to be nonresistant and still serve the state. Had the Mennonites not done so in a large variety of ways? Many had given their lives; none had betrayed the fatherland.[10] The conference, weary of debate, appointed a commission to formulate resolutions to clarify the issues. The commission consisted of the *Kommission für Kirchenangelegenheiten* (Commission for Church Affairs), the presidium of the conference, and two members at large, B. B. Janz and Peter Fast. Two resolutions emerged. The first advocated the right of private interpretation concerning nonresistance. The second reaffirmed the conference's belief in nonresistance as the highest Christian ideal. Both proposals were accepted by a large majority.

The conference failed to solve the question which had forced its convocation; it did little more than recognize the *status quo.* Charitable and broad-minded as its decision to leave the matter of nonresistance to private interpretation appeared to be, it nevertheless marked the continuation of a doctrinal cleavage in Russian Mennonitism. Allowing a radical minority complete freedom of action it ultimately placed the survival of the majority in jeopardy. The *Selbstschutz* mentality rapidly entrenched itself. The implications of the Lichtenau decision were not immediately apparent; for the *Selbstschutz* had limited significance during the German occupation. In the event of a German retreat, however, the path for radical action had been cleared.

With the withdrawal of the German troops, the Mennonite colonies were once more left exposed to the prevailing anarchy and terror. The threat of roving robber bands loomed darkly on the horizon. How could the Molotschna colonies defend themselves? In the Halbstadt volost a special congress with representatives from most of the villages meeting in Rückenau adopted the proposal to mobilize all men between the ages of thirty and thirty-seven. Opposing views were not tolerated. When a delegate from the village of Rosenort protested the procedure, the chairman of the meeting demanded his expulsion. In the ensuing recruitment no concientious objection was tolerated. The same procedures characterized a public assembly in Gnadenfeld, where a similar resolution was passed. Militarism was the order of the day.

Nestor Makhno

The *Selbstschutz* rapidly graduated from a passive to an active military role through a "baptism by fire" caused by the ruthless partisan army of Nestor Ivanovich Makhno, son of a Russian peasant born in the village of Gulyaypole, about forty miles northeast of the Molotschna. As a boy he struggled to make his living

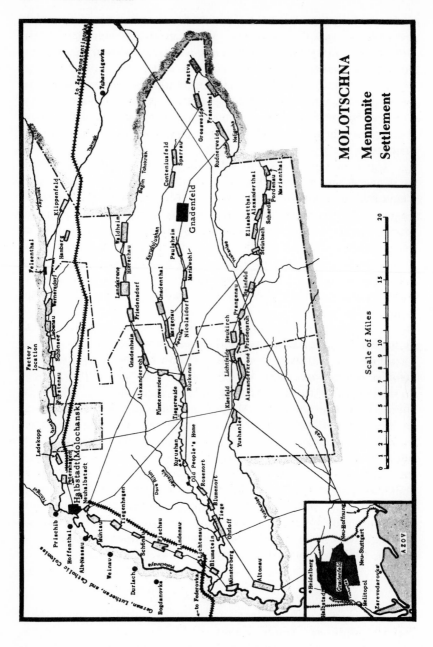

MOLOTSCHNA
Mennonite
Settlement

as a shepherd for the German landowners of the area and developed a vengeful hatred for his exploiters. After the Revolution of 1905 he joined the anarchistic-communistic elements in Russia. In 1908 he was sentenced to death for revolutionary activity, but because of his youth the sentence was commuted to life imprisonment. The October Revolution of 1917 brought freedom and his return to South Russia. Before long he was leading a small army of workers and peasants against the German armies in the Ukraine. By 1918 he headed an independent partisan group whose anarchistic fury was directed against the landlords and the German invaders. Makhno managed to win the support of the peasantry in a large area north of the Sea of Azov. Throughout 1919 he carried on a bitter struggle with General Denikin's White Army in southern Russia. When the Red Army penetrated the area in the summer of 1920, Makhno concluded an alliance with them. The Bolsheviks subsequently broke faith and Makhno, though surrounded several times, managed to escape to Rumania. He subsequently went to Danzig, to Berlin, and finally to Paris where he died of pneumonia in 1934.[11]

Since Makhno's depredations directly affected the major Mennonite settlements of Chortitza and Molotschna, *Selbstschutz* involvement was unavoidable. Initially, the activities of the marauders brought varying degrees of hardship. As a result of their movement through Chortitza, the area was subjected to a severe typhus epidemic. It was in the Molotschna that Makhno first encountered sharp resistance. Organized bands under his leadership first overran the villages of the German colonists in the Prischib volost which adjoined that of Halbstadt. The *Selbstschutz*, determined to halt the invaders, now chose a fringe village in the Halbstadt volost to make its stand. Blumental, situated about thirty miles north of Halbstadt, was strategically located, as it controlled the approach to the Prischib, Halbstadt, and Gnadenfeld volosts. Here Lutherans, Catholics, and Mennonites stood shoulder to shoulder to ward off the bandit attacks.[12] A second front was established in the eastern Molotschna near the villages of Waldheim-Ostrakovka. *Selbstschutz* defenses were reinforced by the northward advancing White Army contingents of General Denikin.

White Occupation (Fall 1918 - March 1919)

During the summer of 1918 the leader of the White Army in the south, General Denikin, sought to strengthen his position in southern Russia by invading the Kuban. He managed to evict the Bolsheviks from its capital, Ekaterinodar, by August 16. Shortly thereafter he entered Novorossisk and before long the Crimea came under White control. Having successfully broadened his base, Denikin was ready for an attempt to link up with the White Army in the east. White troops soon captured Melitopol. As the northward expansion continued, White officers took over the administration of the Halbstadt and Gnadenfeld volosts and made a determined effort to assimilate the *Selbstschutz* into the White Army. In view of the German withdrawal and the increased Makhno threat most of the *Selbstschutz* units welcomed the civil order brought by White occupation. *Selbstschutz* munitions and supplies, depleted after the German withdrawal, were replenished by a sizable shipment of arms from the White arsenal in Sevastopol.[13]

Several joint military exercises strengthened the bonds between the *Selbstschutz* and the White Army. Particularly significant was a direct encounter with the Makhno forces in the large Russian village of Tchernigovka to the east of the Moloschna settlement during October 1918. The anarchists had captured the village. The Whites ordered the Gnadenfeld and Halbstadt *Selbstschutz* detachments to the scene. They were joined by the Waldheim unit. In Tchernigovka the *Selbstschutz* directly engaged the enemy while White guardists took up covering positions. Makhno was driven from the village and almost apprehended. The victory substantially raised the status of the *Selbstschutz* among the colonists.[14] Simultaneously it united the White Army and the militant Mennonites in a common project. Before long White officers exercised considerable influence upon the *Selbstschutz* executive committee. At least one unit allowed itself to become officially inducted into the White Army and together with its new colleagues engaged in a number of questionable exploits. In the end the degree of assimilation or cooperation mattered little. The *Selbstschutz* had identified itself with the White Army, a body which was regarded as a counter-revolutionary element by the Bolshevik regime. In the eyes of the government this association implicated the entire Mennonite constituency in the south.

Several of the *Selbstschutz* leaders became apprehensive about their close affiliation with the White Army. A special meeting of representatives from both the Halbstadt and Gnadenfeld volosts was held in Halbstadt to consider the problem. The regional White commander, Colonel Malakov, was also invited. Despite his protests

Malakov was persuaded to agree to a special resolution defining the status and nature of the *Selbstschutz*. It pictured the organization as an independent body dissociated from any political affiliations and from any standing army, which existed solely for the purpose of defense against roving robber bands. The agency was to be dissolved the instant civil order was reestablished and public safety assured. The declaration with its signatures was then presented to the White officers in the area.[15]

The Terror (March-July 1919)

Early in 1919, the White position in the Molotschna became increasingly unstable. The strength of Makhno's army gradually increased and his commando raids intensified. Denikin, convinced that no major offensive was possible at this time, gradually allowed his forces to retreat southward. The *Selbstschutz*, though it had successfully defended the Molotschna against Makhno for three months, began to retreat. A new danger loomed. The Thirty-third Division of the Red Army was rapidly approaching the Molotschna. Makhno, fearful of losing his power, allied himself with the Bolshevik forces under General Dovenko. The *Selbstschutz* was no match for the new force. Between March 6 and 10, 1919, it made its last stand. Blumental, Hochheim, Heidleberg, and Friedrichsdorf fell to the Makhno forces in quick succession.[16] Panic seized the Molotschna. White Colonel Malakov dispatched a terse message to all the villages: "Citizens! Everything is lost; let each one save himself as best he can!" A mass flight southward began during the night of March 9, 10.[17] But all escape routes had been cut off. The Red Army took fearful revenge upon anyone who dared to resist it. Faced with possible annihilation the colonists resorted to spiritual weapons. Under the leadership of a church elder in Elisabethtal, Molotschna, special prayer meetings were organized in a number of villages. Almost simultaneously Red troops entered Gnadenfeld. On March 11, 1919, two villagers courageously went to Dovenko and pleaded for mercy. They received a harsh response: "You cursed renegades. For 400 years you refused to take up arms—now for this wretched Kaiser Wilhelm," etc. At the risk of their lives the men continued to plead for the villages. Dovenko finally consented to spare the villages, but granted his soldiers the right to plunder for three days and ordered the execution of all captured *Selbstschutz* participants.[18] A revolutionary tribunal was set up in Melitopol, which in the course of a few months executed one hundred persons, among them a number of Mennonites. Particularly shocking was the arrest and execution of Peter Wiens, secretary of the *Mennozentrum* in Halbstadt.[19] During the same month a special delegation headed by B. H. Unruh presented the Halbstadt resolution regarding the nature and function of the *Selbstschutz* to military authorities. Again the Mennonites were promised protection provided they surrendered all arms within three days.[20] The ensuing Bolshevik rule was filled with terror and hardship, but the life of the constituency at large was spared, for the presence of the Red Army tended to curb the worst Makhno excesses. Plundering, violence, and rape were nevertheless widespread. There was now an excuse to justify such atrocities, for the *Selbstschutz* had fought against the Red Army. Its collaboration with White Army officers was also known. These facts were not forgotten.

The Chortitza settlement was especially hard-pressed by the Red Army occupation. Advance regiments had penetrated the area as early as January 1919. Before long the secret police, the *Cheka,* were ferreting out supposed counterrevolutionaries. Several leaders were executed. The nationalization of all the means of production and distribution brought agricultural and industrial activity to a standstill. By the spring of 1919 the shortage of seed wheat and draft horses became crucial, although food was still in fairly good supply. The problem of housing and feeding the occupation army, however, was becoming increasingly burdensome. Denikin's White offensive in the late spring of 1919 brought renewed tragedy to the settlement. White artillery fire, directed against Red tanks in the vicinity of the village of Einlage, severely damaged the houses and factories in the area. An uneasy peace returned to Chortitza and the other Ukrainian Mennonite colonies as Denikin's forces continued northward. No end was in sight for the violence and destruction afflicting the colonies.

CHAPTER TWO

The Continuing Destruction

The White Resurgence and the Blumenort Episode (July - November, 1919)

After freeing Chortitza the White Army became concerned with maintaining public order. To protect the colonies as well as the Dnieper-Nikopol railway White officers trained and equipped a detachment of about one hundred men known as the Chortitza *Otrad*. Many of the Mennonite young men willingly cooperated with Denikin. Late spring also saw the advance of the White Army into the Molotschna area. In early June 1919, Halbstadt was recaptured by Denikin's forces. By July the entire region was in White hands. The lull in the fighting after the passage of the front lasted only three months. During the fall of 1919 a surprise attack by about 6,000 Makhno supporters penetrated Denikin's defenses in Kherson province and overran Zagradovka and Chortitza, reaching the Molotschna by October. A period of unprecedented terror ensued. The invaders openly declared their intention of liquidating the colonists. Displaying a black banner they rode into village after village, plundering, raping, and killing. Because of the cold, troops were quartered in homes. As a result of the ensuing unsanitary conditions a severe typus epidemic struck the Chortitza settlement, resulting in many deaths among both the military and the civilian population.[1]

In the Molotschna a plan for counteraction was secretly drawn up to terminate Makhno terror. The scattered adherents of the disbanded *Selbstschutz* were gathered together with the purpose of attacking the Makhno center in Orloff.[2] Several units of this group reached the village of Blumenort during twilight on Sunday, November 10, 1919. The entry of the armed men was almost unnoticed. Coming across the fields and back roads they reached the farmyard of one of the more prosperous farmers in the village. Convinced that the presence of the men meant trouble he implored them to leave. "What do you want here? This will only bring great catastrophe. Depart at once and leave us alone." The men refused and demanded that their horses and wagons be hidden in the large barn on location. The barn doors had barely closed when a cry for help came from the village. "They are taking our brother! Come and help us!" Several of Makhno's men were abducting one of the villagers. The newly arrived partisans had not reckoned with this emergency. Seizing their rifles quickly they fired at the would-be abductors. Only two of the mounted bandits escaped. The *Selbstschutz* unit left the village almost immediately after the carnage while the villagers fearfully awaited the avengers.[3]

They were not slow in coming. An armed troop arrived in Blumenort early the next morning to punish the villagers, whom they considered collectively responsible for the death of their comrades the night before. Pleas of innocence were ignored. A number of hostages were incarcerated in the basement of the former village store. Near noon a larger regiment bearing black banners entered Blumenort. One of the younger men of the village attempted to explain the real situation to the regimental commander. Momentarily he appeared to listen to the suppliant. Then a Russian woman accompanying the group shouted, "If they [the Mennonites] are on the receiving end they feverishly object, but our people don't matter; they can be shot to death!" The protest was electrifying. A rifle shot brought down the fleeing petitioner. The killing had begun. Armed horsemen began murdering any villagers they found. The imprisoned hostages were cut down with sabers, gunfire, and hand grenades. By Monday evening at least a score of bodies awaited burial. The villagers began to dig. a mass grave. They could not hold a service, for by Wednesday a new horde of revenge seekers arrived from Melitopol and passed through Altonau,[4] Orloff, and Tiege, finally arriving in Blumenort during twilight. Their path was marked by violence and murder. In Blumenort several more villagers lost their lives and a number of farms were put to the torch. Finally on November 14 the situation stabilized sufficiently to allow for the mass burial of the victims. About one week after the Blumenort massacre most of the men who had participated in it were killed by a Cossack regiment in the area.[5]

Banditry and violence in the Zagradovka volost assumed particularly gruesome proportions. A bandit attack between

Nestor Makhno

The mass grave for the victims of the Blumenort massacre, November 1919.

November 29 and December 1, 1919, brought destruction, violence, and death to six villages.[6] Hardest hit were the villages of Tiege and Münsterberg. Tiege was subjected to a siege of fire, plunder, rape, and murder which left eighteen dead and four farms completely destroyed, while in Münsterberg a massacre claimed over 100 lives and showed no pity for the newborn infant nor the aged grandfather. Many bodies were never recovered since the entire village was reduced to ashes. Only the arrival of a Denikin regiment saved the volost from further depredations.[7]

Red Army Occupation (December 1919 - June 1920)

In the last months of 1919 violence again plagued Mennonite colonies. In mid-October, when it appeared likely that Petrograd and Moscow might fall to the Whites, a successful Red Army counteroffensive forced a rapid retreat. A part of the Ukraine was reoccupied by December and a communist regime headed by Christian Rakovsky assumed power in Kharkov. During the first months of 1920 the Whites were gradually driven from the Rostov vicinity. What remained of Denikin's beaten army found itself trapped in the port of Novorossisk. British ships aided in the evacuation of his troops to the Crimea. Here Denikin resigned his command in favor of General Peter Wrangel.

The presence of Red troops in the south brought continued hardship to the Mennonites, especially in Chortitza. Most of the inhabitants of the settlement were suffering from disease and malnutrition. Still in the clutches of a typhus epidemic the colony possessed no resources, human or material, to facilitate its recovery. The Molotschna brought some relief to Chortitza by establishing first-aid centers for the treatment of typhus victims and by sending food. Hundreds of orphans had to be placed in private homes, most of which could ill afford the burden of feeding another mouth. By June 1 about 300 Mennonites had perished from typhus in the villages of Chortitza and Rosenthal alone.[8] At least 100 women and girls who had suffered violence at the hands of the anarchists were under treatment for syphilis. Simultaneously the threat of a smallpox epidemic hung over the community.[9] More settled conditions returned to the area in early summer. Bolshevik rule brought a degree of stability, and most colonists were content to abide by its injunctions in return for protection from the Makhno bands. But the breathing spell was of short duration. Near the end of July a new White offensive under General Wrangel was edging toward Chortitza.

By March 1920, all the Ukrainian Mennonite settlements were in a state of despair and decline. A particularly graphic illustration of the extent and intensity of the catastrophe was Chortitza: its population declined from 18,000 in the fall of 1917 to approximately 13,600 in mid-March 1920. The reasons for this decline were easy to isolate. The typhus epidemic of the winter of 1919-20 alone claimed over 1,000 victims. During 1919 only 130 children were born in the district whereas an estimated 900 persons died. The massacres of the marauders further contributed to the population decline. A labor force of about 3,000 normally employed by the district had vanished by 1920.[10]

Though agricultural in character, the district was virtually devoid of livestock, agricultural equipment, and grain by 1920. Records from the fall of 1917 listed over 400 farms with more than five horses. By March 15, 1920, there was only one such farm. Not one out of the 400 farms which possessed five or more cows in 1917 had as many as five by March 1920. Between October 7 and December 25, 1919, some 2,000 horses and 1,400 cows had been destroyed in the Makhno raids, and most of the remaining stock was requisitioned by the Red Army of occupation. Likewise most of the agricultural machinery had been destroyed or stolen. The Makhno era saw the confiscation of almost 200,000 pud of grain. By March 15, 1920, the entire Chortitza district possessed only about 140,000 pud. Of this, 37,000 pud were requisitioned by the Red Army, 60,000 pud were used as seed grain, and the remaining 43,000 pud were consumed by the district population.[11]

The Molotschna and Zagradovka settlements were subjected to similar pressures. As yet, however, disease was not as widespread nor was food in such critically short supply. But Red occupation meant quartering of troops and requisitioning of scarce food, horses, and wagons. Many of the Mennonites were compelled to drive supply wagons to the front, usually at great personal risk. The presence of large numbers of troops created unsanitary and crowded living conditions, which threatened an epidemic.

The Wrangel Offensive (June - November 1920)

In the late spring of 1920 General Wrangel began the last White offensive of the civil war. Moving northward from the Crimea the attack did not progress far beyond an east-west line running through the Molotschna. Although the front did not extend to the Memrik settlement to the east nor to the Zagradovka colony in the west, both settlements were subjected to a requisitioning of supplies and equipment. The Molotschna lay in the direct path of Wrangel's offensive. For weeks the line of battle seesawed back and forth over the region, some villages changing hands as many as twenty times. Most of the transfers were accompanied by severe fighting and artillery bombardment. In the midst of this havoc the villagers were usually forced to shelter and feed the soldiers of whatever side happened to occupy their territory. The war completed the ruination of the settlement. Between January and April 1920, the Halbstadt volost lost an estimated 3,291,188 rubles in movable property stolen, confiscated, or destroyed.[12] The final phase of the civil war in the Ukraine left the area completely destitute. A partial return of public order came with Wrangel's defeat by the Red Army. In many localities, however, unrest and lawlessness persisted.

Terror, banditry, anarchy, and civil war were accompanied by an invasion of disease and famine against which the colonists in their weakened physical condition were defenseless. The new invaders spared no one. The typhus epidemic, which had already plagued Chortitza early in 1920 and from there spread to other localities, claimed more lives than either war or anarchy. Doctors and ministers, because of their close contact with the patients, frequently succumbed. Family after family was torn asunder. Hard on the heels of the ravaging disease came famine. In the spring of 1921 most of the Ukraine was struck by a severe drought which lasted until the fall of 1922. Except for the timely arrival of American relief a large percentage of the colonists would have perished.

Prospects for any sort of economic recovery in most of the Ukrainian Mennonite colonies were very dismal by 1921. The lack of draft horses and seed grain excluded any sizable planting operations in the spring. Because many of the colonists were forced into transportation and maintenance service by occupying troops, such grain as was sown was often planted by moonlight. A relatively dry winter during 1920-21 left the land with little reserve moisture. Spring rains encouraged good seed germination. The heat and drought of subsequent months, however, caused a crop failure of such severity that the harvest rarely produced sufficient grain to replace that sown in the spring.

The burdensome obligation of quartering troops ended officially

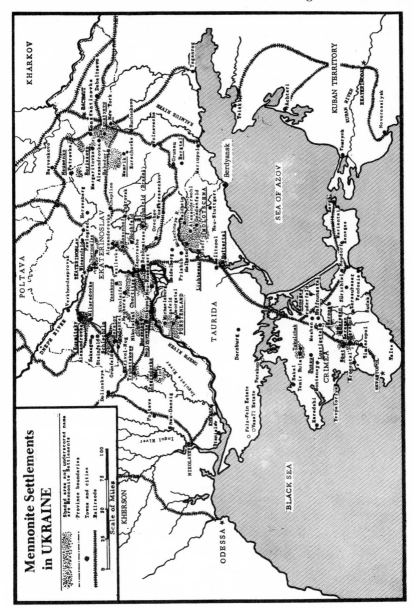

Mennonite Settlements in UKRAINE

on March 3, 1922, but many of the soldiers remained in the colonies much longer. Meanwhile the settlements were also plagued by hordes of beggars, starving and persistent intruders who hoped to cheat approaching death by relying on the generosity of the colonists.[13] Although the colonists were on the verge of despair during the winter of 1921-22, the promise of a helping hand from abroad fanned the remaining spark of hope for a better future. The spring of 1922 partially lessened the grave food crisis, when Alvin J. Miller of the American Mennonite Relief opened food kitchens and distribution centers in the various settlements.

Future Prospects in the Ukraine

By early 1922 the Ukrainian Mennonites had survived most of the major crises which threatened their existence, though the cost in terms of men and materials had been very high. For the present, survival depended on foreign benevolence. Generally speaking, the Mennonites were not responsible for the adverse circumstances prevailing in 1922. The traditional Russian attitude toward its minorities, the ethnic origin of the Mennonites, their prewar economic well-being, their geographic location directly in the path of the civil war, the German occupation, the formation of the *Selbstschutz*—all of these issues contributed to the destruction of Ukrainian Mennonitism.

When the Bolsheviks regained final control of the Ukraine late in 1920, several adverse facts concerning the Ukrainian Mennonites were public knowledge. First, the Mennonites had identified themselves with the German occupation forces. Such action was, to be sure, rooted in a German cultural affinity and the promise of relief from the prevailing anarchy; it in no way involved a repudiation of Russian citizenship. Some of the members of the *Selbstschutz* had, however, actually marched with the Germans. The thin line many had drawn between this flirtation with the enemy and actual treason was not understood by their Russian compatriots when the German Army withdrew from the Ukraine in November 1918.

The Ukrainian Mennonites were also implicated in the eyes of the Bolshevik regime by their identification with the White Army. Their settlements were located in territory frequently held by the antirevolutionary forces. A loose organic connection with the White Army had been established through the activities of the *Selbstschutz*, at least one of whose units directly joined the White cause. Particu-

larly unpardonable was the fact that the *Selbstschutz* had on one
occasion mistakenly engaged Red Army units instead of the Makhno
bands. Even though Red Army officers spared the colonies, they vowed
to execute *Selbstschutz* members. It was difficult to dispel the notion
that the Ukrainian Mennonites were supporters of the counterrevolu-
tion. Another adverse factor was the position of the Mennonites as a
national minority. Before the Revolution this minority was characterized
by wealth, privilege, the use of the German language, nonassimilation,
religious nonconformity, refusal to bear arms, and on occasion, the
exploitation of the Russian working class. The Mennonites had only
partially been integrated into the Russian cultural and ideological
structure. The presence of German and White troops in the
colonies only added to the indictment already in existence.

As a national minority the Ukrainian Mennonites now faced
the task of regaining the confidence of the Bolshevik regime in
Kharkov and of proving their loyalty to the Soviet system. The
assignment was almost an impossible one. If the Mennonites were
guilty of nonidentification in old Russia, they were even more guilty
under the Soviet system. A deep-seated ideological antithesis separated
them from their new rulers. Economically, their commitment to a
capitalism based on private initiative clashed with socialism. Reli-
giously, their theism and pacifism conflicted with atheism and militarism. Administratively, their practice of local autonomy interfered with the designs of a political party determined to change the
essential fabric of the nation. Nationally, their strong sense of
identity in language, culture, and ethnic derivation clashed with
established Russian patterns. Ukrainian Mennonite leaders, clearly
recognizing that survival depended on reconciliation, began to search
for a solution. Almost instinctively they sought to implement an
operational principle which had brought official recognition of
Mennonite separatism in the past—their agricultural and economic
achievements. Such an appeal might hopefully catch the attention
of a materialistically oriented regime. If the Mennonites could
contribute significantly to the economic reconstruction of the
devastated south, the new government might allow them to continue
as a separate national entity. The Soviet government gradually
responded negatively. As this answer became more and more evident
in the religious, cultural, educational, and economic life of the
constituency, the Ukrainian Mennonites gravitated toward the only
alternative—emigration.

The tragedy of Civil War and Revolution.

The Mennonites in the RSFSR

The experiences of the Mennonite settlers in the Crimea as well as in Eastern European and Asiatic Russia were not unlike those of their coreligionists in the Ukraine, varying only in time of occurrence and in intensity. In the end, however, the social upheaval of the Bolshevik revolution spared none of the scattered Mennonite colonies in greater Russia.

The massive nationalization schemes decreed soon after the October 1917 Revolution, while not immediately implemented in all regions, contributed to a spirit of apprehension in the colonies which was economically disrupting. The broad land concessions promised the Russian peasantry laid the basis for disorder and conflict, particularly in the large and well-developed settlements. Old forms of local government and civil order were destroyed without provision for alternative programs for the promotion of public safety. In consequence, every Mennonite colony, whether in Siberia or European Russia, suffered its tragic experiences.

The destruction of the existing order had particularly grave consequences for the Terek Mennonite settlement in the Caucasus, which was founded at the turn of the century. The colony was surrounded by nomadic tribes descended from the Tatars and natives of the region. Forbidden to carry arms prior to the revolution, they had now been armed and actually became a major military force in the area. Since even in normal times they had been inclined toward robbery and plunder, the arming of these tribes was equivalent to officially sanctioning their activity.[14] By late January 1918 it was apparent that these elements were planning a systematic plunder of the entire settlement. A public assembly to discuss the emergency was convened on February 1, 1918, which decided to evacuate the settlement immediately. In at least one village the inhabitants escaped only an hour before the arrival of 500 bandits. After a dangerous and frustrating trek the refugees finally managed to reach the Mennonite colonies in the Kuban.[15] From here many journeyed to the Ukraine to await eventual evacuation to Canada.

The Russian harvest in 1917 was far below normal. In the spring of 1918 bread riots broke out in many Russian cities. To meet the emergency the Bolsheviks ordered all grain not needed to feed the peasants turned over to the government and set up the infamous "Committees of the Poor" in all villages of Russia to force the wealthy peasants to turn over their grain. Ruthless requisitioning of agricultural products continued even after these agencies had been replaced by the village soviets in the autumn of 1918. Many government authorities viewed the resulting chaos as a part of the class struggle. In short order the large-scale requisitions threatened the existence of prosperous farms including the many Mennonite settlements. Even carefully hoarded seed grain was not safe from the depredations of local officials, or from master bandits exploiting the existing chaos. Hardly had the requisitions ended when a natural produce tax, payable in kind, was instituted. This sum, usually assessed well before harvest, frequently bore little relation to the actual foodstuffs harvested.

In most of Russia the winter of 1920-21 was cold and dry. Little rain fell in the spring of 1921. In many instances fields were not even sown because no seed grain was available. In addition, there were grasshopper plagues and hailstorms as well. Few settlements escaped famine. By January 1922 such middle Volga colonies as Trakt, Alt-Samara, Neu-Samara, Orenburg, and Davlekanovo were virtually without bread.[16] In Neu-Samara and Orenburg there were between 5,000 and 6,000 starving people.[17] Except for the timely arrival of American aid, a large segment of the Mennonite population in this area would have perished. Similar conditions prevailed in the Kuban[18] and the Crimea.[19] The forces of disruption did not spare the Siberian settlements of Omsk, Slavgorod, Barnaul, and Pavlodar. In 1919 two Americans from Reedley, California, M. B. Fast and W. P. Neufeld, personally escorted a large relief shipment to the distressed Mennonite colonies in Siberia.[20] In subsequent years the struggle for survival intensified. Crop failure and famine were still prevalent in many Siberian Mennonite villages as late as the spring of 1924.[21]

The Mennonites in the RSFSR as of 1922 were victims, as was most of Russia, of the massive social upheaval caused by revolution and civil war. As a minority they were less numerous and geographically more scattered than the Ukrainian Mennonites. They were less suspect than their brethren in the south since they did not identify with the German occupation nor the White Army and made no attempt to form a *Selbstschutz:* they were therefore accorded a more charitable treatment on both a local and a national level. Certain irreconcilable tensions nevertheless existed. Economically the RSFSR Mennonites adhered to the old order. They were opposed to government interference in their educational and religious concerns. The basic conflict was not over

Mennonite
Settlements
in
EUROPEAN
RUSSIA

Scale is in Kilometers

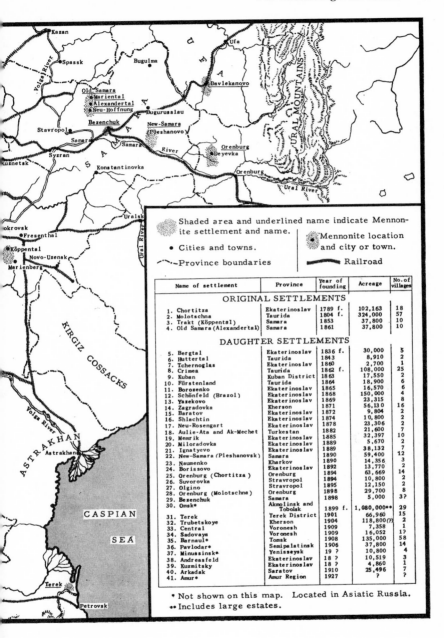

Shaded area and underlined name indicate Mennonite settlement and name.

Mennonite location and city or town.

• Cities and towns.

⌁ Province boundaries

Railroad

Name of settlement	Province	Year of founding	Acreage	No. of villages
ORIGINAL SETTLEMENTS				
1. Chortitza	Ekaterinoslav	1789 f.	102,163	18
2. Molotschna	Taurida	1804 f.	324,000	57
3. Trakt (Köppental)	Samara	1853	37,800	10
4. Old Samara (Alexandertal)	Samara	1861	37,800	10
DAUGHTER SETTLEMENTS				
5. Bergtal	Ekaterinoslav	1836 f.	30,000	5
6. Huttertal	Taurida	1843	8,910	2
7. Tchernoglas	Ekaterinoslav	1860	2,700	1
8. Crimea	Taurida	1862 f.	108,000	25
9. Kuban	Kuban District	1863	17,550	5
10. Fürstenland	Taurida	1864	18,900	6
11. Borosenko	Ekaterinoslav	1865	16,570	6
12. Schönfeld (Brazol)	Ekaterinoslav	1868	150,000	4
13. Yazekovo	Ekaterinoslav	1869	23,315	8
14. Zagradovka	Kherson	1871	56,130	16
15. Baratov	Ekaterinoslav	1872	9,804	2
16. Shlachtin	Ekaterinoslav	1874	10,800	2
17. Neu-Rosengart	Ekaterinoslav	1878	23,306	2
18. Aulie-Ata and Ak-Mechet	Turkestan	1882	21,600	7
19. Memrik	Ekaterinoslav	1885	32,397	10
20. Miloradovka	Ekaterinoslav	1889	5,670	2
21. Ignatyevo	Ekaterinoslav	1889	38,132	7
22. New-Samara (Pleshanovsk)	Samara	1890	59,400	12
23. Naumenko	Kharkov	1890	14,356	3
24. Borissovo	Ekaterinoslav	1892	13,770	2
25. Orenburg (Chortitza)	Orenburg	1894	63,669	14
26. Suvorovka	Stravropol	1894	10,800	2
27. Olgino	Stravropol	1895	12,150	2
28. Orenburg (Molotschna)	Orenburg	1898	29,700	8
29. Bezenchuk	Samara	1898	5,000	3?
30. Omsk*	Akmolinsk and Tobolsk	1899 f.	1,080,000**	29
31. Terek	Terek District	1901	66,960	15
32. Trubetskoye	Kherson	1904	118,800(?)	2
33. Central	Voronesh	1909	7,358	1
34. Sadovaya	Voronesh	1909	16,052	1?
35. Barnaul*	Tomsk	1908	135,000	58
36. Pavlodar*	Semipalatinsk	1906	37,800	14
37. Mimussinsk*	Yenisseysk	19 ?	10,800	4
38. Andreasfeld	Ekaterinoslav	18 ?	10,519	3
39. Kuzmitsky	Ekaterinoslav	18 ?	4,860	1
40. Arkadak	Saratov	1910	25,496	7
41. Amur*	Amur Region	1927	?	?

* Not shown on this map.   Located in Asiatic Russia.

** Includes large estates.

the preservation of superficial social, cultural, and religious values but the transformation of a historic commitment to a way of life. As in the past, they endeavored to use economic achievement as a justification for the continuation of old agricultural and economic patterns. A serious attempt was made to adapt to new agricultural forms in the hope of retaining some degree of local autonomy. In half a decade, however, it became apparent that there would no toleration of minority distinctiveness. Many observers in the various colonies were convinced that Russian Mennonitism had reached the point of no return as early as 1922. For them, survival depended on emigration from Russia.

The Studienkommission

Late in 1919, despite the prevailing civil unrest, the Molotschna settlement called a general meeting of village representatives in Rückenau to seek solutions to their urgent problems. After some deliberations the assembly voted to send a special commission to North America and Europe to explore emigration possibilities and evaluate potential settlement areas. Known as the *Studienkommission* (Study Commission) its elected members were A. A. Friesen, chairman, B. H. Unruh, Secretary, and C. H. Warkentin, and somewhat later, J. J. Esau. The delegates left Russia on January 1, 1920, by way of the Crimea and Constantinople. Eventually the *Studienkommission* became the link between the Russian Mennonites and their coreligionists in Europe and North America. The Rückenau proceedings marked the first step in the creation of the organizational framework for facilitating the later emigration. The *Studienkommission* arrived in Europe during April 1920 and sought aid for their constituency from the Mennonites in Holland, Switzerland, and Germany. Thereupon they left for America arriving in New York on June 13, 1920. Following a tour of both the United States and Canada, B. H. Unruh returned to Germany while A. A. Friesen and C. H. Warkentin remained in America.

CHAPTER THREE

Attempts at
Internal Consolidation (1921)

Mennonite leaders in the Ukraine were not slow in taking the initiative once a degree of stability returned to Russia. Major questions needed answers. What did the future hold for the Mennonites in Russia? Was it possible to retain a sense of identity and self-development or would assimilation be enforced? Would old economic and religious practices be tolerated? How would nationalization and the redivision of the land influence the Mennonite settlements? The most pressing immediate problem, survival, became crucial late in 1920 and early in 1921. Despite disheartening circumstances the Mennonites in South Russia aggressively sought a solution for their difficulties. Before long an agency was created to negotiate with the Bolshevik government. The record of its interaction with the new regime became the story of the Mennonite dialogue with communism.

The Coming of the Americans (September - November 1920)

In America the Russian catastrophe was the direct cause of the formation of a new Mennonite relief agency. In response to the reports and pleas of the *Studienkommission* a special meeting of representatives of all existing Mennonite relief organizations assembled in Elkhart, Indiana, on July 27, 1920. The delegates voted to form a Mennonite Central Committee (MCC) whose first task involved the planning of the Russian relief program. On September 2 the MCC dispatched a relief unit to Russia, composed of Arthur Slagel, Clayton Kratz, and Orie O. Miller. They disembarked at Constantinople on September 27. Since southern Russia was still in the grip of civil war, Constantinople was selected as the base for contact with Russia. It was also a reasonably stable site for communication with America. In Constantinople the relief unit was able to collect information about Russian conditions from such agencies as the American Embassy, the American Red Cross, the Russian

YMCA, and several small Russian relief organizations.

On October 1 Miller and Kratz left Constantinople on an eventful journey which would take them into war-torn Russia. Arriving at Sevastopol they were accorded a warm reception by the American General McCully and officials of the White government. They were supplied with available reports on current conditions and promised free transportation of men and material. The position of General Wrangel of the White Army seemed reasonably secure; therefore Miller and Kratz decided to go as far as Halbstadt. On October 8 they left for this city, arriving there on the evening of October 11. Almost immediate contact was made with the organization and committees representing the Russian Mennonites and the details of the proposed American relief program were mapped out. The relief unit also proceeded to Alexandrovsk, but a visit to Chortitza was canceled because of an obvious weakening in Wrangel's front line just twenty miles to the north. When a general retreat became evident by October 16, Clayton Kratz returned to Halbstadt while Miller journeyed back to Sevastopol. It was the last time that Miller saw Kratz, who shortly thereafter was apparently captured by the Bolsheviks and possibly liquidated or sent to Siberia.[1] All subsequent inquiries made by Miller produced no trace of him.

Meanwhile on October 21, 1920, the first shipment of American relief supplies reached Drindge, approximately seventy miles from Constantinople, where it was stored in the warehouses of the Near East Relief organization. Plans for the shipment of relief supplies to the colonies via Sevastopol were formulated and preliminary arrangements for their receipt were made by Miller at the location.

By October 26 Miller was back in Constantinople. Together he and Slagel made final preparations for the first shipment of supplies to Russia. Although poor communications made it impossible to ascertain the state of affairs in the Russian Civil War, a small Greek freighter was nevertheless dispatched to Sevastopol with relief goods on November 9. Slagel accompanied the shipment. On the very next day rumor in Constantinople reported Wrangel's retreat and probable defeat. Plans for the sending of relief by American and other agencies were altered to provide for the rescue of refugees. When the freighter carrying Slagel and the relief goods reached Sevastopol, the evacuation was already in full progress. In view of the impending conflict the captain at once sailed for the neutral port of Constanza in Rumania and after a month the cargo was returned to Constantinople. Over a year elapsed before the relief unit reentered Russia. In the interval it devoted itself to caring for incoming refugees. Although as far as material aid was concerned the American effort to reach the Russian Mennonites had been a complete failure, the American visit was nevertheless of moral aid to them, for they knew they could count on American help as soon as political circumstances allowed its entry.

The Organization of the VMSR (Verband der Mennoniten Süd-Russlands—*Union of Mennonites of South Russia*)

As the Mennonite constituency in the Ukraine gradually recovered its equilibrium after the Civil War era, it became more and more concerned with reasserting its nonresistant position. The appeal to force had ended in catastrophe. Still surrounded by political instability and general political caprice the Mennonites made a determined effort to once more apply a historic precept of their faith. Ultimately the issue of religious toleration and freedom of conscience was determinative. The future of the Mennonites in Russia depended on the attitude adopted by the Soviet government toward these questions.

Faced with the problem of charting a future course for Ukrainian Mennonitism the *Kommission für Kirchenangelegenheiten* (KfK) (Commission for Church Affairs) called a conference at Alexanderwohl, Molotschna, on February 19, 1921, with representatives from sixty villages. The assembly was particularly concerned with the induction of Mennonite young men into the Red Army. From two representatives from the Kuban, Elder Wilhelm Dyck and J. Derksen, the assembly learned that the Mennonites in the RSFSR had already made some headway in presenting their interests to the central government in Moscow[2] through the work of two Mennonite spokesmen in Moscow, Peter F. Froese and C. F. Klassen. Shortly after the Revolution a number of the pacifist followers of Leo Tolstoy approached Lenin directly to request exemption from participation in the military forces since they objected to the shedding of blood. Lenin was receptive to the idea and passed an order to that effect through the Central Executive Committee on January 4, 1919. The new law allowed the Tolstoyists and other pacifist Christian groups to organize a special council to which anyone desiring exemption from military service for religious reasons might apply. The council reviewed each application and then recommended worthy candidates for exemption. Until 1921 the Tolstoyist council operated with considerable success. On learning of the Tolstoyist council, the

Alexanderwohl assembly, after some discussion, decided to create an agency which would concern itself with the young men then in the Red Army. B. B. Janz of Tiege was elected to head the new organization; A. P. Fast of the same locality became secretary, and H. Bartel of Orloff treasurer.[3] The new union was known as the *Verband der Gemeinden und Gruppen des Süden Russlands*. A shortened form, *Verband der Mennoniten Süd-Russlands* (Union of South Russian Mennonites), was commonly applied to the agency.

A special committee was appointed to define the rights and obligations of the new organization. B. B. Janz, as a member of the special committee, was uneasy about the escapist attitude of some of the other members of the committee, one of whom commented: "We will have accomplished a great deal if we get our young people by these Reds." Similar sentiments were expressed by a former supporter of the *Selbstschutz*. But when Janz presented the committee's proposals to the assembly, they were accepted without revision. When the convention was about to close, Janz requested the floor and declared:

> This assembly gives us the task to go and intercede before the Soviet government and insist that all Mennonite young men are nonresistant. But all of us and the government know what has happened through the *Selbstschutz*. It will be extremely difficult to assert that we are nonresistant. Furthermore, we ourselves do not know if we really endorse this view. Perhaps we want to assume such an attitude now, but if another situation develops we will shoot again. If we really want to adhere to nonviolence in the future, then now is the occasion to confess. What has happened has unfortunately happened, but we are sorry that it did. This must be settled here today.[4]

The presiding officer, Elder Plett, requested the convention to respond to Janz's challenge. Tempered by the events of the recent past many delegates reaffirmed their belief in the principle of nonresistance. When the assembly was about to vote on Janz's question, a delegate demanded that those with opposing views speak to the issue. Janz maintained that a decision on nonresistance was imperative if the constituency wished to make any concrete presentations to the Bolshevik government. If the delegates were not prepared to endorse such a position, it would not be demanded. "But if this is the case," Janz concluded, "I must resign from the leadership of the organization and request you to elect a new chairman." Sentiment overwhelmingly favored a positive response to the nonresistance issue. When all was again in readiness for the vote, the same delegate who had spoken earlier demanded that the opposing views be heard and proceeded to air his own position. An atmosphere of tension returned to the assembly. In view of their disunity Janz again suggested the delegates look for a different chairman. A period of silence followed. Dramatically chairman Plett brought the question to a vote. "Everyone who favors that we strive for nonresistance with all our life and being please indicate." A unanimous affirmative vote ensued.[5]

The Alexanderwohl assembly had made a solemn vow. The new *VMSR* executive could henceforth assert that the constituency it represented had pledged to uphold nonviolence. A certain feeling of uneasiness nevertheless prevailed, for in clarifying its intentions the assembly had expressed little regret for its past misdeeds. The agency it had created was expected to do much more than simply list noncombatant young men. It was expected to chart the future course of Russian Mennonitism. A people's destiny was placed into its hands.[6]

The newly elected chairman of the *VMSR* was a little known teacher from Tiege who attracted the attention of the Alexanderwohl convention by his quiet dignity and his ability to penetrate into the heart of complex issues. His friends knew him as a man of broad sympathies and great courage. He possessed a keenly analytical mind and a persistence bordering on stubbornness. Deeply committed to the faith of his fathers, he seemed to personify the corporate ideals of Russian Mennonitism. Janz was capable of astute diplomacy. He frequently displayed a rare quality which allowed him to press his advantage in an encounter until he arrived just a shade short of the breaking point. His appointment, however, left some unanswered questions. Was he really equal to the task? Was there anything connected with his quiet dignity capable of influencing an officialdom often more impressed by brazenness, exaggerated self-confidence, radicalism, and emotional appeal than by rational analysis? Janz would be providing answers to these questions until 1926.

The *VMSR* immediately faced the task of obtaining an officially sanctioned legal status for itself. The process began at the local level with an application to the regional authorities in Alexandrovsk. These officials rejected the appeal, informing the Mennonite representatives that while the existence of a formal religious agency was permissible, it enjoyed no legal rights whatsoever. Janz was convinced that such an organization was of no worth and decided to strive for a civil-economic institution recognized by existing law and featuring a broad functional base capable of meeting all the constituency's needs.

In a shabby wagon drawn by two emaciated horses Janz left for Schönwiese, situated close to Alexandrovsk, to get help from the legal consultant of the Halbstadt volost, Belosvetov, who had in the past served many Mennonites as a notary in the registration of land titles. This jurist, well informed of Mennonite religious and civil traditions, was commissioned to formulate the legal structure of the *VMSR* on a narrow ethnic basis. The completed plan called for a south Russian union of all Mennonite groups and villages, each village to send two representatives to a central assembly. This democratically constituted body then acted as a sort of governmental unit for its constituency. For the benefit of public authorities the scheme suggested socialistic tendencies as it was symbolic of the cooperative tradition in Russian agriculture.[7]

One major obstacle stood in the way of an all-Mennonite union in the south, namely, the head of the Halbstadt volost, Bagon, whose vindictive reign of repression and brutality gave no hope that he would endorse the registry of the organization. A more favorable situation existed in the Gnadenfeld volost where a Mennonite, Abraham Dürksen, was in charge, who consented to endorse the agency after an official representative congress had ratified its constitution. The organizational assembly of the *VMSR*, held in the village of Margenau on January 3 and 4, 1922,[8] discussed and adopted the proposed constitution. The *VMSR* was to facilitate Mennonite survival in Russia in its agricultural, commercial, industrial, and nationalistic aspects. Most of the delegates in attendance, however, were far more interested in emigration. Not long after the Margenau Congress, Dürksen, true to his word, authorized the *VMSR* in the Gnadenfeld volost.[9] The way was now open for negotiating the registration of the Mennonite *Verband* with authorities in Kharkov.

A Trip to Moscow

By mid-July 1921 several difficult problems confronted the *VMSR*. The question of exemption from military service was still unsolved. None of the young men inducted into the Red Army had yet been released. Economic reconstruction in the colonies was virtually impossible since local officials continued to use caprice and terror and the threat of famine was mounting. Prospects for the entry of Alvin J. Miller and the AMR supplies seemed remote. A satisfactory solution to these problems appeared highly unlikely at the local level and consequently the *VMSR* decided to send chairman Janz and an assistant, H. Wiebe of Steinfeld, to Moscow to secure the entry of the American relief supplies.

Through liberal financial concessions to the regional *Cheka* (GPU after February 1922) both the tickets and official sanctions for the journey were procured. Janz and Wiebe boarded the train to Moscow at Melitopol in the face of acute danger, for rifle shots traversed the length of the incoming train to keep undesirables from boarding. Assisted by well-tipped porters, they managed to slip on board. The train was filled to capacity with young and argumentative disciples of Lenin. The cleavage between the political views of their fellow passengers and their own was soon apparent. Since publicity of any sort was undesirable, Janz and Wiebe remained mute. After an uneventful journey broken only by periodic food stops, the *VMSR* representatives finally disembarked at the Kursk railway terminal in Moscow.[10]

The two men immediately made their way to the Red Cross headquarters in Moscow where they made contact with RSFSR Mennonite representatives P. F. Froese and C. F. Klassen. Wiebe took ill soon after his arrival in Moscow. Janz was left alone with the task of securing the entry of American relief supplies. Assisted by P. Froese, he proceeded to the Commissariat of Foreign Affairs where an interview with vice-commissar Maxim Litvinov was arranged. Janz presented to Litvinov an English petition from Alvin J. Miller requesting the entry of American aid. Litvinov carefully studied it and promised to pursue the matter. The *VMSR* chairman had no choice but to let the matter rest.[11]

In consultation with Klassen and Froese, Janz decided to pursue another problem facing the *VMSR*, namely, the economic ruin of the southern colonies. He appealed to Peter G. Smidovich, an influential member of the party's Central Executive Committee, who as a revolutionary during czarist times occasionally found himself in prison with evangelical Christians incarcerated for nonconformity. Smidovich had apparently gained a sympathetic understanding for religious minorities. When informed of the widespread devastation in the south he showed a keen interest and asked many detailed questions about the status of the Mennonite colonies. He promised to take prompt action on the matter and requested Janz to return on the next day. At their next meeting he gave Janz a copy of a memorandum drafted by the Central Executive Committee in Moscow and directed to the Ukrainian Commissariat of Agriculture in Kharkov. The document stipulated that the central government did not wish to see the historic minority cultures of Russia destroyed and asserted that Moscow did not expect the commissariat to proceed with the land division in the Mennonite colonies as these still had a future cultural value and provided worthwhile models for overall agricultural development. Smidovich turned a copy of the brief over to Janz and instructed him to present it to the Commissariat of Agriculture in Kharkov.[12] Janz could hardly believe his good fortune. For the present the colonies were saved from a capricious redivision of the land.

Their mission successfully accomplished, the *VMSR* representatives left for Kharkov to present Smidovich's memorandum to Ukrainian authorities. Because of illness Wiebe left Kharkov for the Molotschna. In order to avoid the publicity of another congress no replacement for Wiebe was selected. The responsibility for the welfare of the Ukrainian Mennonites now rested squarely upon Janz's shoulders. Soon after his return to Kharkov he proceeded to the Commissariat of Agriculture with the Moscow document and was courteously received by a deputy of Commissar Dimitry Manuilsky. Janz handed the memorandum to the somewhat surprised deputy, who promised to give the matter careful consideration. When Janz arrived at the same office on the next day, he was promptly granted an interview with Commissar Manuilsky. Possessed of a broad political and economic awareness, the commissar supplied Janz with a variety of information of value to him.[13] He did not commit himself on the future of the Mennonite colonies, however.

Negotiating a Contract

Throughout the first months of 1921 the Mennonite relief unit in Constantinople continued to seek access to Russia. In late January Alvin J. Miller arrived in Constantinople to negotiate with the Soviet government to secure the entry of relief workers and relief goods. A preliminary contact with a representative of the Soviet Commissariat of Foreign Trade stationed in Constantinople was of little help, though it did provide Miller with an introductory letter to the Foreign Trade Commissariat in Moscow.

In April Slagel and Miller launched a bold and eventually successful campaign to enter Russia. Joining a group of merchants interested in exploring commercial possibilities in Novorossisk, they left Constantinople by ship on April 6, arriving at the Russian port four days later. The presence of relief workers on board the ship was not as self-evident to Soviet port authorities as the presence of the merchants. Since the officials at Novorossisk possessed no authority to grant the Americans entry permits, they referred the matter to their superiors in Rostov. In the interval Slagel and Miller were given freedom to inspect the revolution-ravaged city. Within a week they were summoned to Rostov. Officials, wary of the extent of their authority, wired Moscow for further instruction. The reply informed Slagel and Miller that the entire problem of American Mennonite Relief had been turned over to the Commissariat of Foreign Affairs and would soon be decided. In the end the two were denied permission to travel to Moscow and so forced to return to Novorossisk. No permission for the entry of relief supplies into Russia was granted.[14] The endeavor was nevertheless partially successful. While in Novorossisk, Slagel and Miller chanced to meet A. J. Fast, who had been sent by the Kuban Mennonites to inform the Americans of the impending catastrophe that threatened to engulf all of Russia. They were now more determined than ever to penetrate into Russia.

A Moscow entry was agreed upon. Internationally a new development contributed to the success of the venture. The American Relief Administration (ARA) headed by Herbert Hoover had been requested to provide foodstuff for Russia. Contract negotiations between the ARA and the Soviet government were soon under way. Miller hastened to the London office of the ARA, where he met Lyman Brown, head of the ARA in Europe, and acquainted him with conditions in Russia as well as the nature and purpose of American Mennonite Relief. Brown displayed a genuine interest in the activities of the AMR and honored its intention to function as an independent relief agency within Russia. It was agreed that Miller begin negotiations with the Soviet government on behalf of the AMR only after the ARA contract had been signed.

The difficult process of obtaining a Russian visa was greatly simplified for Miller through the instrumentality of the Friends International Service Committee, already operating in Moscow and on good terms with the Soviet government.[15] The London office of this organization supplied Miller with a letter of introduction to the chief of the Soviet diplomatic mission in that city. Miller was courteously received by the Soviet representative, who took a very encouraging interest in the activities of AMR. After presenting a

report of his activities in Russia as well as a memorandum outlining the conditions under which AMR proposed to operate,
Miller received not only a visa but also a special introductory
letter to the Soviet Foreign Office.[16]

Following a brief stopover in Geneva to attend an international conference of relief organizations, Miller proceeded to
Riga, Latvia. He rode on the same train as the first contingent of
the ARA headed by Philip H. Carroll and arrived in Moscow on
August 28, 1921. At the Windau railway terminal the delegation was
met by a representative from the Foreign Affairs Commissariat and
one from a special committee appointed by the Central Executive
Committee to combat the famine. Miller was lodged in the Savoy
Guest House located in the heart of the city.

In Moscow, Miller faced the formidable task of negotiating a
relief contract with the Soviet government on behalf of AMR. His
first step was to contact the head of the Anglo-American division
of the Foreign Commissariat, G. Weinstein, who requested a brief
outlining the nature and purpose of the AMR. The document
presented by Miller affirmed the close working relationship
between AMR and the Friends Service Committee, an agency
already well known to the Soviets, and emphasized that AMR
wished to aid all the destitute living in the regions of the Mennonite settlements. The Ukraine was chosen as the area for work,
for a good railway linked Sevastopol and Kharkov, and the
Ukraine appeared most seriously threatened by famine. The AMR
was furthermore prepared to cooperate with any of the relief units
sponsored by the ARA, and asked that his agency be accorded
the same privileges granted the ARA.

Weinstein hesitated to act upon Miller's request. Upon the
advice of the director of the Friends relief program in Russia.
Arthur Watts, Miller tried to circumvent Weinstein's bureaucratic
delay by proposing a limited relief project for the Crimea to the
Commissar of Health. The commissar, however, refused to accept
the proposal, but gave Miller a letter of introduction to George
Chicherin, then Commissar of Foreign Affairs. Miller was now
directed to Vice-Commissar Maxim Litvinov, who had signed the
relief contract with the ARA. Miller's experience with Soviet
bureaucracy was not yet at an end. The party's Central Executive
Committee had appointed a special agency to negotiate with foreign
relief organizations, the Central Commission for Combatting
Famine. Miller was now sent to its chairman, Leo Kamenev. On

his third attempt he was granted an interview.[17]

Once acquainted with the proposals of the AMR, Kamenev revealed a genuine and helpful interest. In a letter addressed to Miller (September 15, 1921) he promised to protect American relief supplies, free them from custom duties, and facilitate their transport in Russia.[18] With Kamenev's cooperation, work on the contract began almost immediately. Negotiations were complicated by the arrival of J. Koekebakker in Moscow, who had been sent as a representative of the Dutch *Algemeene Commissie voor Buitenlandsche Nooden* (General Committee for Foreign Emergencies) to negotiate a contract with the Soviet government for the entry of Mennonite aid from Holland. Since the Soviet officials objected to a separate agreement with the Dutch Mennonites, the initial draft of the AMR contract was altered to accommodate the *ACBN* and signed by the Moscow government and AMR on October 1, 1921.[19]

The agreement pledged the AMR to use its facilities to aid the needy civilian population, particularly women and children, "regardless of race, religion, or social or political status." Relief efforts were to be concentrated in the Crimea and the provinces of Taurida and Ekaterinoslav. Relief workers promised not to engage in any "political, commercial, or journalistic activity, whatever." The Soviet government promised to facilitate the transportation and storage of relief supplies, guaranteed their safety once in Russia, and allowed complete freedom as to their distribution. All relief supplies and the items necessary to their distribution were granted duty-free entry.

One obstacle still had to be circumvented. Though Leo Kamenev had signed the relief contract on behalf of the Ukraine, Miller soon found that it applied only to the RSFSR. The historic roots of Ukrainian nationalism had not been cut by a common devotion to the communistic \creed.[20] Miller's introduction to Ukrainian separation occurred most pleasantly and unexpectedly through the offices of Janz, chairman of the *VMSR*, who had, unknown to Miller, been sent to Moscow in an official capacity. He had been commissioned by the Ukrainian Commissar of Foreign Affairs to invite Miller to Kharkov for the purpose of negotiating a separate relief contract with the Ukrainian government. Why had Janz come to Moscow a second time?

Moscow Again

When a telegram from P. F. Froese arrived announcing that

A. J. Miller had reached Moscow, there was considerable excitement in the famished Mennonite colonies. They decided to send Janz to Moscow. In July a new menace, typhus, had begun to stalk the land, making rail travel in the current congested condition very dangerous. Nevertheless Janz again risked his own welfare on behalf of his constituency. He stopped at Kharkov to determine whether the Commissariat of Foreign Affairs was interested in aiding the distribution of the American relief supplies in the Ukraine. Commissar Kovalev asked Janz to return to his office before the next train departed for Moscow and then assured him that the Ukrainian government welcomed the presence of Miller and the AMR supplies. Kharkov authorities envinced an obvious sense of national pride in making such a decision independently of Moscow. Janz left with the gift of a return ticket entitling him to a special compartment on the Kharkov-Moscow express and a letter empowering him to invite Alvin J. Miller to the Ukrainian Republic for the specific purpose of negotiating a contract for the entry of American aid.[21]

In negotiating his contract with Moscow officials Miller had been assured that its provisions were applicable in all Soviet republics including the Ukraine. Not long after Kamenev had signed the contract, Janz appeared at Miller's door in the Savoy Hotel as the authorized representative of the Ukrainian Socialist Soviet Republic, carrying Kovalev's letter requesting Miller to consult with the Kharkov regime on the question of relief work. Kovalev had instructed Janz to inform Miller that a separate relief contract must be negotiated in Kharkov if the Mennonite colonies were to receive American assistance. Froese, Klassen, Janz, and Miller met to plan their strategy. To expedite the sending of relief to the stricken Ukrainian Mennonites they decided that Miller should accompany Janz to Kharkov. Before leaving Moscow for the south, Miller and Janz bought heavy overcoats as protection against the October cold in the unheated railway coaches.[22]

In Kharkov Janz and Miller found quarters at the home of a Jewish physician, Dr. Bassin. A leading citizen of Kharkov, Bassin had been a member of the Communist Party, but was expelled because of alleged bourgeois leanings. In addition to his Mennonite guests, Bassin occasionally had to provide lodging for members of the secret police. The resulting integration was a curious one— atheist Bassin, humanitarian Miller, pietistic Janz, and the dreaded *Cheka*.

Before and after the arrival of the 50 Fordson tractors supplied by MCC.

At the Commissariat of Foreign Affairs, Miller conversed with Kovalev through an interpreter and presented his proposals. Then he together with one or two other members of the Commissariat proceeded to the offices of the All-Ukrainian Central Executive Committee. Because of transportation difficulties Janz was unable to accompany Miller. Negotiations were carried on with B. Yermoshtchenko who substituted for CEC chairman Petrovsky. The contract which Miller offered the Ukrainian government was similar to the Riga agreement signed by the ARA and the contract negotiated with Moscow by Miller for AMR. One obstacle marred the smooth progression of the talks. Christian G. Rakovsky, the chairman of the Council of Peoples Commissars in the Ukrainian SSR, refused to grand diplomatic immunity to Mennonite relief workers, promising them only such protection as was accorded Red Cross workers. He nevertheless expressed satisfaction with Miller's promise that the aid granted the Mennonite colonies would be extended to all in the immediate area, regardless of race or religion.[23]

After some further consultation with both Yermoshtchenko and Rakovsky, the contract was drafted in its finalized form. Its terms allowed the AMR complete freedom as to the areas of operation, but was forbidden to engage in any political, economic, and religious activities. The size of its staff in the Ukraine was left to its own discretion. Article fifteen of the contract was particularly gratifying as it provided for the exclusion of local officials from representation in the regional relief committees. Provision was also made for the delivery of private parcels sent by donors abroad to their friends or relatives in the Ukraine. The completed contract was signed by B. Yermoshtchenko, C. G. Rakovsky, and A. J. Miller on October 20, 1921. An identical contract was simultaneously signed on behalf of the Dutch Mennonites.[24] At Janz's prompting, Miller indicated that his agency was willing to supply not only food but also aid in economic reconstruction by supplying tractors to replace the horses lost in the revolution and civil war.

B. B. Janz felt that the signing of the contract was an opportune time to define the role which the *VMSR* could play in the proposed reconstruction. Such a step he hoped might raise its status in the eyes of the Ukrainian government, and eventually lead to official recognition and endorsement of its activities, which would strengthen the position of the entire Mennonite minority in the Ukraine.[25] Miller's good relationship with the Ukrainian government was utilized to obtain another interview with Yermoshtchenko on the subject of economic reconstruction. Janz was also present at the meeting. The prospect of possibly obtaining badly needed agricultural machinery from the AMR pleased the Bolshevik leader; he even favored the suggestion that such an agency as the *VMSR* could best supervise the use of such machinery. As yet Miller was unable to give any concrete promise of machinery aid. The interview nevertheless served to focus attention upon the activities of the *VMSR* and on the willingness of the Ukrainian Mennonites to do their part in building up the country. The contact between Yermoshtchenko and Janz proved valuable when the *VMSR* later sought government ratification of its charter.[26]

Optimism ran high when the news of Miller's success in Kharkov reached the colonies. Daily bread as well as adequate clothing for the approaching winter was more than they had hoped for. But the jubilant spirit was short-lived. Bitter disappointment set in when bureaucratic obstinacy and inefficiency caused delay after delay in the arrival of the badly needed relief supplies.

CHAPTER FOUR

Old and New Horizons in the Ukraine

The Petition to Emigrate (December 17, 1921)

Mennonite participation in the rebuilding of the economic life of the Ukraine was particularly welcomed by Dimitry Manuilsky, the Commissar of Agriculture in the Ukrainian Soviet Socialist Republic. Painfully conscious of deteriorating conditions in the south he was willing to promote any scheme which promised economic recovery. The *VMSR* program provided him with much-needed moral and material support. Manuilsky promised Janz full government cooperation if his organization was able to obtain 50,000 to 100,000 pud of seed grain from abroad for the coming year. But he did not specify the conditions under which the grain would be brought in nor who its recipients were to be.

Manuilsky's offer nonetheless provided the *VMSR* with a unique opportunity to solidify the position of the Ukrainian Mennonites.[1] Mennonite landholders were naturally essential to economic reconstruction and had little chance of leaving their farms. But the rapidly increasing Mennonite refugee population were only consumers, not producers. Might not the government be persuaded to allow these to be repatriated to Germany or Holland? For the moment the issue had to remain dormant. Close cooperation with the government in relief and reconstruction was the order of the day. To facilitate the efficient execution of Miller's contract an All-Ukrainian Mennonite Relief Committee was organized. When the venture was officially sanctioned, Yermoshtchenko and Manuilsky were invited to become members six and seven respectively. The move was a calculated one. The approaching winter threatened a famine of catastrophic proportions in the Taurida, Ekaterinoslav, and Volga regions. Inadequate though they were, Mennonite relief supplies served as a continuous reminder of the good intentions of the *VMSR* and its foreign benefactors.

Circumstances forced the VMSR into a somewhat ambiguous position. While eager to further the welfare of the Mennonite farmers, it could not ignore the intensifying emigration sentiment in the colonies. The Margenau Congress (January 3 and 4, 1922) of the VMSR clearly expressed these sentiments as they had crystallized in the fall and early winter of the previous year. In the face of the dim prospects for any economic recovery in the near future the VMSR leadership decided that some preliminary investigation into emigration possibilities must be undertaken. Perhaps the central authorities would not be averse to a limited exodus of displaced colonists. By removing surplus population from the settlements two basic problems might be solved: the alleviation of famine and the creation of conditions which would ensure a future livelihood for the area. It also seemed reasonable to confront government officials with the question of a limited repatriation at a time when they were most favorably inclined to other VMSR operations. In late 1921 the VMSR drafted a petition requesting permission for the refugee and landless Mennonites to emigrate.

The petition was presented to the Central Executive Committee of the Ukrainian Communist Party on December 17, 1921, by B. B. Janz.[2] The VMSR was painfully aware of the implications of such a course of action. The Mennonite constituency bared its inmost thoughts to those in power and invited definite political action, especially since the petition clearly revealed Mennonite dissatisfaction with prevailing circumstances. The document began by asserting that Russia provided no hope for the future development of the Mennonite colonies, then listed the circumstances which warranted such a conclusion: the poor prospects for a continued existence based on agriculture because of banditry and the destruction of farms, the poor harvest of 1921, the requisitioning of grain, and the complete lack of agricultural equipment. The prospect of American relief, they said, had a negative influence as it encouraged robbery and murder by the neighboring populations by creating a myth of abundance within the colonies. The quartering of soldiers in the area, they argued, had exhausted all available food supplies; precious seed wheat was being consumed, and cattle and horses slaughtered. The caprice of local officials threatened to deprive the farmer of any resources which were still at his command to ward off the famine. The petition to emigrate further contended that an intolerant nationalism in southern Russia had begun agitating for the expulsion of all foreigners, creating severe hardships for the colonists.

Legally, the Mennonites were outside the law, for officials had refused to sanction the charter of the *VMSR*. In essence this implied that they had been refused the right of agricultural reconstruction. Since the entire cultural framework of this minority was dependent on a free agricultural system, its survival as an ethnic minority group was out of the question. The petition boldly presented its request that the Mennonites be allowed to return to their original homeland in Holland and to their relatives in America. These people had fulfilled their function as model farmers for the past one hundred and thirty years. Their removal represented only a minimal population loss. If they remained in Russia, many of them might succumb to the famine. Current circumstances all indicated that the potential of the group for future agricultural reconstruction was extremely limited.

Terror in the Molotschna *(December 1921 - January 1922)*

Mennonite success in the official negotiations with the Moscow and Kharkov governments was in sharp contrast to the reign of terror within the colonies. Bolshevik authorities were still apprehensive about the Ukraine. It was here that the new government had encountered the stiffest resistance from counterrevolutionary elements. The South had been the last stronghold of the White Army, hence the South was collectively guilty of treason. The Mennonites had severely compromised their traditional nonresistant position through the activities of the *Selbstschutz;* this would become more and more evident as negotiations with the government proceeded. In the fall of 1921, in a ruthless search for arms hidden by the insurrectionists, weapons used by the *Selbstschutz* participants were found in many of the Mennonite villages. To ensure the surrender of arms the authorities resorted to such severe measures as beatings and the execution of hostages.

Meanwhile in the village of Rückenau, Molotschna, an informal meeting of fifteen or twenty men was held which had direct implications for Janz's work in Kharkov. They discussed the possibility of repatriation to Germany, a procedure allowable under the terms of Brest Litovsk. As a result of the meeting, 137 private petitions for emigration were addressed to the German government. H. Kornelsen of Alexanderkrone was selected to take them to Kharkov and to facilitate their processing with Janz's help.[3]

Kornelsen provided Janz with a firsthand report of the terror and violence still prevalent in the colonies. They finally decided to

lodge an official complaint with higher party officials in the
Ukrainian capital. After several revisions the final draft of the
memorandum was signed by Janz for the *VMSR*. The proposed
course of action was a risky one. The possibility of government
reprisals loomed. The day when the document was to be presented
to the Commissariat of Justice, Janz spent in Shuravlevsky Park in
Kharkov uneasily weighing the consequences of his action. In the
evening he returned to his lodging with the memorandum still in
his possession. For some time he left the grievance brief in his
files. Finally, just before he left Kharkov to return home for Christ-
mas, Janz took the courage to deliver the petition to the Commissariat of Justice.[4]

To his surprise he was respectfully received by the commissar's
representative and promised an investigation of the matter. Returning to the bureau next day he encountered an unexpected development. The Commissariat of Justice, angered by the prevalence of
terror and caprice in the South, had sent a telegram to responsible
authorities ordering them to terminate all violence and begin
immediate investigations into the situation. Janz even received a
copy of the telegram. This development left Janz in a dilemma.
On the one hand, it promised an end to the terror; on the other,
it would most certainly evoke the wrath and perhaps revenge of
local officials. Since his activities were probably well known to
these individuals, he was somewhat apprehensive of his own safety
as well.

The festive season was hardly over when Janz received a
summons to the district governmental offices in Tokmak to attend
to some routine administrative matter. Here he was surprised to
find two members of the Kharkov government. One of these was
Makar, the chairman of the Committee for National Minorities in
the Ukraine. The ensuing discussion almost immediately focused on
the terror. In Makar's eyes the entire minority had participated
in counterrevolutionary activity. The weapons of the *Selbstschutz*
had been found in a number of the colonies. If violence had
occurred and if hostages had been shot, the reason for such action
lay in the Mennonite refusal to surrender arms. The violence and
radicalism of a few had compromised the position of the many in
the eyes of the Kharkov regime.

Makar was nevertheless willing to carry out an investigation of
the terror. Addressing himself to Janz he said:

We will now come to you in the villages and want to hold

hearings at a number of suitable locations in your settlements, where every citizen is free to come and present his grievances. You, however, must be personally present at every hearing so that the people have confidence [in us], otherwise they will say nothing. . . . We will begin in Halbstadt.[5]

Central authorities conducting a hearing together with the chairman of the *VMSR!* The proceeding provided room for both optimism and fear. It could provide officials with a convincing picture of the southern disaster. Conversely, it could become a subtle instrument of treachery in the hands of Soviet officials. The settlers, confident that Janz's presence meant an honest hearing, might express their dislike of the Bolshevik system. The material gathered in this way could easily be used to charge the colonies with counterrevolutionary activity. Potentially Janz was an unwilling instrument of deception, compelled by circumstances to betray the people he hoped to help.

There was no turning back. The investigation commission began its sittings in Halbstadt. Trustful because of Janz's participation in the hearings, the colonists came and expressed their grievances. With tears people from all walks of life told their tale of woe and suffering. The obvious sincerity of the settlers was everywhere apparent. Whether in Tiege or Waldheim their stories pointed to past and present injustices.[6] Makar, however, still refused to interpret their experiences as the sufferings of the innocent. Only once did the National Minority Committee chairman express his feelings directly. Following a day of hearings he remarked to Janz: "I find that from the Soviet standpoint this event is not particularly serious. If the people do not surrender their weapons, what else can we do?"[7]

The investigation of the terror came to an indecisive close, and more settled conditions returned to the colonies. Makar never publicized the findings of the commission. In all probability it had done little to change Makar's view that the Mennonites constituted a counterrevolutionary segment in the South. In a late July (1922) edition of the official Ukrainian party publication, *Communist,* Makar criticized the religious hypocrisy of the Mennonites and listed the number of weapons confiscated from them.[8]

Janz suspected that Makar's sojourn in the South had done little to insure the future stability of the Mennonite settlements. His suspicions intensified when, upon returning to Kharkov in mid-February, he was refused any information as to the outcome of the hearings. There was no alternative but to resume the tasks at hand: the registration of the *VMSR* charter and the emigration question.

The Decision to Emigrate

A tense atmosphere prevailed at the first congress of the *VMSR* held at Margenau on January 3 and 4, 1922. Solutions to the current domestic crises had to be found. There was some encouraging news: the arrival of aid from the AMR was imminent, and further-more two additional agencies, the ARA and the German Red Cross, had promised relief for the Ukraine. But the mood of the meeting remained sober and realistic. Most of the representatives realized that the relief efforts were designed to meet the current emergency and functioned only on an interim basis. Beyond the question of immediate survival the delegates saw a much greater one: was Soviet Russia a permanent home for the Mennonites? The question was never formally raised on the conference floor, for the congress was attended by a government representative. Indirectly the problem found expression in three proposals presented by chairman Janz. The first suggested the formation of an All-Ukrainian Mennonite Relief Committee. The second advocated the distribution of existing supplies in the Molotschna area by the *VMSR*. Additional material might be obtained by dispatching a special commission abroad. The third and most significant proposal endorsed the settlement of the starving segments of the Mennonite population in Holland and America in order to lessen the food crisis. The delegates consented to all three proposals without hesitation. The action gave voice to the then dominant concerns of the Ukrainian Mennonites—survival and emigration.[9]

The convention came to a close on the evening of January 4. The delegates, deeply conscious of the precarious conditions prevail-ing in their various constituencies, once more fixed their attention on the mounting catastrophe. They spoke in terms of "saving society" rather than alleviating famine in isolated areas. Their apprehensive-ness concerning a Mennonite future in Russia took the form of another resolution stipulating that the only long-term solution for the starving Mennonite population lay in leaving Russia. The resolution specifically authorized the chairman of the *VMSR* to take the steps necessary to ensure the realization of emigration.[10]

Responding to the directives outlined by the Margenau conven-tion, the executive committee of the *VMSR*, meeting at Tiege on

January 10, outlined a course of action. It appointed the foreign relief commission. Since B. B. Janz's administrative responsibilities had been increased by the convention's assignment to investigate emigration possibilities, he was granted an assistant in the person of Philip D. Cornies. A prominent Mennonite educator, Cornies had held a teaching position in Klubnikovo, Neu-Samara, until 1905, when he transferred to Rosenort in the Molotschna. With his diplomacy and mastery of the Russian language he made an invaluable contribution to the *VMSR*. Soon after his appointment Cornies joined Janz in exploring the possibilities of a Mennonite exodus from Russia. Though prospects for emigration were as yet nonexistent, it was decided to commence a listing of Mennonite refugees in the event that permission for such a venture might be granted.[11]

The proceedings were indicative of the contradictory policies pursued by the *VMSR* from this point onward. On the one hand, it demonstrated a loyalty and public mindedness through a spirited participation in the economic reconstruction of the South, a role which was recognized by the governmental authorization of its charter in April 1922. On the other, the same agency had already submitted a petition for emigration to the Central Executive Committee of the Kharkov regime which implied that no material betterment was possible.

Another meeting of the *VMSR* executive was held in Orloff on February 7, 1922. R. C. J. Willink of the Dutch *ACBN* was also in attendance. The emigration question was the main issue on the agenda. Willink had brought with him some of the reports of the study commission which suggested available settlement sites for the emigrating Russian Mennonites. All attending the meeting were tense. They were convinced that Russian Mennonitism had arrived at the crossroads. The emigration question had to be accepted or rejected in principle. There were no prospects for economic betterment. The social and moral fiber of the people had been gravely weakened by continual civil unrest. The Mennonites had lost confidence in their government. The nationalization of the land, discrimination against minorities, the unrelenting horrors of revolution, civil war, and banditry—all this had undermined the self-reliant spirit of the colonists. A tranquil religious life was likewise impossible under prevailing conditions. A tragic chapter in Russian Mennonite history was being written. The sense of finality and hopelessness was overwhelming. It was time to vote on the issue. "Shall we remain in Russia?'' The *VMSR* executive responded with a unanimous "No!''[12] The decision to emigrate was made. It eventual implementation would take years—years filled with suffering and hardship, but worst of all with endless disappointment.

The Registration of the Charter

Emigration was at best a long-range solution to the problems facing the Ukrainian Mennonites. The *VMSR* consequently concerned itself with current emergencies. Basic to the question of survival was the problem of economic reconstruction. Was such a venture feasible in Bolshevik Russia? No progress was conceivable in this area unless a variety of projects were initiated by an officially recognized agency; therefore the *VMSR* had to become a legally sanctioned entity. A draft charter had been read to the delegates at the Margenau Congress. The assembly approved the document and authorized Janz to commence negotiations for its official sanction and registration. Some favorable preliminary contacts had fortunately been made. Miller signed the AMR contract with B. Yermoshtchenko in October 1921. At Janz's request Miller arranged an interview for Janz with Yermoshtchenko. The *Verband* chairman was thus enabled to discuss the problem of economic reconstruction with the Ukrainian leader, who viewed Mennonite participation through the *VMSR* with considerable favor.

After the interview Yermoshtchenko left Kharkov on a government assignment and did not return to the city until March 10, 1922. During this interval Janz had sought to register the *VMSR* charter and petitioned the government for emigration. Prior to Yermoshtchenko's return, both the charter and the emigration question had been placed on the agenda of the Central Executive Committee meetings, but the items had apparently never been discussed. Janz was now in an awkward position. On the one hand, he desired to maintain the integrity of his earlier contact with Yermoshtchenko in hopes of utilizing his influence on behalf of the charter. On the other, he could not hide the fact that the same group that advocated reconstruction now desired to leave Russia. It was difficult to justify both positions. Should Janz invite the displeasure of Yermostchenko and advocate emigration or dash the hopes of his constituency by urging reconstruction?[13]

Janz's fears appeared unjustified when Yermostchenko met with him and Cornies, on March 13. The discussion centered only about the charter. But no assurance was given that it would be approved.

The Ukrainian official observed that if the Commissariat of the Interior refused to act, the matter became the business of the Central Executive Committee, and that if the new organization received sanction, the retention of the name "Mennonite" might be allowed.[14]

Janz had less reason to be optimistic when he was summoned to meet with N. Skrypnik, the Commissar of the Interior, in order to discuss the registration of the charter more fully. Though courteously received, it became obvious at once that the commissar was not interested in sanctioning the charter. Placing his foot on a nearby chair, he proceeded to criticize the document. He granted that the desire of a national minority for an independent existence in Russia was a valid one. The agency (*VMSR*) under which this minority hoped to function, however, smelled strongly of counter-revolution. General Denikin's White Army had been called the Army of Southern Russia and the resistance to the Bolsheviks had been concentrated in this area. Any name even vaguely suggesting the events of the recent past was out of the question.[15]

Janz agreed to leave out the words "Southern Russia" in the title. "Why not," he suggested, "use the title 'Mennonites of the Ukraine'?" Skrypnik immediately objected. The word "Mennonite" was a religious expression and could not be used as the official title of a minority group in Soviet Russia. Janz tactfully countered the objections. After all, he argued, this was the only term which correctly designated this historic group, which had existed as a national and well-defined minority within Russia for the past one hundred years, always with the name "Mennonite" applied to it. It might be confusing and misleading to call the group by a new name. Repeatedly the commissar asserted that no name having any sort of religious connotation could be tolerated. To arouse the wrath of the Ukrainian leader meant courting danger. Janz, however, instinctively felt he had good reason to persist, for the Ukrainian Mennonites had been largely responsible for the arrival of American relief in the south. The American Mennonite Miller had even recognized the sovereignty of the Ukrainian government by signing a separate relief contract with it. The interview came to an inconclusive end. The commissar gave no promise that the charter would be considered for registration.[16]

The problem of the charter was now turned over to the Central Executive Committee for final decision. Though it was scheduled for consideration by the committee on April 5, more pressing issues had forced its postponement. When Janz inquired as to its status on April 8, he was informed that the final decision on the charter as well as the entire Mennonite question would be made on April 12. Prospects were not rosy. A number of government members opposed the charter on the grounds that it contradicted Ukrainian state sovereignty because it seemed to suggest a state within a state.[17]

On April 13 Janz went to the offices of the Central Executive Committee to inquire about the outcome of the deliberations. In the hall he chanced to meet Petrovsky, the chairman of the CEC, who immediately demanded of Janz, "What are you still doing here? You know it's not possible." The implication was unmistakable. Janz left. The future seemed extraordinarily bleak. Despair intensified as he envisaged subsequent developments—the liquidation of the *VMSR;* exile or emprisonment for its leaders; revenge for Mennonite assertiveness. The approach of Easter brought no change in the situation. On Good Friday, Janz learned of the official rejection of the charter by the CEC.[18]

Anxious to escape the depressing atmosphere of his cramped quarters and hopeful of finding some comfort in the message of Easter, Janz went to worship with some Russian evangelicals in Kharkov on April 16. Having ministered to the group on an earlier occasion, he was immediately asked to address the congregation. Though protesting that he had come to seek, not give, comfort, he was nevertheless persuaded to preach the morning sermon. In presenting hope to others he regained his own. His inner spirit revived. A confidence emerged that all would be well. Optimistically Janz returned to his work on April 19.[19] The subsequent developments were as unexpected as gratifying. When Janz returned to the offices of the CEC, he again unexpectedly met none other than chairman Petrovsky, who tersely communicated a directive to Janz: "Go to the Commissariat of the Interior. Comrad Manzev is there. He will look after you." The news came as a shock. Manzev had replaced Skrypnik as the much feared head of the Ukrainian *Cheka!* No benevolence could be expected from this man who not long before had brutally crushed an insurrection in the Caucasus.

Manzev received Janz with unexpected cordiality.

Yes, I know the Mennonites well—there is little among them that resembles the state church, they are democratic, more

rationalistic—one can find many points of contact with
them—one need not fear in allowing them an organization.
They might in fact retain control of most of their institutions.
Furthermore, protection against capricious local officials will be
provided.[20]

All this hinged upon one condition. The word "Mennonite" must
be deleted from the official title of the organization. Manzev asserted
this with a firmness Janz hesitated to resist. He explained to the
commissar that the lack of definite historical proof prevented the
Mennonites from identifying themselves with any specific national
group. Though they spoke German, many of them probably
orginated in Holland. Manzev paused for a moment, then suggested:
"Would it not be possible for you to consider yourselves of
Dutch descent?"[21]

The *VMSR* head was allowed forty-eight hours to revise the
charter. He was assisted by a government jurist. Change after
change was made. Janz finally complained that the charter no
longer sounded like the original document. The Vice-Commissar of
the Interior insisted on additional changes. Mennonite-controlled
institutions as well as the village assemblies must be disbanded.
Janz appealed to Manzev on the institution question and to
Skrypnik on the assembly issue. He was upheld on both counts.
On April 25, the charter was approved for an organization
calling itself *Verband der Bürger Holländischer Herkunft* (VBHH)
(Union of the Citizens of Dutch Lineage). An impossible task
had been accomplished.[22]

Soon after the registration of the charter a shift within the
Communist Party structure transferred Manzev to Moscow. By
chance Janz visited his office on the day of his departure. Silently
he listened to the commissar's farewell address to his subordinates.
Waiting for the opportune moment amid the hustle and bustle,
Janz boldly approached Manzev, congratulated him on his new
appointment, wished him success, and observed: "Your departure
means a loss for the Ukraine as well as a personal loss for me,
particularly in view of our recent collaboration in the registration
of the charter." Apparently deeply touched Manzev answered:
"Everything will continue to progress here. There are other decent
men with whom it is possible to work. If you are ever in difficulty,
however, come to see me."[23] The opportunity to claim this promise
lay in the not too distant future.

The Meaning of the Charter

According to the charter of the new legalized *VBHH* its primary function concerned the restoration of the Ukrainian Mennonite colonies to their former level of economic prosperity. This task demanded the revitalization of agriculture, the advancement of general education, and the maintenance of welfare institutions and insurance agencies.

The organization was granted a broad range of economic concessions. Commercially it had the right to deal in any raw materials or manufactured goods essential to its program. It could participate in any financial and credit operation and even draw on foreign capital if necessary. Agriculturally it could initiate cooperatives, maintain storage facilities, utilize existing transportation systems, and exploit certain lands for experimental purposes. Industrially the *VBHH* could begin the production of such items as it needed for the success of its program. In the social sphere it was given a free hand in the operation of benevolent and cultural institutions. The organizational structure of the *Verband* provided for varying levels of authority. The village chapter was subordinate to that of the district, which in turn was responsible to the general assembly. The *VBHH* was also free to join analogous organizations. In all of its operations it was recognized as an official legal entity;[24] and it maintained an office in Kharkov, Butovsky 4.

The ratified charter was of deep significance to the Mennonite constituency in the Ukraine. It distinguished the Mennonites as the first noncommunist national minority to obtain such broad privileges. The potential economic importance of the charter was far-reaching. The Mennonites were allowed to continue independent farming, but their landholdings were reduced to a maximum of thirty-two dessiatines. In their agricultural operations they were free to pursue such commercial contacts as were most profitable at home and abroad. Schools and benevolent institutions generally remained under the control of the *Verband*. In addition the organization was free to associate with other groups of a similar character. Its executive officers were elected by its constituency. There was no forced integration with the Russians or with any other minority groups in the vicinity. In brief, with the ratification of the *VBHH* charter the Ukrainian Mennonites were provided with a unique opportunity to survive as an economic and cultural group.

Was the Ukrainian government sincere in sanctioning a

charter for a group basically opposed to its political doctrines and policies? In an immediate sense the question could be positively answered. The liberality of the government was partly determined by the newly launched New Economic Policy (NEP) which sought to release a part of the socialistic economy to private initiative. The desperate situation in the south reflected an ineptitude which the Kharkov regime sought to minimize by stressing economic reconstruction. Any group was welcome to participate in such a venture.

The ratification of the charter climaxed a trend of events which was essentially in contradiction to public opinion in the colonies during the first half of 1922. Most of the Mennonites saw no future in Russia and little purpose in reconstruction schemes. It was therefore not surprising that the Margenau Congress was predominantly concerned with emigration. The idea was adopted as a fundamental operational policy by the *Verband* executive on February 7, 1922. Why then the emphasis on reconstruction? Several issues determined this strategy. Regardless of what portion of the Mennonite population chose to leave, there were those who preferred to stay behind. For these people the charter created a legal basis for the needed assurance of a livelihood. *Verband* leaders realized that the approval of the charter was an emergency concession by Kharkov authorities and that few of its broad provisions were practicable, particularly if local conditions improved. The charter and the agency it authorized represented a bid for time during which emigration and reconstruction possibilities might be more fully explored. In either case, the *VBHH* became a means of sustaining Ukrainian Mennonitism through its current crisis.

In part the *VBHH* represented the continuation of the General Mennonite Congress concept. The first GMC was called shortly after the February Revolution in 1917 to meet in Orloff between August 14 and 18, 1917. Delegates from all the major settlements attended. The congress attempted to define the political, economic, and cultural adjustments which now faced the Mennonites. It was the intention to make the congress a permanent institution, in a sense as a counterpart to the *Allgemeine Mennonitische Bundeskonferenz* (General Mennonite Conference) which governed religious matters. A second congress was held in Orloff, September 19-21, 1918, but the intensifying civil chaos prevented any all-Russian Mennonite assembly from meeting in subsequent years. Because the anarchy and destruction caused by the civil war made a new civil-economic agency an absolute necessity, it could well be argued that the *VBHH* constituted a regional revival of the congress idea.

Organizationally each Mennonite settlement in the Ukraine constituted a local chapter of the *Verband*. Branches like those of Halbstadt, Gnadenfeld, or Chortitza had their own organizations. The annual meetings of these groups, usually called *Rayon-Versammlungen* (Rayon Assemblies), elected officers to implement the policies decided upon by the central organization. All the local chapters sent delegates to the general congress which met annually. If circumstances warranted it, special sessions of the *VBHH* could be held more frequently. The structure assured that local chapters enjoyed a high degree of autonomy in finding solutions to their own problems.

The name of the newly approved organization, *Verband der Bürger Holländischer Herkunft (VBHH)* (Union of Citizens of Dutch Lineage), caused some consternation among members of the Study Commission. A. A. Friesen in Canada, though certain that the new name meant little in America, was fearful of its misinterpretation by German officialdom. Germany and Russia were drawing closer together; hence a closer identification with Germany seemed potentially advantageous for the Russian Mennonites.[25] B. H. Unruh was more outspoken in his criticism. "There is indeed much uneasiness about the name of the *Verband*," he wrote with reference to Germany. "If only one had a good historical conscience in the issue. Don't be displeased with me but I cannot rid myself of a certain feeling of shame. . . ."[26] Neither Friesen nor Unruh fully appreciated the serious predicament of their Russian brethren. For B. B. Janz in Kharkov there was little choice but to accept Manzev's suggestion that the Mennonites think of themselves as of Dutch descent. A name with religious overtones was out of the question as far as Bolshevik authorities were concerned. In order to obtain any concessions whatever the Russian dictates had to be accepted. The new name simply designated an economic organization among the Mennonites; it was not concerned with ethnic origins or a confession of faith. The name was of minimal importance. Naturally this fact was not easy to communicate to the Mennonite constituency outside Russia.

The Batum Tragedy

Constituency action with regard to both emigration and reconstruction was occasionally supplemented by individual and somewhat irrational efforts, not organically related to the later government-sanctioned exodus. A mass flight to Batum on the Black Sea symbolized the radical expedients which some Mennonites adopted in order to survive. The act was an elemental response to impossible living conditions. It was simply emigration by flight, without a serious assessment of the consequences. Late in 1921 a number of destitute families from some of the villages in the Gnadenfeld and Halbstadt volosts sold their few remaining belongings and departed for Batum, where, it was rumored, emigration passports were readily obtainable. The first group of forty arrived in Batum toward the end of February 1922. The size of the group gradually increased to some 350. After their arrival they learned that they could not get exit visas after all. A tragic sequence of events resulted in death for many of the refugees and untold hardships for those who survived.[27] Malnutrition, inadequate housing, and the extremely damp climate contributed to an outbreak of malaria affecting about 95 percent of the refugees. An almost simultaneous outbreak of typhus claimed fifty-two lives. By the fall of 1922 some of the refugees were able to get visas and leave for Constantinople, then Germany and America. Because of lack of funds and other complications some remained in Batum until well into 1923.[28] These were supported by the AMR through the auspices of the Near East Relief agency. Generally speaking, the Batum episode was unrelated to the organized emigration in the Ukraine except that the agencies in Canada and the United States looked after the eventual resettlement of refugees. During 1922-23 the Study Commission was particularly committed to the rescue of its countrymen from "that place of death," Batum.

CHAPTER FIVE

Why Emigrate?

The complexity and diversity of the formative forces of any migration movement should not be minimized. The calculated departure of an ethnic group from a region it has inhabited for more than a century is never adequately explained by a single cause, nor even by a listing of its multiple causes.

Several general observations are valid with regard to the origins of the Mennonite movement out of Russia. Geographically the Mennonite settlements in Russia were widely separated; hence the emergence of any organized emigration planning among them was initially regional rather than national, and therefore the early efforts were sporadic and individualistic, several villages in a given region combining to authorize someone to act on their behalf. Such a course of action was often dictated by the intensity of local stresses or the aggressive leadership assumed by one of the villagers. Chronological variations must receive careful attention. In areas of extreme hardship and suffering such as the Chortitza and Molotschna settlements an active emigration concern emerged as early as 1919, but not until two or three years later in some of the Eastern Russian and Siberian settlements.

The role of prominent personalities was a powerful one. As these individuals gradually came to lead the movement, it increasingly took on the stamp of their characters. These men were often able to define the reasons and motives for exodus more precisely and pragmatically and thus became its local spokesmen, providing many uncommitted members of the constituency with a sense of direction.

The forces forming the emigration were both variable and subjective in character. The strength of the emigration sentiment at any one time often depended on local conditions. Fluctuation might result from a recent rainfall or the release of official pressure, both of which renewed hope for economic recovery. In general, the movement gained in momentum and scope as the government's intolerance of the Mennonite minority became more appparent. While there was, to be sure, some vacillation and shift in emphasis in the reasons for emigration, these were not universally applicable. Each would-be emigrant had his own personal reasons for wanting to leave Russia. Few of the emigrants carefully assessed their motives or consciously classified their reasons for departure. Although this nebulous sub-jective commitment to emigration cannot be concretely tabulated, it constituted a massive force behind the Mennonite flight from Soviet Russia.

The emigration motives changed during the period of flight. In 1925-26 the Mennonites listed many of the same reasons for emigra-tion as in 1922. By 1926, however, some of the pressures crucial in 1922 had dwindled into non-importance, while others had become more significant. Human suffering figured heavily in determining emigration readiness in 1922. Four years later this consideration was minimal and had been supplanted by long-range ideological and social con-siderations.

The Constituency Viewpoint

There is accurate and detailed material on the dialogue on the emigration question between members of the constituency which helped to crystallize public opinion for emigration. Particularly signif-icant in this regard was a project initiated by *VBHH* chairman B. B. Janz during the summer of 1922, in asking prominent Ukrainian Men-nonite leaders to officially record their reasons for endorsing or rejecting the emigration. These reports were incorporated into *VBHH* records and secretly sent to Germany via diplomatic mail. Many other individuals communicated their reasons for exodus through private letters, published by the American Mennonite press.

Most of the writers in 1922 gave as reasons for the emigration the national and social tensions existing in Russia. Many saw in the acts of violence committed against the Mennonite colonists the continuation and intensification of the antiminority policies of pre-revolutionary Russia. While loyal to the land which their fore-fathers had made arable, the Mennonites could not forget the hate campaigns of the czarist press, the injunctions against German language and culture in 1914, nor the land liquidation laws of 1915. There were no developments on the local level between 1917 and 1922 which give evidence of a substantial reversal of minority discrimination. A deep distrust of Russia deepened![1] As one settler wrote in June 1922,

The Mennonites no longer have a fatherland in Russia. We already had ample opportunity to realize this prior to the war, but now, through war, civil war, and violence, we have reached the conclusion and conviction that we are only tolerated guests in Russia.[2]

The majority of the Mennonites agreed with this viewpoint. They had suffered for their cultural separatism and would continue to do so. Ultimately russification and assimilation were inevitable. "The events of recent years have brought us to the point where we see in every Russian—not individually but as a representative of his nation—our oppressor, tyrant, and enemy."[3] The Mennonite sense of identification with Russia had been destroyed. By 1922 the chasm was unbridgeable.

Another basic reason mentioned by most observers in 1922 was the economic devastation of the colonies. The infamous Committees of the Poor had confiscated such land from the Mennonites as they felt entitled to. Most farmers lost their entire inventory in the process, leaving them no animals or machines with which to work the land. The balance of the time-proved Mennonite agrarian structure was seriously threatened by the infusion of a native Russian population, which frequently had no appreciation for the progressive methods of the colonists. Simultaneously the control of the individual volosts usually passed to people incapable of formulating an intelligent economic policy. Government procrastination in drafting a decisive land policy further contributed to the despair of the Mennonite farmer. There was no role for him to play in the new Russia, or even the possibility of such a role emerging in the future. He might struggle to survive, but without land, machinery, and cattle his efforts had no sense of direction. There was no inspiration in useless labor.[4]

The widespread economic devastation coupled with the physical violence, disease, and arbitrary policies prevalent between 1917 and 1922 poisoned the social and moral atmosphere in the colonies. Observers in 1922 complained of the widespread dishonesty, ethical relativism, covetousness, and extreme selfishness among the Mennonites. A continuous preoccupation with the question of survival had subjected all other values to this drive. "We are so saturated [with moral degeneracy], so sick, that in most cases when we defend our rights we do not ask if the methods employed are right or not; for us it is taken for granted that all means may be used."[5] The colonists were "physically and spiritually exhausted."[6] Children raised in such an atmosphere and deprived of religious instruction in the process would not be future assets to the settlements. There was only one solution: both adults and children must be taken out of such an environment.

Religious motives for emigration were also given in 1922. In every segment of Mennonite society there were some who were deeply convinced that an ideological compromise with communism was impossible. The social and moral foundations for a religious Mennonite reconstruction were missing and would not be supplied in years to come.[7] The curtailment of religious freedom was typified to the colonists by the forceful conscription of Mennonite young men into the Red Army—this despite the existence of contrary legislation decreed by Lenin on January 4, 1919. While some Mennonites were released during the course of 1922, the lawless acts of local officials led many to question the sincerity of central authorities in granting such a privilege. In subsequent years the nonresistance question came to symbolize a conflict which would ultimately decide whether freedom of conscience and religion existed in the new Russia. By 1925 and 1926 the basic forces behind emigration had regrouped and centered around this one issue.

Opinions expressed in private letters during 1922 did not differ substantially from the viewpoints expressed by constituency leaders. The chief concerns of the majority were economic and material in nature. Their letters reported drought, crop failure, a perennial shortage of bread, and the lack of clothing and adequate housing. There were no prospects for future economic reconstruction. Many of the letters were consequently appeals for financial help. A few private letters focused upon the loss of religious freedom and the necessity of leaving Russia "because of our children and our faith." Ideological factors, however, generally were not listed as reasons for emigration in private letters until after 1923. Improved economic prospects after the fall of that year allowed the colonists to become less anxious about survival, and encouraged them to reflect upon the broader issues of a future existence in Russia.

Many of the reasons for emigration listed by individual Mennonites found support in official memorandums and resolutions adopted in the interests of the Mennonite population as a whole. In most cases these were simply listings which made no interpretive analysis of the problems. The *VBHH* Grigoryevka Congress, meeting on February 25, 1925, tallied such issues as compulsory military service, the land question, the ban on religious instruction, and general economic ruin as reasons for the Mennonite exodus.[8] The reports of the *Kommission für Kirchlicheangelegenheiten* during 1924 and 1925 isolated the lack of religious freedom as the major motive behind the emigration.[9] The American Mennonites, on the basis of reports from abroad, saw forced assimilation, the land question, and the lack of religious freedom as the major reasons for the emigration.[10] The Mennonite World Conference meeting in Danzig from August 31 to September 3, 1930, heard several analyses of the emigration movement in retrospect. Though more detailed and formalized, the reports did not offer a substantially different picture from that emerging from the constituency itself in 1922. The speakers, C. F. Klassen,[11] D. Toews,[12] and B. H. Unruh,[13] all cited the loss of freedom of conscience as the fundamental cause of the emigration. This view was doubtless shared by the attending delegates.

The formal and the informal listings of the undercurrents initiating the emigration which were formulated during and shortly after the actual movement, made no relative value judgments on the factors involved, nor did they analyze the degree of application each found. The average emigrant could not evaluate his intense personal experiences; therefore he simply listed the major experiences which he felt forced him to leave his homeland. In most cases the often fine distinction between cause and effect was ignored. Despite the fact that the Mennonites made no precise distinction between the various forces exerting pressure on them, a gravitation toward certain common denominators did seem to exist during various stages of the emigration movement.

Bread Alone

Some settlers found it difficult to determine whether they were victims of a widespread emigration sentiment or were acting upon intelligent conviction and in accord with their conscience. The majority thought they were leaving because of religious convictions, but their real reasons were probably more economic and social in nature. The Ukrainian Mennonites were just emerging from years of violence and civil unrest, with little prospect for economic rebuilding. A large refugee population burdened the colonists. Famine had been a serious problem until food kitchens were opened by the AMR; but even with American help the food shortage remained critical.

During the second half of 1921 and throughout 1922 the pleas sent by the *VBHH* to its friends in America consistently referred to economic devastation of the colonies, suggesting that America help by sending food and facilitating emigration out of Russia. By March 1922 the real crisis was an economic one. *VBHH* letters spoke of the waves threatening to engulf the Mennonite population in the Ukraine, of the beginning of a time of dying, of prospects of rotting cadavers. There was only one solution—leave Russia![14] Regardless of changing circumstances, "our people have resolved to leave and in the main will remain true to that resolve."[15] There were references to the dark future, the night, the catastrophe.[16] "It will be easier to begin a new settlement in a free, quiet, provisioned land, than to attempt reconstruction in a completely exhausted, totally ruined and starving one."[17] Emigration was an elemental survival tactic which, though ultimately aimed at achieving freedom of thought and religion, had as its primary object the conservation of life. All other processes were subordinated to a basic struggle for existence. At the height of the crisis the Russian Mennonites responded to destruction, plunder, violence, and famine much like human beings anywhere—by attempted flight. A blind escape into the vastness of Russia was meaningless. The Mennonites, however, had concerned, sympathetic friends in America. The existence of Russian Mennonitism depended on rapid evacuation. Janz never tired of pleading with American leaders and the Study Commission for prompt and decisive action.[18] Even the question of land allotment, which had caused much consternation among the colonists some years earlier, was forgotten. "In the south no one is interested in land: bread and emigration are the poles about which interests revolve."[19]

In April 1922, when the first American relief shipments reached the colonies and the strong hand of brotherhood from abroad promised not only bread but also material aid for the rebuilding of the colonies, a spirit of optimism gradually returned to the settlements. Survival as a primary force behind the emigration slowly modified to include such additional long-range considerations as private landownership and religious freedom. Two developments influenced the prevailing emigration sentiment toward the end of April. On April 24, 1922, the Kharkov government granted permission for the evacuation of the Mennonite refugees in the Ukraine to Paraguay. The next day the charter of the *VMSR* was officially registered with authorities in Kharkov and the name of the organization changed to *Verband der Bürger Holländischer Herkunft* (Union of Citizens of Dutch Lineage); the *VBHH* was a legally sanctioned agency for economic reconstruction in the south.

The severe physical and economic circumstances which had

kept the interest in emigration at an all-time high until the spring of 1922 slowly improved. The permission to leave Russia strengthened the resolve of those who had decided to depart regardless of changing conditions. Their reasons for exodus were based on the actual and potential loss of treasured moral, ethical, and religious values. For those whose interests in resettlement mainly resulted from economic chaos and social instability, the opportunity to engage in government-sanctioned economic reconstruction was enough to dampen their desire to emigrate. Some felt that a renewed dialogue with Bolshevism was possible, at least as far as agricultural problems were concerned.

Such views were certainly not shared by B. B. Janz. He felt that any concessions granted the Mennonites were at best temporary and should be utilized to facilitate the exodus of as many colonists as possible. A basis for economic recovery nevertheless had to be erected for those who remained behind. Janz gave himself to both tasks. At no point in his career as leader of the *VBHH*, however, did he believe that economic reconstruction was really possible in Soviet Russia. For him the violence of the past, the threat of russification and assimilation, the destruction of the old forms of land tenure, the closing of charitable institutions, the militant dogmatism of the new regime, and the loss of religious freedom made a Mennonite future in Russia impossible. These views were not shared by all of his colleagues in the *VBHH* executive. The introduction of the New Economic Policy (NEP) in March 1921 allowed the forces of private initiative to reassert themselves. The arrival of American aid in the spring of 1922 further encouraged the colonists to think seriously of reconstruction. Some even thought that the NEP marked the beginning of a moderate socialism which might restore property rights.

This "land consciousness" had its roots in the events of the recent past. Already in July 1921, P. G. Smidovich, a member of the Central Executive Committee, had assured B. B. Janz that forbearance and restraint would characterize the redivision of Mennonite land in the Ukraine.[20] The Kharkov Commissariat of Agriculture subjected itself to the Moscow directive. In response to this apparent concession the *VMSR* Margenau Congress (January 3 and 4, 1922) endorsed a resolution advocating the redivision of all land still in Mennonite possession among all the Mennonites in the Ukraine, refugees and landless included.[21] Subsequent negotiations by Janz in Kharkov revealed that the government had chosen to forget its earlier promises. In March and April 1922, the Ukrainian Commissariat of Agriculture decreed that Mennonite land must be divided according to universally observed norms, with no special concessions.[22]

A resolution adopted by the *VBHH* Landskrone Congress (May 29-31, 1922) mildly censured the government's agrarian planning, stating that Mennonite agriculture could not survive under present land norms nor without the right of private property and private initiative.[23] As prospects for economic recovery improved, the land question once more became a sensitive issue among the Mennonites of the Ukraine. According to the land division scheme at least one half to three quarters of the land once belonging to the settlements was to be taken over by Russians.[24] Despite widespread unrest the land question was not resolved during the summer and fall of 1922. Local officials were particularly arbitrary in their treatment of the Mennonites. The Mennonites presented a special petition concerning this situation to the Central Executive Committee in Moscow.[25] It was passed on to the Federal Committee for Lands, which recommended to the Commissariat of Agriculture that no changes be made in existing laws to accommodate the Mennonites.[26] Further attempts at negotiation in the following years were equally futile. The Mennonite farmer had to be content with a small acreage, the title of which belonged to the state.

What influence did the land question exert upon the emigration movement? In 1922 the land question had little direct bearing on the proposed exodus except insofar as it was a source of general unrest. As yet emigration was only possible for the refugees and the landless. There was no legal provision allowing for the exodus of the discontented farmer. Group emigration purposely bypassed the landed colonist in the interest of using him in economic reconstruction. Toward the end of 1923, private or individual emigration became the only legal method of exodus, all group emigration being prohibited. The colonists could, however, leave upon approval of their private applications by authorities. Up to this point the wealthier elements of the Mennonites had despaired of ever leaving Russia. Now individual emigration by personally paying the fare with private capital opened up new possibilities. As a result there was a widespread stirring.[27] Discontent created by the land question now expressed itself in a mass application for private exodus. The accumulation of discontent over the land question in 1922-23 had a decisive influence on the emigration movement between 1924 and 1926.

The land question was naturally of no consequence to the destitute refugees in the Chortitza and Molotschna regions, where land was simply not available for them. Their only future lay abroad. It might therefore be argued that the land question was a dormant emigration motive for those who actually departed in 1923, except in the sense that the availability of land might have influenced their decision to leave their homeland.

Not by Bread Alone

The advent of individual emigration brought a fundamental shift in emphasis within the forces influencing the Mennonite exodus from Russia. In most cases the motives for leaving became more personal and subjective. In the group emigration of 1923 the reason for the movement was the evacuation of the obviously destitute. The possibility of private emigration added a more personal and broader base to the forces behind the emigration. Now the economic reasons for emigration were usually eclipsed by social and religious ones. Many of the emigrants leaving after 1923 had considerable personal possessions, which they willingly sacrificed by selling at a fraction of their value if only they were permitted to emigrate. For these individuals Bolshevism clashed ideologically with their cultural and religious values. Ultimately such questions as freedom of worship, the religious instruction of children, and freedom of conscience with regard to the bearing of arms proved more crucial than the question of economics.

The contribution of the nonresistance question in actually initiating the emigration was of a secondary nature, appearing on the scene only after emigration sentiment had become well-defined by other forces. The anarchy of civil war, banditry, and Red Army occupation had a purging and sobering effect on even the more radical *Selbstschutz* advocates. By 1922 the Ukrainian Mennonites had resolved to reassert their peace witness more decisively and endeavored to inject it into the prevailing political and ideological structure by active negotiation with the Bolshevik government in Kharkov. Though Lenin's decree of 1919 provided for exemption from military service on the basis of conscience, its actual local implementation was difficult. In lengthy official negotiations with the Kharkov government B. B. Janz was promised an important concession in the form of an alternative service program exempt from military jurisdiction.[28] Two representatives from the Mennonites in the RSFSR, P. F. Froese and C. F. Klassen, also attended the deliberations. As the Mennonite project passed through various government agencies, however, its provisions were increasingly restricted. Toward the end of 1924, after lengthy and exhaustive negotiations, it was evident that freedom for the Mennonite conscience was not obtainable in Russia.[29] Imprisonment and forced labor were not infrequent for young men of military age.[30]

How did this problem affect the emigration movement on the local level? The Russian Mennonites could ascertain the government's attitude on the military question only from the policies adopted by local officials. Most of the colonists were not aware that the Mennonite alternative service project received a sympathetic and tolerant hearing in Moscow during 1923 and 1924. Those who were better informed questioned the Soviet promise to grant the concessions. The majority of the colonists only knew that their plea for religious toleration was not being acted upon, and interpreted government procrastination as an outright rejection of their request. By 1924 the provisions of Lenin's January 4, 1919, decree of exemption were largely ignored. Many of the colonists became convinced that the Soviet government simply refused to sanction their way of life and the precepts of their faith. Their only choice was to leave Russia.

By 1925 and 1926 the majority of the settlers desired to emigrate. Many had no alternative but to remain in Russia. These men and women were willing to adapt to the political and economic demands of communism but refused to give up their freedom of conscience. A farmer writing to the Canadian *Mennonitische Rundschau* probably best summarized the feeling of his constituency:

> Certainly we have not offended those in authority. It is only that we do not wish to, and cannot, leave religion. Up to this point we can commit ourselves to communism; that is, we can share possessions with others and work communally. To join the circle of the ungodly, however, is beyond our ability—then we must flee if possible.[31]

CHAPTER SIX

Blighted Hope

Freedom to Depart

The winter of 1921-22 inaugurated the first great famine of the
the Soviet period. By January 1922 the situation had become critical in most of the Mennonite settlements. The continual delay in the
arrival of American relief supplies intensified the despair. On March
1 Janz reported:

A time of dying is now beginning for us Mennonites! . . . In
Russia there are a few that are living, many that are vegetat-
ing, and the vast hungry South is dying. What a smell from the
cadavers will rise towards heaven by May![1]

The worsening circumstances steadily augmented the already widespread desire for emigration.[2] Refugees increased in number. All the
while there was no response to the emigration petition of December
17.

Some of the despairing refugees finally decided to take matters
into their own hands. A petition of uncertain origin, requesting entry
into Germany and representing 117 families, arrived at the German
Foreign Office. Nothing came of the matter. Since this private action
might have serious negative implications for the *VMSR* emigration
negotiations, B. B. Janz took up the cause of the petitioning families.
Adding another two hundred refugee families to those of the original
petition, Janz presented the list to the Dutch *ACBN* with the request
that everything possible be done to facilitate the exodus of the refugees from Russia.[3]

Meanwhile a significant move was made by the executive of the
VMSR. A second petition requesting repatriation was prepared and
presented to the Central Executive Committee of the Ukrainian
Communist Party. The document was of a character similar to the one
drafted in December 1921. Both petitions considered not only the

exodus of refugees but also a general emigration of the Mennonite population. In view of this they were directed to the chairman of the Committee for National Minorities, Makar. A preliminary meeting relative to the petition was held between Janz and Makar's deputy, Andrei Ivanov, on March 2. Since Makar had left for Moscow, the discussion produced no concrete results.[4] Makar's participation in the emigration negotiations was extremely important. He had also headed the investigation commission touring the colonies during December and January and was consequently well informed of the situation. Shortly after returning to Kharkov from the south he had suffered an attack of pneumonia and was incapacitated until the end of February. Just before leaving for Moscow, Makar personally notified Janz of the likelihood that both the refugee and landless Mennonites would be permitted to leave Russia, but that a large-scale exodus would not be allowed.

R. J. C. Willink, as the representative of the Dutch *Commissie* in Russia, now took up the cause of the refugees which B. B. Janz had brought to his attention. In a brief addressed to the Commissariat of Foreign Affairs he requested that the government state its position in principle toward a Mennonite expatriation.[5] After a brief consultation between Willink and foreign commissariat official, the matter was referred to the Foreign Commissariat for further study.[6] An indication of the response to both Willink's and Janz's petitions came on March 16 when Janz was granted an interview with Andrei Ivanov, still representing Makar who had become seriously ill with typhus after his return from Moscow. Ivanov clearly stated his position: "Give us proof that some country is willing to receive you. Let them inform us how many they will take!" Janz had no recourse but to furnish such proof—he had to convince the Kharkov government that there was a country that would accept the Mennonites.[7]

Only one alternative remained. On July 22, 1921, the Paraguayan Congress had passed a decree authorizing a Mennonite entry. Though aware of Paraguay's generosity, the reports of the Study Commission had made the *VMSR* executive extremely hesitant in committing itself to a concrete program. Now Janz felt compelled to investigate this possibility more fully. Ivanov's proposal was straightforward. If the Mennonite emigrants received an entry permit from any foreign country, the Ukrainian Commissariat of Foreign Affairs would automatically grant them an exit visa.[8] Any further negotiations meant consigning the refugees to Paraguay. Janz was extremely reluctant to do this. He hoped that the Dutch government might somehow intervene. "If, for example," he wrote to B. H. Unruh, "the three hundred families whose names were submitted to the Dutch *Commissie* received entry permits [for Holland] a beginning would have been made."[9] Janz's predicament was a very obvious one. He was being forced to send the emigrants to an unknown land. A tactical delay was out of the question as Kharkov officials were becoming impatient. Not sure of the long-range implication of his action, Janz finally presented the Foreign Commissariat with the official document signifying Paraguay's willingness to receive the Mennonite colonists.

On April 24, Janz was notified that the Foreign Commissariat had sanctioned the emigration of the Mennonite refugees to Paraguay. He was requested to compile lists of those eligible to leave. Long hours of clerical labor finally completed the first list containing 2,744 names.[10] April 24 symbolized the successful pursuit of two strategies, emigration and reconstruction. In achieving his goals up to this point Janz had stressed that the nonproductive elements among the Mennonite settlements must be eliminated through emigration.[11] Material aid could then be directly channeled to the agricultural producer. The economic logic of the proposal appealed to Kharkov authorities. The reverse was true of the operational philosophy of the *VBHH* officially created out of the *VMSR* on April 25, 1922. Its interest in the buildup of the south was a means to an end. The *VBHH* support of the government program was primarily intended to evoke a more lenient emigration policy. An important fact was not lost sight of, however: cooperation with central authorities was essential to the welfare of those Mennonites who remained in Russia.

A Question of Destination

Despite Paraguay's willingness to accept them, the destination of the prospective emigrants was by no means certain. Paraguay did not appeal to the *VBHH* executive nor to the constituency. In part this attitude had been crystallized by P. C. Hiebert, who in his tour of the Ukraine had sought to convince the colonists of the limited possibilities in Paraguay.[12] Momentarily the emigration movement appeared self-contradictory. People were preparing to leave their native land completely unsure of their destination.

The enigmatic character of the proceeding was particularly apparent to B. B. Janz. On May 6 he presented the completed emigration lists together with the necessary accompanying documents to the Foreign Commissariat. As already indicated, the list contained

2,774 names. Janz anticipated no complications in the processing of the list, for an official of the Commissariat informed him that the emigrants could count on almost immediate departure and asked whether transportation was available. Janz replied that he had informed his benefactors in the West of the number of emigrants preparing to leave and that he had requested transport, bed, and board for them. The official seemed satisfied with the explanation and promised that full particulars regarding the emigrants would be issued within a week.[13]

The implications of the interview were clear. Even if allowance was made for bureaucratic exaggeration and inefficiency, the first group would be ready to sail by the end of May. A ship, a port, and temporary accommodations had to be procured by June 1. The situation was ironic: a group of progressive emigrants were free to go where they pleased, but there was only one backward country ready to receive them. In Russia *VBHH* authorities were free to select and recommend prospective emigrants to central authorities. Unofficially at least 20,000 would be allowed to leave. Abroad, a hardworking Study Commission had explored every potential settlement site with little success. There was an additional disheartening circumstance. Since Kharkov authorities refused to contribute to the evacuation cost, foreign capital would be needed to transport the refugees through Russia and pay the cost of their subsequent harbor sojourn. Amid all these uncertainties *VBHH* officials also faced the ominous prospect that the government might suddenly cancel its endorsement of the emigration.

What was Janz to do? All of the alternatives he envisaged had become unfeasible. He had counted on the willingness of the Dutch government to aid the Russian Mennonites, but a recent letter from B. H. Unruh informed him that no help of any sort could be expected from that source.[14] Many different countries had received consideration—Mexico, the United States, South Africa, even Surinam Dutch Guiana] in South America. In each case the results were negative. Only Paraguay remained. All the members of the Study Commission as well as the majority of the *VBHH* leaders were hesitant to recommend Paraguay.

From Germany Unruh endeavored to inject a new perspective into the emigration question. "Why," he questioned, "had the *Verband* never considered the English domains—Canada, for example?" Janz, in contrast to some of the members of his constituency, had always been somewhat apprehensive about Canada. In several of his letters to the Study Commission he mentioned its harsh climate, the limited privileges promised by the government, and also the scattered manner of settlement which he felt might destroy the Russian Mennonite concept of community. If, however, the choice lay between Paraguay and Canada, Canada should certainly receive priority. Letters from A. A. Friesen in Canada substantiated the reports that the Liberal Party would repeal the Order-in-Council (June 9, 1919) barring Mennonites from entering Canada.

Since the émigré constituency in Russia was not averse to Canada as a settlement site, *VBHH* leaders began to seriously consider this nation. Although the Kharkov government had granted exit visas with Paraguay in mind, the colonists were under no obligation to go there. Passports had been granted on the general assumption that at least one country was willing to accept the emigrants. Their actual destination was of little importance to the government. It had nevertheless assumed that since the country in question was small only a limited number of *bona fide* refugees would emigrate. The possibility of entry into Canada could broaden the scope of the movement. If a large and rather neutral country now offered to receive a substantial number of Russian Mennonites, the Kharkov regime might relent and endorse a more massive emigration.

Despite uncertainty of the destination of the emigrants, the *VBHH* executive proceeded to draw up plans for actual embarkation. Since the exodus had been authorized by the Ukrainian government, it seemed wise to use only Black Sea ports. If the territory of the RSFSR were involved, Moscow authorities would certainly place obstacles in the way. An investigation of available southern ports proved disheartening. Berdyansk and Sevastopol were badly silted. Odessa was too far away in view of the inadequately functioning railway system. For the moment Theodosia appeared to be the most suitable port of embarkation.[15] Arrangements were carefully made for the movement of baggage. Fearing the capriciousness of border officials Janz persuaded the government to approve a specific list of articles which the colonists could remove duty free.[16]

But by mid-May it was obvious that the point of departure would be Odessa rather than Theodosia. Odessa presented some difficulties. The emigrants had to be transported by rail to Alexandrovsk, then by barge to Odessa. At a special meeting held in Alexandrovsk on May 13, and attended by Janz, Miller, C. E. Krehbiel, and P. C. Hiebert, the *VBHH* was informed that the former warehouse of the International Harvester Company at Odessa might be used to house the emigrants. The AMR tentatively promised to supply the transients with food. On May 19 Janz returned to Halbstadt with Krehbiel to complete arrangements for the departure from Odessa.[17] Emigration leaders were generally optimistic, for it now appeared certain that Canada had decided to allow the Russian Mennonites to enter as agricultural settlers.[18]

The constituency was informed of the recent developments between May 29 and 31 when a *VBHH* Congress was held at Landskrone. As at the Margenau Congress, however, the delegates were primarily interested in emigration. After hearing progress reports on the state of affairs in both Russia and abroad, the representatives passed a resolution to the effect that an expanded emigration policy was unavoidable since there were still many who had no prospects of sustaining themselves as farmers.[19] The congress directed a special appeal for continued support in the emigration movement to the Canadian Mennonite Board of Colonization.[20]

The Intensifying Crisis

On June 2, 1922, the Liberal government in Canada repealed the Order-in-Council barring the entry of Mennonites. In southern Russia meanwhile preparations for departure intensified. By July 20 the third emigrant list had been submitted to Kharkov authorities for visa processing. In a short time 4,000 people might be ready to sail, and by late fall perhaps 10,000 or even 15,000. The colonists could not be restrained. People were liquidating their personal property by the thousands. If only the actual exodus could be protracted and gradual, lest authorities become uneasy![21] Such a fear proved groundless. July came and went and not a single emigrant left Russia. Why the delay? Had the Americans become fearful of the undertaking? Were the costs too high? Every delay placed the movement in greater jeopardy. To be sure, the Kharkov regime was still benevolent, but in Russia change came suddenly, sometimes overnight.[22]

On July 22, 1922, an article entitled "Who Are the Mennonites?" appeared in the official Kharkov party publication *Communist*.[23] Written by Makar it seemed to portray the official findings of the investigation commission that had toured the Zaporozhe region during the last two months of 1921. The verdict was not good. Makar charged the Mennonites with hypocrisy and inconsistency. While claiming an inheritance in the world to come, they were enjoying more than their share of earthly happiness since the majority were well-to-do. Similarly their nonresistance had been compromised by the *Selbstschutz* episode as well as the large quantity of arms confiscated from them. Benevolence and generosity, basic teachings in their religion, had not been put into practice. Did the article express the attitude of only one man or of the government? Was it intended to intimidate the emigration efforts of the *VBHH*? It might be a bad omen for the Mennonites in the future, for, they feared, permission to leave Russia might suddenly be revoked.

The urgency of an immediate emigration became more apparent with the passing of August. Crop failure caused by drought and excessive heat increased the prospect of widespread famine. No reduction of the natural produce tax was in sight. Young men continued to be conscripted into the army. There was no hope of increasing the size of land allotments. Janz commented, "If one has a number of children, if one has learned to know thoroughly the current principles of the entire system, then one's heart cramps in infinite grief."[24]

The abiding conviction that there was no future for the Mennonites in Soviet Russia sustained Janz in his frequently discouraging encounters with government officials. Some success had accompanied his efforts. By August 14 lists containing the names of 17,121 prospective emigrants had been presented. Exit permits had been readily obtainable, persons on the third list receiving these on August 1. The plan called for the submission of several lists each week. Permits were usually granted two weeks later. The sense of urgency seemed overwhelming. Worsening conditions dictated that at least 10,000 to 13,000 refugees should leave before winter. Even more crucial was the departure of the first 3,000 or 4,000 whose exit permits were valid for only a short period. An application for renewal might bring complications and unpleasant questions.[25] Why were the negotiations abroad so slow? Had not the *VBHH* executive approved Canada as a place of settlement?[26] Was Janz's continual urging, pleading, even cajoling of no avail?

The extreme tension of his work gradually exhausted Janz. He seriously began to think of submitting his resignation at the next *VBHH* Congress. He had to consider his family—six children whose father was always absent and who was nearing collapse from overwork. Wasn't it time to look after himself and his family? Why should he who worked so hard that others might emigrate leave last of all; in fact, risk not leaving at all? How much longer would government officials tolerate his presence and his persistence in seeking concessions for his people? Was there not a place of rest for him in far-off Canada?[27]

The necessity of removing the surplus refugee population from the Mennonite colonies became more evident in the late summer of 1922. Widespread crop failure promised a worsening of the famine. Thus far the AMR had not been able to feed all the starving Mennonite population in the Ukraine. AMR operations in the south between April and August had frequently left well over 5,000 people unfed.[28] Even a limited exodus might produce a more favorable balance, particularly in view of the critical shortages winter would bring. With the refugees gone the settled population could commence the work of reconstruction.[29] Reconstruction prospects were optimistic. Information arrived in Kharkov from B. H. Unruh that there were excellent prospects of sending 75,000 pud of seed grain to Russia. Though meaningless for the thousands of refugees in the colonies, the anticipation of adequate spring seed was a great encouragement to those with no hope of leaving Russia.[30]

Meanwhile by September 10 the first of eleven prospective emigrant lists of 1,200 names had been approved. Over 15,000 persons were ready to depart. The railways were prepared to transport a shipload of emigrants per week. All was in readiness for the commencement of the exodus. Eager emigrants became restless and impatient. There were frequent inquiries as to the arrival of the ships and possible departure dates.[31]

The prevailing atmosphere was suddenly subdued by a communiqué of optimism and expectation from the CPR; it was prepared to evacuate 3,000 emigrants during the current year.[32] The news came as a blow to B. B. Janz. At least 15,000 people were prepared to leave at a moment's notice! Why the unreasonable restriction? Janz sent a letter direct to the CPR office in Moscow.[33] in which he retiterated the fact that the Canadian Order-in-Council had been repealed, the site of settlement clarified, and the contract signed for the first list of emigrants. Thousands of refugees had liquidated all their personal belongings. Winter accommodations were not available. Could not a widespread evacuation of these refugees begin immediately? Not long after he had sent the letter Janz left for Moscow to learn the reasons for the delay. Here complex and frustrating problems awaited his attention. When the Osterwick Congress of the *VBHH* met on September 22 and 23, 1922, it completely bypassed the emigration question, taking cognizance of it only as a means of reconstruction.[34] They considered emigration as a settled matter, only technicalities remaining to be solved. Few seemed to recognize the illusory calm before the storm.

In the Web of Circumstance

The rude awakening came not from Kharkov officials, as Janz feared, but from an accumulation of circumstances in Moscow, in the Ukraine, and abroad. The first harbinger of the setback came in September when it became apparent that only a small number of the prospective emigrants would be able to leave before winter. Janz hoped that a Ukrainian-centered movement might still be possible with either Odessa or Nikolaev as embarkation points. The real reasons for the delay he felt lay with the CPR. But unknown to him a complex pattern of events at home and abroad had prevented the CPR from initiating the transportation of refugees.

One of these was the outbreak of cholera in the Ukraine. Though the disease was not widespread, an exaggerated report reached the office of Colonel J. S. Dennis, director of the Department of Colonization and Development for the CPR. On September 5, 1922, members of the Canadian Mennonite Board of Colonization met with Dennis in Saskatoon and decided to contact Owen in Moscow to investigate the matter. Owen's reply pointed out that all the southern ports were quarantined because of cholera, and furthermore, the current Turkish-Greek dispute interfered with shipping through the Dardanelles. The evacuation of the refugees would have to wait until spring.[35]

The Study Commission members in both Germany[36] and Canada[37] also urged a realistic appraisal of the proposed emigration in view of certain circumstances which made a fall exodus rather doubtful. Many issues were still not clarified. The port of embarkation had not yet been selected. No official Canadian government documents pertaining to the emigration had yet reached Russia. The emigrant lists had not been sent to Canada. Finally, the emigrants would have to meet the health standards outlined by Canadian law. Russian Mennonite leaders must count on submitting themselves to all legal formalities. They had to realize that though a solid foundation had been laid for emigration, official processes were tardy and time-consuming.

In Moscow P. F. Froese and C. F. Klassen, working on behalf of the emigration of the Mennonites of the RSFSR, had also encountered a number of impediments. A special meeting with Peter G. Smidovich of the Central Executive Committee took place on September 22 and 23, 1922. During the interview Froese and Klassen stressed that a basic prerequisite for reconstruction in the Mennonite colonies required the removal of the refugee population. Smidovich promised to give them every consideration once all the preparations for such a movement were completed. His endorsement of a limited emigration led to further conferences with the People's Commissariat of Foreign Affairs. The talks isolated an innocent-sounding problem which would soon become a major obstacle. The Foreign Commissariat wanted a guarantee from the country receiving the emigrants that all the people leaving Russia would be accepted and not compelled to return to Russia. Was documentary proof of this intention available?[38] The absence of Canadian representation in Moscow made this a complex issue.

Two other questions confronting the RSFSR Mennonite representatives in Moscow were whether the Canadian authorities would require medical certificates from the emigrants as they had in the Ukraine and which port of embarkation was available in the RSFSR. The second question was the more pressing. The ports of St. Petersburg, Riga, and Libau in Latvia had their drawbacks. St. Petersburg and Riga were closed in winter. Libau, while ice-free the year round, was in foreign territory and connected to Riga by a narrow-gage railway, compelling emigrants to change trains there.[39] The problems encountered by the Moscow delegation anticipated the issues with which the entire emigration movement would soon have to grapple.

Froese and Klassen had also become aware of another threat to the proposed exodus, namely, outright government opposition. While in the Russian capital they had conferred with a representative of the North German Lloyd. Naturally solicitous on behalf of his firm, the agent outlined the administrative formalities as well as the technicalities related to the removal of the Mennonite refugees. He anticipated delaying tactics from two government departments—the *GPU* and the Commissariat of Foreign Affairs.[40]

Janz became aware of the complex web of circumstance frustrating emigration efforts during the month of October. A telegram reached Janz at Tiege in the Molotschna on October 2 which informed him that the CPR was willing to bring out 3,000 people via Libau and asked whether the organization could cover the fare from the various localities in Libau. For Janz the telegram had fearful implications. To the Study Commission he wrote, "Apparently the way, like that of the children of Israel, shall not be the closest one, but will once again be fought through a desert of difficulties."[41]

This "desert of difficulties" was no mere figure of speech. What Janz had feared was becoming a reality. The Ukrainian emigrants might have to traverse the territory of the RSFSR. All the carefully laid plans for a southern exit were useless. How to make the impatient emigrants understand? Where could they be housed for the winter of 1922-23? What of the cost of the long journey to Libau? Were reduced rates available? Complications of one kind or another could be expected in Latvia. By spring the attitude of Kharkov officials might have radically changed.[42] The new development was extremely disconcerting. Just two weeks previously, at the Osterwick Congress, Janz had consented to serve another year. Had he made a serious error?

CHAPTER SEVEN

The Meeting of the Ways

In Moscow a curious sequence of events unified all the emigration leaders in a common cause. On October 14, 1922, P. F. Froese and C. F. Klassen took part in an important conference with A. R. Owen who had returned to Moscow the day before, bringing a copy of the contract which the Canadian Mennonite Board of Colonization had signed with the Canadian Pacific Rainway. He also informed Froese that two ships, the *Montreal* and *Scandinavian,* were standing by in English waters awaiting further orders. The two vessels had a combined passenger capacity of 2,647. Two other ships, the *Sicilian* and the *Pretoria,* were also being readied. Accommodation for an additional 1,400 persons was now available. Two things were necessary: a port and 3,000 emigrants. Since even empty vessels were costly, immediate action was essential. Owen and Froese agreed that Libau was the only available port. After the meeting Owen wired this information to London.[1]

Froese cabled Janz to come to Moscow at once, for the emigration issue tolerated no delay. Janz immediately responded. Following a brief stopover at Alexandrovsk he proceeded to Kharkov, where he sought to discuss the new developments with officials of the Commissariat of Foreign Affairs. He received no cooperation. One of the officials sarcastically commented, "Let your friends open the Dardanelles. Telegraph Lloyd George to allow your emigrants to pass through."[2] The officials in the agency supervising the actual evacuation proved more accommodating and saw little difficulty in the northern route once the diplomatic formalities had been dispatched in Moscow.

There was no choice but to leave for the Russian capital. Since the permits for the exodus had already been issued in Kharkov, the Foreign Commissariat in Moscow viewed the matter as a purely technical procedure and directed Janz to the government department supervising the movement. With this the emigration efforts of the Ukrainian and East Russian Mennonites joined hands. The representatives of both groups met in the same government offices. Government agencies proved most accommodating. They promised to provide sufficient rolling stock to ensure the departure of an emigrant train from Alexandrovsk to the Russo-Latvian border station of Sebezh every five or six days and set a specially reduced fare amounting to one-half the price of a fourth-class ticket for all emigrants. If desired, warm food would be made available at three or four points along the way. The concessions were dependent on one condition: the Latvian government must grant transit visas in order to enable the emigrants to reach Libau.[3]

Janz and Froese now conferred with Owen regarding the port of embarkation. Though officials were not strongly opposed to the use of a southern port, Janz felt it best to agree to a northern evacuation for several reasons: Since most of the southern harbors were badly silted, vessels could easily be damaged. The CPR, moreover, had made preparations for a northern departure and was ready to do all in its power to ensure the comfort of the refugees. Finally, the prospect of a well-ordered and reasonably fast rail journey, at reduced fare and in heated cars, could not be ignored.[4]

The decision to use a northern port as an embarkation point was not without its problems. Transit visas from RSFSR and Latvian officials were not immediately available while the first exit permits granted by the Ukrainian government were about to expire. Simultaneous negotiations with Moscow and Kharkov were essential. Furthermore, how much time would the emigrants have to liquidate and prepare for the exodus once the administrative formalities had been completed? Janz's hope to conclude diplomatic processes within a week was futile. Financing the long trip from Alexandrovsk to Sebezh presented a major problem. Despite the fare reduction the great distance made the journey too expensive for most of the destitute refugees. The emigrants also had to count on paying approximately $11.50 per person to cover the cost of the Latvian transit. Janz sought to avoid the administrative difficulties of a foreign loan by requesting a credit advance from the CPR with which to pay the Soviet government. Owen refused the petition. Janz then sent a plea for transit funds to the CMBC. By return telegram the board guaranteed $35,000 but for expenses in Latvia only.[5] Not long before, the CMBC had informed him that no more than 3,000 emigrants could be accepted in Canada before winter. Janz was determined that at least these should leave and that the long-awaited trek out of Russia begin.[6]

By November 6, the plans for the departure of the first group of 774 emigrants were almost completed. All that remained was the renewal of the exit permits in Kharkov. Since no credit was available, the outgoing colonists had to rely on their own resources. The departure date for the first group was set at December 1. For the five-day journey the government promised to provide one railway car for every twenty-five people. Each unit would be heated. Every person over the age of sixteen planning to emigrate was required to possess an exit permit as well as a certificate from the *VBHH*, which recognized him as a *bona fide* emigrant. The CPR steamer *Sicilian* was scheduled to take the first group from Libau to Southampton, where they would board another steamer for the trip across the Atlantic. Because the first echelon would be representative of the entire group in the eyes of officials, Janz was particularly concerned that the emigrants be in good health. In order to avoid a price depression due to mass liquidation the *VBHH* also ordered the establishment of a local emigration committee in Chortitza to supervise the gradual sale of the emigrants' personal effects.[7]

A Will but No Way

The plans for the departure of the first group were barely completed when new complications arose. On November 8, Janz had ordered the Chortitza emigration committee to commence the liquidation of the emigrants' personal property. The next day the order had to be rescinded, for two major obstacles had arisen. As Froese and Klassen had already learned, the Foreign Commissariat insisted that no emigrants rejected by Canadian health authorities return to Russia, and that doctors from the Canadian Department of Emigration were barred entry to the Soviet Union as a retaliation against similar action taken by the Canadian government in connection with a Soviet delegation.[8] Though mere by-products of international tensions, these problems brought emigration proceedings to a complete standstill. There was no way of preventing anyone medically unfit by Canadian standards from leaving Russia for Latvia with the first group of emigrants. When subsequently rejected in Latvia, however, these individuals could not return to Russia.[9] The emigrants naturally wished to leave as family units. Filial affection tempted many to include medically unfit members. The ravages of revolution and famine were everywhere. Disease and malnutrition affected almost every family.

The emigrants were landless refugees, many of whom had been saved from starvation by AMR kitchens. To insist that every family exhibit the highest standards of health therefore seemed unreasonable to the emigrant.[10] Such logic was difficult to communicate to the foreign immigration authorities. In the end the rigid application of Canadian health standards to the Mennonite emigrant population was to cause untold heartaches and difficulties.

In an attempt to facilitate the medical inspection Janz telegraphed the CPR office in London requesting that a Russian doctor be allowed to process the emigrants. On November 23 a dispatch rejecting the proposal arrived in Moscow.[11] By now the dilemma was painfully apparent. Winter had come to Russia and the prospective emigrants had not left. The Canadian doctors could not come to the colonies; and once in Latvia the medically unfit could not return.

A momentary ray of light broke through the gathering storm clouds. On November 24, a representative of the British Mission in Moscow informed Janz that Kharkov had granted entry permits to two Canadian representatives. A Ukrainian government official in Moscow confirmed the information. Janz also learned that Owen had been granted permission to travel to Kharkov and Odessa in order to investigate the possibilities of a southern exodus.[12] Owen's southern sojourn brought no real progress. While the port of Odessa appeared most reasonable for a winter exodus, the continuing tensions in the Dardanelles prevented its use.[13]

Meanwhile the anxiety and frustration of the prospective emigrants increased. In mid-December two delegates sent by the southern emigrants to Moscow to confer with Janz informed him that the continual postponement of the departure date was having serious repercussions in the colonies. People who had carefully guarded their travel funds were now forced to make a crucial decision. Should these resources be utilized for seed grain or not? Those who had no livelihood wondered how long AMR resources could continue to sustain them. Some feared an increase in the natural products tax. Every week more and more people registered their intent to emigrate. Janz wrote: "In other words it [the emigration] has become an elemental tumult, the dams are bursting. The people have made up their minds and are ready to struggle with death and life."[14]

In the hope of partially alleviating the intensifying dilemma Janz tried to find a solution to the problem of the Latvian rejects. Wishing to modify the attitude of the Foreign Commissariat on the matter he submitted a petition on December 13, urging that the medically unfit be allowed to return to Russia from Latvia within two weeks. The *VBHH* guaranteed that the returnees would not become a burden to the government. The petition was directly channeled to Foreign Commissar Litvinov, who delegated his economic-legal department to investigate the request. On December 21, Janz learned that the petition had received a favorable hearing and might be approved if sanctioned by the *GPU* and Commissar Litvinov. Such action ensured the commencement of the emigration within two weeks. However, this prospect of success had some drawbacks. Even if relatively few returned to Russia, the treasury of the *VBHH* would be severely strained. The task of resettling destitute refugees back in the country they so desperately desired to leave would not be a pleasant one. But first and foremost, the movement of emigrants had to be initiated. In the interval alternative projects could be explored[15] to maintain the medically unfit outside of Russia.

Despite all the efforts of emigration leaders the year 1922 ended in disaster. On the very day that Janz had learned of the pending approval of his petition a telegram from Montreal informed Owen in Moscow that all imigration into Canada had been postponed until spring.[16] In the Mennonite settlements the successful registration of the *VBHH* charter stood in contrast with the obstacles encountered in the implementation of its economic provisions. Similarly the authorization of the emigration in both Kharkov and Moscow witnessed a series of disappointments. Because of the widespread devastation, the government initially endorsed thousands of exit permits. Then when the exodus was about to begin, the southern ports proved too shallow, and a cholera epidemic broke out. An emigration route in the north had barely been settled when the question of medical examinations blocked the way. The instant this problem appeared to have been solved, the entire project was postponed by Canada until spring.

This frequent ebb and flow of hope and despair had a detrimental influence on the émigré constituency. For almost a year many of the refugees had been in temporary lodgings, expecting to depart at any moment. Since they had to finance their journey through either southern or northern Russia, they carefully hoarded their savings, only to see the ruble ruined by inflation. In the spring another decision became necessary. Should available funds be invested in seed grain in the hope of achieving a fall return? The array of problems destroyed all confidence in the future and gradually undermined the moral and spiritual fortitude of the refugees. For some the elemental drive of self-preservation over-shadowed any interest in the welfare of the community.[17]

Inaction and Action

For the Moscow representatives of both the Ukrainian and RSFSR Mennonites the prospect of a spring departure was undesirable. Thousands of refugees were gravely disappointed.[18] Apparent hopelessness rapidly gave way to impatience and discontent. The situation was crucial in other respects. The government agency which had authorized the emigration might be dissolved. A growing resentment against the emigration movement was discernible in both Kharkov and Moscow, which might cause an abrupt policy change at any moment. An increase in rail fares appeared imminent. In Canada, opponents of the CMBC might force the organization to break its contract. The continuous delay was doubtless exasperating to CPR officials. The doctors of the Canadian Immigration Department still were not allowed to enter Russia. Furthermore, Janz's petition to the Commissariat of the Interior for a fourteen-day return period for the medically disqualified in Latvia was disallowed.[19] As a consequence the Foreign Commissariat insisted that no emigrant could return to the Soviet Union once he had crossed the country's borders.

In Moscow CPR agent Owen did all he could to aid the beleaguered emigration representatives. At his suggestion the Canadian Immigration Department was asked to agree to the use of a doctor from the British Trade Legation in Moscow or the American doctors there. The request was rejected. Only Canadian doctors were acceptable.

Janz, Froese, and Klassen meanwhile embarked on a twofold course of action. They asked the American Mennonite Colonization agencies to request the Canadian government to allow all Russian Mennonites to enter, irrespective of their physical condition. The Americans refused to present such a petition because the plan demanded a basic change in Canadian immigration law. It was further decided to contact a German delegation in Moscow about the possibility of transferring the medically unfit to Germany. Exploratory talks soon confirmed that the German government was not interested, largely on account of the critical domestic situation in Germany.

Endless obstacles and hindrances! Only one thing was certain. The Mennonites could not stay in Russia. An exit had to be found. B. B. Janz wrote:

> It is dark. Nothing to see, nothing to feel, nothing to calculate, no support, no foundation, no future; what one sees and hears, recognizes and assesses is all factual material for a negative conclusion, for negation. For a long time I have worked, hoped, striven—with one word *believed*. Most of the more serious people in our congregations have given support and unitedly struggled until the present day. The small chest with our whole hope and faith floats as a last wreck upon the billows of the Russian flood, and appears destined and compelled to sink in it.[20]

By January 1923 American reactions directly affected the well-being of the Russian Mennonites. Throughout 1922 a rising wave of opposition had been discernible among the Mennonite constituencies in Canada who were preparing to receive their brethren from abroad. Dissatisfaction was expressed by individuals, small groups, and the Mennonite press. The efforts of a militant minority soon produced considerable hostility to the proposed movement.[21] An exaggerated press version of this antagonism reached Russia and, combined with the news that the exodus had been postponed until spring, was extremely depressing to the emigrants. Anxious colonists in Chortitza convoked a special meeting to reevaluate their prospects. On several occasions they had already delegated J. P. Klassen to visit Janz in order to obtain a firsthand progress report. Klassen returned from his last visit on December 27, 1922. A special convention of emigrants in the Chortitza volost was held on January 2, 1923. The emigrants themselves now made two proposals—first, to explore more fully the settlement possibilities in Mexico,[22] and second, to dispatch a representative to America to investigate the difficulties.

A telegram was sent to Janz requesting his participation in such a mission. He discouraged the undertaking. Not only was it impossible for him to leave his post, but such a venture by one group was illegal since it possessed no privileges outside the *VBHH*. No funds for such an undertaking were available in Russia and would have to come from America. This Chortitza episode represented a natural but naive reaction to hopeless circumstances. It totally disregarded the fact that all permits had been obtained through the *VBHH* and that this agency was indispensable for anyone wishing to leave Russia. It was an evidence of the growing selfishness which disregarded community welfare in the interest of self-preservation. In December 1922 a similar plea for action had come from the emigrants of the Gnadenfeld volost.[23]

The panorama of general dissatisfaction and growing desperation which confronted *VBHH* leaders during the first months of 1923 did not blind them to the problems and tasks facing them. Would a large-scale emigration from Russia be endorsed by the American Mennonites? How many emigrants might they accept in 1923? What other possibilities were there? What of the medical rejects in Latvia? Was Mexico open to them? Would public opinion in America be favorably influenced through the arrival of a new representative from Russia?[24] Solutions frequently came gradually and painfully.

Toward a Philosophy of Emigration

Throughout 1922 the *Verband* consistently dealt with the emigration problem as a current emergency faced by many technical problems. There was consequently little attempt at formulating a long-range plan or at assessing the historical significance of the movement. The purpose of the agency was pragmatic. It was a means of facilitating the evacuation from Russia and of providing for those would have to stay. The work had been extremely frustrating. The *VBHH* executive spent many hours drawing up memorandums or engaging in seemingly fruitless discussions. Were these efforts justified? Did they not represent a useless struggle against overwhelmingly powerful circumstances? Was emigration absolutely necessary to the future of the Russian Mennonites? For both the *VBHH* leadership and its constituency answers to these questions became more and more urgent.

On January 1, 1923, B. B. Janz presented these issues in a letter addressed to the leaders of the Mennonite conferences and organizations in America.[25] The document outlined a working philosophy for future emigration efforts and provided a penetrating résumé of the problems confronting the Russian Mennonites. The events of the recent past could not be forgotten: the carnage at Blumenort, the murder of prominent Mennonite leaders, the spread of famine. The moral fiber of Mennonite society was becoming subject to decay. There were other discouraging developments. Most of the private schools had been taken over by the state and many of the Mennonite teachers dismissed. Land allotments had been drastically reduced. Integration with surrounding populations appeared inevitable. In Janz's estimation the destruction of the existing cultural-economic pattern was less disastrous than the loss of trea-

sured religious values. For most of the emigrants the retention of
these was all-important.

Certain questions of tremendous importance still remained
unanswered. Was the *VBHH* committing a grave historical error
by its relentless pursuit of emigration? Did not the possibility for
economic and cultural progress still exist in Russia? Were the
difficulties perhaps due to the fact that Russia was in a transition period? Might not the pendulum of revolution swing back to
a more rational position in which individual initiative again played
a part?[26] Surely the Mennonites could play a considerable role in the
construction of the new Russia! Janz disagreed. Economic adaptation
and readjustment was not the real issue. Rather, the Mennonites were
confronted with a governmental policy dating back to the last quarter
of the nineteenth century, a policy rooted in the historical, social, and
cultural pattern of the land, namely, russification. The Mennonites in
the 1870's had left because of increased pressure to conform to the
Russian national image. Except for minor variations that pressure had
never relented. More and more the government formulated its minority
policy according to the will of the masses. In Russia the progressive
element would always pay for the less progressive by both taxes and
conformity.

> Even if this government did not exist and a different one were
> in its place, the picture would not be too much different. And
> if, contrary to all expectations, the state collapses (which I
> certainly do not expect) the time following this would be
> frightful—chaos![27]

Contemporary bureaucratic opinion seemed to confirm Janz's con-
tention, at least as far as the land question was concerned. In
conference with a Kharkov official Janz received a candid analysis
of the Mennonite position.

> We do not move against the masses but with them. These are
> against you. We want peace. If we give you the land (which
> you have possessed for 130 years) the neighboring Russians
> will destroy and murder. What shall we do then? We simply
> cannot help you. We must reckon with the masses.[28]

By 1923 a widespread effort to curb the agricultural basis of Mennonite economic life was imminent. The trend in this direction was
clearly established not only because Russian neighbors were eager
for their share of the colonists' land, but also because Marxist-
Leninist theory demanded its nationalization. A minority of 100,000
could not long survive such onslaughts. If they continued, and there

was every indication of this, there was no future in Russia. Emigration was the only alternative.[29]

The Founding of the All-Russian Mennonite Agricultural Union (Allrussischer Mennonitischer Landwirtschaftlicher Verband)

Revolution, civil war, and banditry had left the Mennonite colonies in the RSFSR in a state of material, cultural, social, and religious ruin. In the interests of achieving a degree of stability and in the hope of effecting some type of reconstruction several sporadic efforts were made by several of the Mennonite groups to obtain a recognized status. Desiring to obtain official sanction for their non-resistant position some of the Mennonite settlements in the RSFSR had commissioned P. F. Froese and C. F. Klassen as their representatives in Moscow. In Moscow these two men made contact with the Moscow United Council of Religious Bodies, led by Vladimir Tchertkov, a staunch adherent of Leo Tolstoy. By appealing directly to Lenin the Council had induced the Central Executive Committee to decree the exemption from military service for such young men as refused to bear arms for conscience' sake. The law became effective on January 4, 1919. Henceforth anyone making application to the Council could, upon its recommendation, legally refrain from bearing arms.

The position of Klassen and Froese in Moscow was considerably strengthened when a Conference of Eastern and Siberian Mennonite Churches meeting at Beryozovka near Davlekanovo in July 1920 certified them as their representatives in Moscow. This additional support did not help the delegates to any great extent. During the second half of 1920 the legal position of the Moscow United Council became more and more imperiled. The home of its chairman was raided by the *Cheka*. Tchertkov himself was spared from exile only by the intervention of Leo Kamenev, an influential member of the Politburo.[30]

Klassen and Froese now appealed directly to the Commissariat of Nationalities, headed by Joseph Stalin. On the basis that the Mennonites were of neither pure German or Dutch extraction Froese and Klassen sought to persuade the Commissariat that the Mennonites must be classified as a minority distinct from the other German colonists. The effort was futile. Froese and Klassen were informed that a German division capable of looking after the Mennonites already existed within the Commissariat. Special consideration was out of the question, particularly since the petitioners were not even members of the Communist Party.

In March 1921, when the Soviet government replaced the economically ruinous War Communism with its New Economic Policy, the easing of pressure in the economic field brought a corresponding breathing spell in other areas. But the NEP came too late to prevent the first great famine of the Soviet era. By summer it became increasingly apparent that a catastrophe was in the making. In response to the growing emergency a Social Relief Committee, headed by several prominent Russians, was formed in Moscow. Froese and Klassen joined this agency, hoping that participation in this humanitarian project would give a certain legality to their other activities in the Russian capital. But any gains by this strategy were soon lost. The Social Relief Committee was forcibly dissolved by the Soviet secret police and many of its members, including C. F. Klassen, were temporarily imprisoned.

The summer of 1921 nevertheless brought a change for the better. In mid-July two representatives from the newly organized *VMSR*, B. B. Janz and H. Wiebe, came to Moscow to negotiate the entry of famine relief supplies promised the Mennonites in Russia by the AMR, to secure the release of Mennonite young men still in the Red Army, and to inform the central government of the widespread economic devastation in the south. Froese, Klassen, and Janz were again able to confer when Janz returned to Moscow in late summer of 1921 on the occasion of Alvin J. Miller's arrival in the city. The identification of the Mennonite representatives with the signing of the AMR relief contracts in both Moscow and Kharkov served to enhance their status and proved helpful in later negotiations.

The release of private initiative in the economic field through NEP soon brought a return of prosperity. With it came a desire for economic reconstruction in the Mennonite settlements. Seed Grower Associations sprang up in Alt-Samara and Köppental am Trakt. In the Ukraine the *VBHH* had its charter ratified by the Kharkov government on April 25, 1922. Another union of a similar nature had been organized in the Kuban area. Its leaders were F. Isaak, C. A. De Fehr, and J. Reimer. In South Russia as well as the vast expanses of Siberia the Mennonite colonists all faced the same basic problems: unification and reconstruction, and failing these, emigration. Many settlers had been totally ruined by revolution and civil war. For these emigration seemed the only alternative. But many desiring to emigrate could not, and these had to be assured a future livelihood in Russia. The successful fulfillment of both tasks, emigra-

From left to right, Peter I. Dyck, B. B. Janz, Philip D. Cornies.

The AMLV executive in 1928. From left to right, C. F. Klassen, vice-chairman; P. F. Froese, chairman; H. F. Dyck, secretary.

tion and reconstruction, needed an extensive organization basis. Such a venture was fraught with some danger. In February 1922 two agents of the secret police had raided the residence of Froese and Klassen and attempted to confiscate the agency files, claiming that they had been sent to liquidate it. Froese protested vehemently and tried to reach the secretary of the All-Russian Central Executive Committee by telephone. This so impressed the visitors that they left after sealing the files. An appeal to Leo Kamenev soon reopened them.[31]

The idea of an economic organization found widespread support among the Mennonites by midsummer of 1922. The officially sanctioned *VBHH* as well as the newly organized Kuban union in the southeast naturally intensified this feeling. In Moscow the possibility of forming a similar agency in the RSFSR was seriously discussed by Klassen and Froese. On October 11, quite apart from these deliberations, a Mennonite Conference met in Alexandertal, Alt-Samara, attended by representatives from Arkadak, Barnaul, Turkestan, Kuban, Trakt, Ufa, and Alt-Samara.[32] It decided to inaugurate an agency similar in character to the *VBHH*, and elected a committee to draft a charter. The committee patterned its charter after that of the *VBHH*. The new organization was to possess both agricultural and commercial functions, although in its charter the agricultural aspect received the dominant stress. In the formulation of the charter every effort was made to ensure that it correctly reflected the economic needs of its constituency. To assure government endorsement it contained no religious provisions. The new association might become a legally constituted body only if it served a constituency and purpose different from any existing agency. The final revision of the charter was completed in Alexandertal between November 20 and 24, 1922.[33]

The Mennonite representatives in Moscow presented the final draft of the charter together with an accompanying memorandum to a member of the Presidium of the Central Executive Committee, P. G. Smidovich. Froese and Klassen were personally received by Smidovich on January 25, 1923. A second interview followed on January 29 at which the Soviet official declared that he agreed in principle to the project. Hereupon the documents were passed on to the Commissariat of Internal Affairs and the Commissariat of Agriculture for further processing. Consultations with representatives from the Agricultural Commissariat were held on February 3 and 5. The Mennonite proposal was endorsed and returned to the Presidium. The Commissariat of

Internal Affairs proved much harder to convince. It suspected that the planned Mennonite Union had both an economic and a religious character. In a special brief Froese and Klassen carefully delineated the agricultural functions of the projected agency and presented the brief to the Internal Commissariat on February 9. By the end of February the Mennonite representatives learned that the charter had been returned to the Central Executive Committee, but that it had not received the approval of the Commissariat of the Interior.[34]

The bureaucratic nightmare was by no means over. The charter was once again discussed with Smidovich on March 13 and 17. It was now sent to the State Secretariat. Again the objection that the *Verband* was both economic and religious in character. On March 19 the charter .was returned to the Codification and Law Project division of the Commissariat of Justice. The head of this division, P. A. Krassikov, had met Froese on a previous occasion and was not unkindly disposed toward him. Krassikov observed that he could not authorize a religious organization with certain economic peculiarities. The Mennonites after all were a religious group. Froese explained:

"Yes, but we are also an ethnic group with particular economic and cultural characteristics."

"But of what nationality are you?"

"We are descendants of settlers from Germany and Holland."

"Well, mention this in your charter."

The desired revisions were made: The organization had only one basic aim, agricultural reconstruction, and would under no circumstances be used for religious purposes. Then too the word "Mennonite" was defined as representing the descendants of earlier colonists from Holland and Germany. By the end of March the Commissariat of Justice was satisfied with the terms of the charter. It was now returned to the Presidium of the Central Executive Committee for final endorsement.[35]

A painful period of waiting ensued. All the other projects under consideration by the Mennonite representatives suffered for lack of an officially sanctioned charter. Smidovich, the spokesman for the charter in the CEC, became ill toward the end of March and spent several weeks in a sanatorium. He briefly returned to Moscow for the 20th Party Congress, April 17-25, but no meeting of the CEC Presidium took place. Smidovich arrived back in Moscow on May 15. The next day the Presidium of the CEC sanctioned the charter of the *AMLV*. Froese and Klassen were informed of the decision two days later. The

The Second Congress of the AMLV at Davlekanovo, June 27-30, 1924. Chairman P. F. Froese can be seen in the second row, third from the right.

task of Mennonite agricultural reconstruction could now begin.

The first congress of the *AMLV* was held in Alexandertal, Alt-Samara, during October 1923.[36] Not only its charter but its operational program was closely patterned after the *VBHH*. Two quite contradictory themes dominated the proceedings in Alexandertal— reconstruction and emigration. According to its charter the *AMLV* purposed to raise the Mennonite settlements in the RSFSR to their former level of economic prosperity. To aid them in achieving this aim the Mennonites were granted a broad slate of privileges. The Moscow regime was sincere in its concessions since the provisions of the *AMLV* charter were in agreement with the terms of the New Economic Policy, but this liberality would end with a change in national economic strategy. Regardless of what the developments might be, the officially sanctioned *AMLV* did offer the colonists a breathing spell for the immediate future. Like their brothers in the south, however, they were not interested in economic reconstruction. Emigration and not reconstruction evoked an eager response at the Alexandertal Congress. The two themes characterized the entire life of the *AMLV* although emigration was not always an obvious feature of its operational policy. In part this already reflected the intensifying government hostility toward emigration later in 1923.

CHAPTER EIGHT

The Man in the Middle—B. H. Unruh

The Study Commission sent abroad by the Russian Mennonites arrived in New York on June 13, 1920. Its members included A. A. Friesen, B. H. Unruh, and C. H. Warkentin.[1] Following a fruitful tour of the United States and Canada the members of the group parted. Secretary B. H. Unruh returned to Germany on November 1, 1920, while chairman A. A. Friesen and C. H. Warkentin remained in America. For a time Friesen lived at the home of M. H. Kratz in Philadelphia. Because of a lack of funds he accepted a temporary lectureship in chemistry at Bluffton College (Ohio) in 1921. In 1922 he moved to Rosthern, Saskatchewan, where he worked in close conjunction with the Canadian Mennonite Board of Colonization in the areas of relief and emigration.

In seeking to serve its Russian constituency the Study Commission attempted to construct as broad an operational base as possible. In Germany, Unruh set up his headquarters in Karlsruhe and became an indispensable connecting link between Russian Mennonite leaders and a number òf foreign governments. One of the tasks of the Study Commission was to seek the aid of the Dutch Mennonites in facilitating the emigration from Russia. Soon after his arrival in Germany, Unruh contacted A. K. Kuiper, a pastor of the Amsterdam Mennonite congregation, and T. O. H. Hylkema, pastor of the Giethoorn Mennonite Church. Hylkema had been in close contact with the Russian Mennonites between 1914 and 1920.[2] Unruh urged the Dutch Mennonite leaders to call a general meeting of their constituency in order that the plight of Russian Mennonites might be presented. Kuiper, hesitant to follow such a course of action, introduced Unruh to Mr. B. Loder, a member of both the Supreme Council of the Netherlands and the Hague Tribunal, created in 1899 to solve international disputes. In the interview Unruh learned that the Dutch government would promise no support for the Russian Mennonites.[3]

Meanwhile Unruh continued his efforts to rouse the Mennonites in both Holland and Germany to action. His work in Holland was particularly fruitful. Working in close conjunction with Hylkema, Unruh drew up a proposal advocating that the then existing *Steuncommissie* (a small committee for the support of Mennonite refugees from Russia) be transformed into a large relief organization. A special meeting to consider the entire problem was held at Amsterdam on December 20 and 21, 1921. In attendance were A. Binnerts (Haarlem), F. C. Fleischer (Winterswijk), T. O. Hylkema, H. Warkentin, O. Woelinga (secretary-treasurer of the *Steuncommissie*), and B. H. Unruh. After considerable discussion it was decided that the *Steuncommissie* would cease to exist as of January 1, 1921, and be replaced by the *Algemeene Commissie voor Buitenlandsche Nooden* (General Commission for Foreign Emergencies). A. Binnerts was elected chairman. The new organization played a very substantial role in supplying relief materials to the Russian Mennonites.

The Russian catastrophe also roused the German Mennonites to action. As early as April 3, 4, 1918, a conference of South German Mennonites was held at the Weierhof in the Palatinate where a plan for resettling some of the Russian Mennonites in Germany's African colonies was discussed. The scheme crumbled with the defeat of Germany. Contact between the two groups was renewed in April 1920, when the Study Commission met with South German leaders at Heilbronn. The formation of a relief agency was accepted in principle. Good intentions were transformed into practical action when a food and clothing crisis among Russian Mennonite refugees already in Germany became apparent. On November 20, 21, 1920, a conference of South German Mennonites convening at Ludwigshafen proposed a union of all German Mennonites for relief purposes. The organization was called the *Mennonitische Flüchtlingsfürsorge* (Mennonite Refugee Aid). Its chairman was Christian Neff. Later it became the *Deutsche Mennoniten-Hilfe* (German Mennonite Aid).

Prospects for intercontinental cooperation were not lacking. On February 17, 1921, Orie O. Miller of the AMR met with the German relief committee in Ludwigshafen. A few days later (February 21) a similar meeting was held with the Dutch committee in Amsterdam. Though most of the discussion centered about the refugees from Constantinople, the groundwork for a large-scale cooperation between the three committees was nevertheless being laid.[4]

Wider Horizons

In accordance with this broad approach to the problems facing Russian Mennonitism, Unruh sought to make contact with religious bodies and denominations whose convictions or interests might make them sympathetic to the plight of the Russian Mennonites. Prior to his departure to America as a member of the Study Commission he had sought to confer with representatives of the Lutheran and Catholic colonists in Russia, who had formed a loosely structured council in Berlin. Religious and policy differences prevented any close cooperation within this group, however.

Unruh was particularly interested in the English Quakers. Besides the similarity of their religious interests to those of the Mennonites was the more important fact that they had already received the permission of the Moscow government to commence relief work in Russia. Together with Hylkema, Unruh explored the possibilities of a visit to England. On February 21, 1921, after a long wait for Unruh's visa, the two finally left for England and remained until March 3. Exploratory though it was, the journey allowed Unruh and Hylkema to establish some valuable contacts, especially with the Quakers. The secretary of the Friends War Victim Relief Committee promised to give the Mennonite relief efforts in Russia, where the committee was already functioning, full support and endorsement. English Baptist leaders further assured Unruh and Hylkema that support for the Russian Mennonites could be found in their constituency. An interview of some significance took place on February 25 when Unruh and Hylkema conferred with the aged Viscount Lord James Bryce, distinguished historian, jurist, and political scientist, who between 1907 and 1913 had been British ambassador to the United States.[5] Though very much interested in the plight of the Russian Mennonites, Bryce felt sure that the British government could do nothing to facilitate the emigration movement from Russia. He nevertheless gave his visitors a letter of introduction to the high commissioners of Canada and South Africa.

On March 3, 1921, Hylkema and Unruh were granted an interview with an assistant to Prime Minister Lloyd George. Two questions were asked of this official. Could the British government do anything to facilitate a Mennonite emigration from Russia? Would it be possible to emigrate to any of the British colonies? Hylkema and Unruh received a typical bureaucratic response. The government might consider the first issue if presented in the form of a memorandum.

Entry into British dominions was a regional affair, however, and could not be determined by the English government. Unruh was convinced that the only dependable source of support was with the Quakers, and perhaps the Baptists.

Upon his return to the continent Unruh pursued a number of projects to promote the cause of his brethren in Russia. For approximately the next two years, Unruh's work was of an exploratory nature in a number of different areas. His role in the emigration movement during this period was sweeping and complex. It demanded a great deal of patience, paper work, and bureaucratic know-how. While essential to the success of the later emigration, it frequently produced no concrete or dramatic results.

Another sphere of Unruh's activity involved negotiations with the governments of those countries most directly concerned with the proposed emigration, Germany and Holland.[6] On March 17, 1921, almost immediately after his return from England, Unruh had an audience with the Dutch foreign minister to discuss the possibilities for Mennonite settlements in Surinam, South Africa, and Mexico. The minister promised government aid in one specific problem: the transfer of the Constantinople refugees to Germany.[7] In Russia the executive of the *VMSR* was thinking primarily of a settlement in Holland. The emigration petitions submitted to the Kharkov government on December 17, 1921, and February 28, 1922, specifically mentioned evacuation to Holland. To accommodate this sentiment Unruh persuaded the *Algemeene Commissie voor Buitenlandsche Nooden* to take the matter in hand. A petition requesting the admittance of the Russian Mennonites to Holland was drafted by chairman A. Binnerts and secretary F. C. Fleischer and presented to the Dutch government. The Council of Ministers rejected the request. Janz had also drafted a special petition on behalf of the *VMSR*, but because of the earlier rejection the *ACBN* refused to submit it to the government. Unruh tried a more indirect approach by requesting the Dutch government to exert diplomatic and moral influence in favor of the emigration. The *Commissie*, uncertain that such a move had any merit, refused to endorse it.[8] Consequently, by the end of April 1922 it was apparent that the Dutch government would not cooperate. Fortunately, a Canadian alternative was already in the making.

A more fruitful field of endeavor was found among the Mennonites of Holland and Germany. Here the organizational preparations for Russian relief were almost completed during the first months of

1921. Orie O. Miller's consultations with both the German and Dutch relief committees in February 1921 did much to facilitate inter-Mennonite cooperation. Meanwhile a trickle of refugees provided an immediate task for the *MFF*. Preparations had to be made to receive Russian refugees from Constantinople and other areas.[9] Through the generosity of the German and Bavarian government twenty-two barracks at the former military camp Lechfeld were placed at the disposal of the *MFF*.[10] The camp was to be of crucial importance for a number of years.

During April, Unruh attended a meeting of the Central Committee for Mennonite Union in Hamburg, a contact which brought with it invitations from the Mennonite churches in northern Germany. In May he addressed the Palatine-Hessian Mennonite Conference on the plight of Russian Mennonitism. Not long after, he toured the West Prussian Mennonite churches. His journey came to a profitable conclusion on July 22 in Kalthof near Marienburg, when the Conference of West Prussian Mennonite Churches endorsed two proposals, one guaranteeing the economic well-being of the Constantinople refugees entering Germany, and the other pledging support for the refugee settlement begun in Mecklenburg.[11] These relief efforts were to be coordinated by the *MFF*.

The Communication Problem

Throughout 1921 Unruh had practically no direct contact with the homeland. In Russia *VMSR* chairman Janz did not use the regular mail services for fear of jeopardizing his organization. Communication was consequently irregular, one-sided, and inadequate. Isolated reports frequently exaggerated or minimized existing conditions. Unruh had little precise knowledge as to the wishes of his constituency and so was unable to plot a precise course of action.

Unruh probably had more knowledge about conditions in other Mennonite settlements than in the Ukraine. While in Hamburg during April 1921 he chanced to meet David Wiebe, an unofficial representative of the Siberian Mennonites. Wiebe insisted that his countrymen wished to emigrate, but only to Germany.[12] In the summer of 1921 Unruh received isolated letters from some of the refugees in the Molotschna. Written by people with limited horizons and based on local experience, these letters were often overoptimistic and presented a false picture of the overall situation.[13] Unruh did learn of the intensifying emigration sentiment in some of the Mennonite settlements. Through Orie O. Miller he was informed that the Mennonites of the Don region and northern Caucasus were exploring emigration possibilities, and had unsuccessfully petitioned the central government in this regard. On August 18 he met their official representative, A. J. Fast, in Ludwigshafen.[14] From other sources Unruh learned that the Kuban Mennonites had unsuccessfully presented an emigration petition to the central government. A significant and objective report by Elder J. Wiens of the Molotschna arrived toward the end of August.[15] Another source of information from the same area came from W. Goerzen, who arrived in Germany via Poland. Goerzen had been authorized to report on the condition of the Ukrainian Mennonites in Germany. Unruh conferred with him in Berlin on October 10 and 12 and again on November 22 in Karlsruhe.[16] On November 29 reports of conditions in Trakt and Orenburg came into Unruh's possession.

An emigration movement could not be launched on the basis of such loose information. During November 1921 Unruh made serious efforts to establish a communications route via Constantinople or Moscow,[17] but with little success. By December he became increasingly convinced that preparations would have to be made for a mass migration. Originally the Study Commission had only been empowered to investigate settlement possibilities. This mandate was not decisive or broad enough. He was not certain that it still had the confidence of the constituency. Though Orie O. Miller crossed the Russian border rather frequently, he refused to carry personal letters lest the relief program be harmed. Unruh had heard of the formation of the *VMSR* but received no clarification as to its purpose or function from chairman Janz. Since Janz had sent a report to the American relief committee,[18] why had he, Unruh, not received any communication? How could the Study Commission work under these conditions? The solution of this frustrating problem came. in the unobtrusive form of a letter addressed to Unruh and delivered via German diplomatic channels to A. J. Fast in Berlin.[19] Its first paragraph listed a significant address: Dr. Sasse, Sumskaya 54, Kharkov. Sasse was the head of a German legation resident in Kharkov. At Janz's request Sasse allowed the *VMSR* to use the services of the German diplomatic courier. The significance of the address could not be overestimated. The eventual success of the entire emigration movement hinged upon it. At last there could be a free exchange of reports and directives.

The Reconstruction Issue

The information contained in Janz's letter of November 20, 1921, presented Unruh with a new and extended problem. He had hitherto been concerned with the worsening circumstances in South Russia, the necessity of relief, and the prospect of an eventual emigration. It now became apparent that the *VMSR*, though not yet officially sanctioned, posed as an agency of economic reconstruction, especially since emigration was still out of the question. Henceforth the Study Commission was to pursue two projects—emigration and reconstruction. With the information came an order. The Ukrainian Commissar of Agriculture had requested the *Verband* to secure 50,000-100,000 pud of seed grain for spring planting from abroad. A successful fulfillment of this order might solidify the position of the *VMSR*.

Up to this point the Study Commission had sought to create a basis for an effective Russian relief program in Europe and America. Simultaneously it had investigated potential credit sources to finance an eventual emigration. Now a third problem was added: the financing of reconstruction in South Russia. Although the matter had been previously discussed as an eventual sequel to the relief program, it had never been the assigned task of the Study Commission. Unruh attacked the problem with characteristic vigor. The matter of credit for emigration had already been discussed with the *ACBN*. Unruh endeavored to broaden the project by including credit for reconstruction. Could not the entire question of credit for the Russian Mennonites be expanded to include those who emigrated and those who stayed? In both cases the quality of the colonists themselves as well as the products which the land produced could be considered adequate guarantees. For the emigrants the settlement land itself might constitute a guarantee. Unruh advocated that a special committee be appointed to investigate the feasibility of his proposals.[20]

The *ACBN* revealed considerable interest in the project. Its secretary, Pastor F. C. Fleischer, immediately contacted the Dutch Ministry of the Interior where he consulted with a representative of the finance department. Fleischer briefly outlined the cultural and economic achievements of the Russian Mennonites and pointed out their historic connection with Holland, and asked whether the Dutch government could extend credit in order to facilitate the economic recovery of these colonists. The answer was explicit and direct: the Dutch government had little confidence in the Bolshevik regime and refused to offer any credit to it. Fleischer then proposed that the government consent to guarantee the five million guilder assets of a philanthropic joint-stock company (*Aktiengesellschaft*) organized and run by the *ACBN*. The company then hoped to use its own assets (tractors, seed grain, etc.,) in furthering the economic recovery of the Mennonite settlements. In this way no funds would be irretrievably invested in Russia. The official promised to study the proposal more closely.[21] The entire project was reviewed at a special meeting held on December 29, 1921, at Frankfurt am Main and attended by Unruh, Fleischer, and Willink. For the moment Fleischer's plan appeared as the best solution to the plight of the Mennonite farmers in Russia.[22] Unruh's negotiations with German manufacturers of agricultural machinery soon convinced him of the soundness of Fleischer's proposals. Bolshevik property concepts made most industrialists hesitant to acquire any fixed assets in Russia.[23]

What constituted a sound operational philosophy with regard to economic reconstruction in the colonies? Unruh reasoned that Russia was in the midst of a transitional period. Real reconstruction could only begin after the political and economic situation had stabilized.[24] Until such a time grandiose plans were out of the question. Both the *VMSR* and the relief organizations in Europe and America had to think in terms of minimal programs. Large-scale credit was simply not available. Under the current conditions only immediate rather than long-term goals were attainable. For the Russian Mennonites reconstruction meant the plotting of survival tactics, not the initiation of a large-scale business operation. By the spring of 1922 these tactics were clearly correct. The colonies needed agricultural machinery and seed grain. Both the *ACBN* and the AMR had decided to supply these items, but only with the intent of meeting the current crisis. The aid provided by these agencies was certainly not sufficient to ensure the economic recovery of Ukrainian Mennonitism. This could take place only if the colonists received credit from abroad for the purchase of seed grain and machinery. But any large-scale business investment in Russia seemed out of the question. Reconstruction consequently depended on personal credit extended to the colonists by individual members of Mennonite congregations in Europe and America.[25] Such funds were guaranteed solely by the integrity and industriousness of the colonists in Russia. Only limited aid could be sent to the colonies in 1922. The situation was frustrating since a good harvest in 1923 required the sending of sufficient seed grain and machinery in 1922.[26]

The successful pursuit of a reconstruction program abroad was

partially hampered by a lack of interest in the project by the Mennonite colonists themselves. For many, reconstruction meant only self-
preservation and survival until such a time as it was possible to leave
Russia. Even Janz's letters were indecisive as to the scope of reconstruction. In view of the fact that the *VBHH* charter was ratified on
the condition that Holland and America supply the colonies with material aid Janz requested that several tractors be sent as evidence of his
organization's good intentions. Simultaneously he emphasized the poor
credit rating of Russian Mennonitism, whose economic future was
extremely unstable.[27] The veritable emigration panic which had seized
the colonies made an honest attempt at rebuilding impossible. "The
future is as dark as the night," Janz wrote. "We are still striving
after a basis for a regulated, secure, and peaceful existence."[28] For
Unruh this situation was extremely frustrating. He was continually
forced to base his strategy on his interpretation of very uncertain
conditions.

Several aspects of the reconstruction question crystallized during
the second half of 1922. The most important of these related to the
program of the *VBHH* itself. The impossibility of immediate emigration
in 1922 forced many colonists toward a more realistic appraisal of
their future economic status. It was further abundantly clear that any
emigration would be a partial movement. Since a widespread threat
of famine made the question of survival of paramount importance, the
VBHH constituency was consequently much more amenable to the
definition of reconstruction tactics. The arrival of the first twenty-
five AMR tractors in Odessa on August 13 provided additional encouragement.[29] Then, too, on August 21 *ACBN* director Willink signed a
contract providing for the shipment of Dutch seed grain to the
Ukraine.[30] The *VBHH*, however, lacked the funds for the purchase
of the seed grain. Since nonuse of its wide range of economic privileges
threatened to discredit the Mennonite agency in the eyes of the government, its executive members negotiated for government approval of a
foreign loan. Such a move was sanctioned by Ukrainian authorities
on September 12 and 13, 1922.[31] By the terms of the contract the
ACBN extended a 50,000 guilder credit to the *VBHH* for the purchase of seed grain. The loan was to be repaid at the rate of one
pud eight and one-half pounds for every pud borrowed.[32] In addition
to Dutch credit for seed grain the *VBHH* also launched an ambitious
project designed to obtain a million-dollar loan from abroad. It called
for the purchase of small ten-dollar bonds by the Mennonites abroad
to mature in five years and pay 5 percent interest. The project was

approved at the Osterwick Congress of the *VBHH* held on September 22, 23, 1922.[33] Ukrainian Mennonitism was gradually committing itself to reconstruction—this without any long-range economic guarantees from a government which had not yet defined its future agricultural policy.

Once the *VBHH* had clarified its reconstruction plan B. H. Unruh's labors in Germany became more purposeful. He was particularly enthusiastic about the small bond venture which he felt represented a transition from a charity to a business base in the relations between the Russian colonies and the Mennonite constituency abroad.[34] Unfortunately when Unruh tried to present the *VBHH* project to the Dutch Mennonites he encountered an uninterested and pessimistic response. Small contributions in the interest of philanthropy were readily available. The Dutch business instinct, however, was reluctant to participate in a large credit transaction without sufficient guarantees.[35] A direct appeal to the chairman of the Dutch National Bank was rejected on the grounds that the intensifying economic depression in Holland and France made this impossible. By March, 1923, both Fleischer and Hylkema of the *ACBN* were taking an active interest in the bond issue, but technical and judicial problems prevented the commencement of sale.[36] Reports from Russia failed to communicate the sense of well-being needed to encourage economic investment. The AMR tractor program was experiencing great difficulty because of the noncooperation of Kharkov regime.[37] Meanwhile 20,000 of the 50,000 guilder seed grain credit promised by the *ACBN* reached Russia. Two difficulties interfered with its use: The funds came too late for the purchase of seed for spring planting, and an uncontrolled inflation had hit the Russian ruble, which brought a rapid loss of purchasing power[38] when the money was changed into Russian currency. The foreign loan was nevertheless highly important, for it represented the only purchasing power available to the colonies. The Kharkov government, anxious to promote agricultural reconstruction in the south, officially approved a foreign loan for the *VBHH* in midsummer.[39]

All these developments only served to make Unruh's work more difficult. He was unable to present the evidence of a growing stability in the Soviet state. Any appeal for financial investment in the Mennonite colonies ran aground on the question of guarantees. European capitalists were not interested in a program which combined business and philanthropy. Despite these handicaps Unruh was able to contact a number of potential investors in Russia. Surprisingly large sums

Rev. B. B. Janz explains his memoirs relating to the emigration to the members of the Canadian Mennonite Relief and Immigration Council, May 28, 1963. From left to right, Rev. J. J. Thiessen; Rev. B. B. Janz; A. A. Wiens; C. A. DeFehr.

P. F. Froese; B. H. Unruh, and C. F. Klassen in later years.

128

frequently appeared available. Though there was no reason to doubt the sincerity of their sponsors, in most cases the transfer of capital was never implemented. When the basis for foreign credit was almost completed during the first half of 1923, inconsistent action on the part of the Bolshevik government discouraged both the *VBHH* and potential foreign investors. In terms of concrete returns much of Unruh's labor was futile. During 1924 and 1925 the projected reconstruction in South Russia was further undermined by the intensifying anti-Mennonite trend evident in the policies of the Soviet government. Circumstances conspired against Unruh's every effort to aid his brethren in Russia. He did what he could; his immense correspondence and extensive travel taxed his physical resources severely. Fortunately some of his work was rewarded with concrete results, especially in the area of emigration. It was in this area that Unruh made his lasting contribution to his constituency in Russia.

CHAPTER NINE

Bureaucratic Complications

A key problem which occupied the *VBHH* leaders during the first several months of 1923 was that of the medical rejects in Latvia. As yet no destination had been found for these people. Increasingly impatient Chortitza refugees called two special assemblies on January 2 and February 5. Both advocated intensive investigations of emigration possibilities in Mexico. During this interval, the *VBHH* executive committee met at Schönwiese and decided to send a special delegate to America in the interests of emigration. B. B. Janz was selected as the first candidate. On February 5 the Chortitza emigrants appointed their own representative, J. P. Klassen, to accompany Janz. Since the Chortitza group was rather interested in Mexico, the *VBHH* executive began to consider whether interest could be combined with a scheme whereby Latvian rejects might be channeled to Mexico.[1] In early February Janz approached both the Mennonite Colonization Association of North America and the Mennonite Executive Committee for Colonization on the issue.[2] The Mexican alternative, however, lost its importance by the pursuit of previous plans and by the discovery of a more plausible solution to the Latvian problem. During February, March, and April, however, no optimistic prospects emerged. To Alvin J. Miller Janz observed:

> The uncertainty abroad causes us much concern. What can be done is not clear to us. Recently we have received reports that the situation is rather difficult, much more difficult than we had imagined.[3]

Negotiations in Moscow

In Moscow increased interest in the emigration by certain government departments raised fears that the movement might suddenly be terminated. It was learned that a special commission had been created in the Council of Labor and Defense (*Sovet Truda i Oborony*), which consisted largely of influential Soviet officials whose primary interest was not emigration but immigration.[4] On February 2, 1923, the Council of Labor and Defense issued a statement that a land area constituting about 220,000 desyatinas had been reserved in the Volga regions for prospective immigrants, perhaps Doukhobors. The declaration, coincided with similar sentiments expressed by the Soviet Foreign Minister Chicherin at the Lausanne Conference. Apparently the immigration propaganda was intended to raise Russian prestige abroad and restore confidence in the Soviet regime. Any group determined to leave Russia certainly did not suit such purposes. Would the Soviet government terminate the Mennonite exodus in the interest of its international image?

Several incidents and circumstances suggested this possibility to emigration leaders. Repatriation from Latvia had been disallowed. While the emigration of enlisted Mennonite men was being tolerated, the privilege had only been granted after persistent appeals by B. B. Janz. In the course of negotiations with government officials, Froese and Klassen consulted with the chairman of the newly formed Soviet Immigration Commission, who referred to the proposed Mennonite venture as purposeless, but admitted that his Commission had not formally deliberated on the issue. Because their information was fragmentary, unofficial, and circumstantial, Froese and Klassen felt it necessary to obtain a more thorough understanding of the matter. Through the courtesy of Sokolov, a member of the Foreign Commissariat, an interview was arranged on February 5 with the Moscow *GPU* representative Garov. To open the discussion Froese and Klassen mentioned the transport of emigrants from the Ukraine to Libau. Garov proved hostile and refused to pursue any of the questions raised on the grounds that he was not empowered to deal with them, but mentioned a decree passed on September 18, 1922, which forbade emigration from the RSFSR for political reasons and new regulations regarding the transit of emigrants which forced the Mennonites to leave individually, not corporately. The new **RSFSR** emigration regulations were in sharp contrast with the arrangements for exodus made in the Ukraine.

Henceforth each emigrant had to obtain individual approval from the Moscow *GPU*. The air of confidence with which Garov spoke was disturbing.[5] There was little doubt that he reflected the attitude of his organization. Though traditionally hostile, the new militancy of the secret police gave evidence of a formidable threat to the emigration movement. Fearful of provoking retaliatory action Froese and Klassen courteously ended the interview. For the present, silence was the best strategy.

Meanwhile the representative from the Chortitza emigrant group, J. P. Klassen, arrived in Moscow. On February 12, Alvin J. Miller, P. F. Froese, and J. P. Klassen held a special meeting with Owen. The discussion revolved about the single question: when might the movement of emigrants begin? Since the opponents of emigration seemed to be gaining, what were the possibilities of beginning the exodus at once? Owen's analysis was precise. The Dardanelles were still impassable, leaving a northern evacuation as the only possibility. For this purpose CPR ships were always available. There was only one drawback. The American Mennonites had not yet declared themselves willing to guarantee the medically unfit in Latvia. This must be done officially and quickly.[6]

A second meeting of considerable importance was held on February 13. Froese and C. F. Klassen met in the offices of the Foreign Commissariat with Sokolov and Garov[7] to discuss the technical difficulties connected with the transportation of the first 3,000 emigrants from the Ukraine. Particularly crucial was the question of the RSFSR exit. Garov was still disturbingly hostile. The fact that the Kharkov *GPU* had already supplied the emigrants with permits did not seem to impress their Moscow counterpart. In the end the Mennonite leaders were forced to agree to several stipulations. The *VBHH* was to draw up a special certificate for every family on the emigration list. A Kharkov representative would then take these certificates to Moscow where every family would be granted a British visa in view of the absence of a Canadian representation in Moscow. The Moscow *GPU* then granted an exit permit to each family receiving a British visa. Furthermore, the cost of the Russian document (one per family) was set at five gold rubles. Photographs of the emigrants, required by the law, might not be needed provided a special *GPU* petition was approved.

The interview convinced Froese and Klassen that the bureaucratic tendencies of the Soviet system bordered on genius. They nevertheless felt that at least Sokolov was sincerely concerned with facilitating the emigration. Sokolov was extremely interested in the number of Mennonites intent on leaving Russia. Aware that the idea of mass emigration could have an adverse effect on the deliberations, Froese and Klassen were careful to point out that a limited emigration was envisaged. These were starving people whose absence might substantially benefit the colonies and enable economic reconstruction to begin. Both officials appeared reasonably satisfied.

One thing became apparent in all the contacts with the Moscow government during the first months of 1923. Moscow was giving orders to Kharkov. Ukrainian independence was gradually waning and with it the emigration arrangements made with that government. From the February negotiations it was reasonably clear that the Moscow *GPU* sanctioned the emigration. Unfortunately they thought only in terms of 3,000 emigrants. The Foreign Commissariat seemed convinced that the Mennonite emigration problem was solved.[8] For the emigration leaders matters were more complex. What might happen later when application was made in Moscow for the exodus of additional thousands?[9] One problem had been eliminated, but the overall situation remained unchanged. As yet not a single emigrant had left. The Latvian medical rejects still had no place to go. Canada had not yet indicated the number of emigrants it could receive in 1923.

The Path to Lechfeld

On January 20, 1923, the *VBHH* instructed its representatives abroad to investigate whether Germany could be persuaded to temporarily accept the medically unfit emigrants from Latvia. In Germany B. H. Unruh and A. J. Fast immediately began to work on their new task. On February 12 they conferred with the German minister for refugee aid (*Flüchtlingsfürsorge*) in Berlin and learned that the government was not opposed to the Latvian rejects entering Germany on the condition that these find shelter at Lechfeld and be cared for by the *DMH* (German Mennonite Aid). Upon receiving lists of the disqualified persons he would see that they obtained an entrance visa to Germany.[10]

Unruh now sought to gain the cooperation of the *DMH*. The steadily worsening economic conditions in Germany made such direct aid difficult for the German relief agency. Hopeful of American assistance, however, it accepted the responsibility. On March 19 Unruh was officially informed of the *DMH* willingness to care for the Latvian rejects.[11] This information was channeled to the ministry for refugee aid. Unruh, Fast, and a *DMH* representative met with German government representatives to complete the plan on April 17. An official declaration of German willingness to accept medically unfit Mennonite emigrants followed. A copy of the document reached emigration leaders in Russia on April 26.[12]

American participation played an essential part in the proceedings.

The *DMH* had only agreed to the Lechfeld resettlement after American Mennonite Relief promised to aid in supporting the refugees. In mid-February Janz cabled the Canadian Mennonite Board of Colonization requesting a financial guarantee covering the cost of transporting refugees to Germany. The board eventually responded with a positive reply. On the strength of these developments Owen advised the London office of the CPR to begin the movement of refugees on April 28. The constant delays before this first definite action, however, caused much turmoil and anxiety among both the emigrant constituency and the *VBHH* executive.

Emigrant Impatience

In mid-April 1923, the Lechfeld solution still appeared rather remote to emigration leaders in Russia. To their knowledge, the German government had not yet declared itself willing to allow these people to enter Germany. At the same time they were waiting for the Canadian Mennonite Board of Colonization to officially guarantee the costs of transporting the medical defectives from Latvia to Germany. A CMBC cable (February 17) indicating its willingness to participate had apparently gone astray. In the Ukraine, exit permits for three and one-half thousand people had expired and renewal was not to be taken for granted. Most of the emigrants saw little change in external conditions between January and April. In late January and early February Chortitza refugees under the leadership of J. P. Klassen had already threatened independent action. Klassen had been sent to Moscow in February and participated in meetings with both the CPR and the *GPU*.

By April the possibility of a split within the ranks was a very real threat. To avert this the *VBHH* executive had given the Chortitza group considerable autonomy, allowing them to revise their lists and even add 300 names. A strong separatistic inclination nevertheless persisted.[13] Another meeting at Rosenthal on April 10 formulated plans for initiating a new emigration movement.[14] Elder Isaak Dueck of the Chortitza congregation and J. P. Klassen were delegated to America to try to create more favorable sentiment toward the emigration movement. Mexico was named as the most desirable settlement site. A mandate was also given to H. J. Andres who would succeed J. P. Klassen as leader of the group in the event of Klassen's journey to America. Janz's appeals for unity lest the safety of the entire movement be jeopardized were dismissed as nonapplicable and inconsequential.

The Chortitza action revealed little understanding of the political and diplomatic complexities that had come to surround the emigration movement. The permission to emigrate could not be separated from the officially sanctioned *VBHH*. The government was tolerating emigration only as an accessory to economic reconstruction. It was on this premise that exit visas had been granted. Legally the launching of a new emigration move would require the dissolving of the *VBHH* and the painful building of a new agency. The Chortitza group simply ignored these facts. In the hope of accommodating Chortitza independence and in the interests of averting a rift the *VBHH* decided to authorize the naming of an additional delegate to accompany B. B. Janz to America. The Chortitza emigrants would have to regard such an individual as their elected representative. Some precautions were necessary lest the somewhat undisciplined atmosphere at Chortitza bring about the election of an unsuitable candidate. What course of action was open?

Late in April, P. H. Unruh, elder of the Alexanderwohl congregation in Goessel, Kansas, and former AMR worker in Russia, was concluding a study tour of the Mennonite settlements in Russia. Unruh had taken an active interest in the entire emigration movement and was well informed on developments in both Russia and America. Unruh, together with a traveling associate, was invited to a meeting of the *VBHH* Council on April 26 and 27.[15] The presence of these well-informed observers injected some realism into the proceedings. Chortitza elements substantially modified their position when informed of the complexities facing the emigration movement. It was soon evident that Unruh was a focal point helpful in the restoration of unity. Since the emigrant discontents still insisted on dispatching an additional delegate to America, and it was also obviously necessary to create a more favorable sentiment for the emigration in America, the *VBHH* Council authorized P. H. Unruh as an additional representative to America, even though the legality of this action was questioned. The Council even went so far as to agree to an important organizational change. The two major emigrant groups on the right and left of the Dnieper River were each empowered to elect one delegate as a member of a newly created *VBHH* emigration department. One of these, the Chortitza representative, henceforth assisted the *VBHH* chairman in all matters related to the emigration.

B. B. Janz considered the appointment of Unruh as a move designed to "prevent a serious split or discord."[16] Up to this point the only communication between the Russian and American

Mennonites had been via letter. Unruh consequently became a "living bond" joining the Mennonites in America and Germany with those in Russia.[17] The appointment nevertheless had the character of an emergency measure. It apparently took no account of the fact that a non-Russian Mennonite was representing a Russian cause and organization, nor did it clarify P. H. Unruh's working relationship to the other delegates abroad. In the end this move, calculated to prevent a split in Russia, caused a serious rift between the Russian Mennonite emigration leaders themselves.

The Departure of the First Group

P. H. Unruh's appointment was designed to facilitate the long-term implementation of the emigration movement. Notwithstanding a concern for the structural solidarity of their own organization, *VBHH* leaders were also preoccupied with completing the technical preparations for the departure of the first group. By March the external problems obstructing the actual emigration had been reduced to two: the CMBC guarantee covering the costs of transporting the medical rejects from Libau to Lechfeld had not yet arrived, and the *DMH* had not yet promised to care for the refugees when they reached Lechfeld. As was so frequently the case in the entire movement, the final impediments to its commencement seemed to be abroad and not in Russia. This was certainly the case with Germany where bureaucratic delays postponed a final decision until April 17. The news that Germany would accept the Latvian rejects did not reach Russia until April 26. The CMBC, however, could not be charged with inefficiency. The board guaranteed the Libau-Lechfeld travel expense at once when they received Janz's plea. The return telegram, dated February 17 and addressed to Janz, read: "Board guaranteeing expense of rejected [in]Latvia." But this message did not reach him. Klassen, Froese, and Owen in Moscow as well as Janz in Kharkov were impatiently waiting for a response. Toward the end of March, Janz, in a downcast mood, wrote: "Have I been disappointed by my American brethren on whom I depended so much? And are my people to be disappointed with me?"[18] More than two weeks passed and still no news. On April 16 Janz commented: "With sorrows, apprehensions, and great impatience we await the guarantee of the Board for the defectives."[19]

Finally the news that Germany was prepared to accept the medically unfit arrived in Moscow. A meeting with Owen was immediately arranged. When Owen heard of the new development, he cabled the

London office of the CPR on April 28 and advised them to begin the movement of emigrants. On May 8 Froese and Klassen learned that all was in readiness. Janz was notified of Owen's decision and requested to come to Moscow at once.[20] He arrived in Moscow on May 20. He was preceded by J. P. Klassen with the final emigration lists on May 9. Janz arrived on a Sunday. On Monday he and Klassen made their way to the Foreign Commissariat to complete the arrangements for the exodus. All the government departments related to the venture were cooperative. Even the *GPU* was still prepared to honor the agreement it had drawn up in February.[21] Detailed arrangements for the departure of the first emigrants were completed in Moscow by mid-June. Janz and Klassen left for the south on June 16. Six days earlier a special thanksgiving service had been held in Moscow. In the intimacy of their quarters the Mennonite representatives in Moscow paused to thank God for His guidance and to ask Him for new strength for the strenuous tasks awaiting them.[22]

The first group of 726 emigrants left Chortitza on June 22. Last-minute complications arose when *VBHH* vice-chairman Philip D. Cornies, who was to accompany the train, was arrested. A scene that was to be frequently repeated |typified ' the departure, families and friends bidding each other a tearful farewell. For some the parting had an overwhelming sense of finality, since their friends and relatives had no prospects of ever leaving Russia. Despite the hopeful anticipation which at times characterized the planned exodus, its actual initiation brought the pain of separation and the insecurity of an unknown future. Community and church relationships, family ties, and bonds of friendship were sacrificed for the conviction that it was better to go than to remain. The first group crossed the Soviet border at Sebezh on July 1. But the worst was yet to come. The medical inspection in Latvia caused grave disappointment for at least ten percent of the emigrants. In the end Latvia contributed to a more intense breakup of family relationships than the Chortitza departure.

The actual beginning of the emigration movement produced a significant change in the social consciousness of the Mennonite settlers in Russia. "Those staying in the colonies feel like remaining migratory birds when the flocks of their kind have departed," observed Janz.[23] Many became unwilling to gamble on a future existence in Russia when directly confronted with the fact that it was possible to leave. Without any official encouragement or direction from the *VBHH* leaders, new emigrant lists were drawn up in addition to those originally ratified, even though no new lists could be accepted for processing. Since emigration had finally become a reality, many settlers firmly resolved to leave Russia, and resolutely began work on this arduous and dangerous task.

> . . . the people have had enough. Now after they have seen a few leave they only want to depart. It is an elemental movement outward. The people are not concerned about the precious articles they leave behind, even if they must depart poor and naked.[24]

CHAPTER TEN

An Array of Problems

The Arrest of Philip D. Cornies

The first group consisting of 726 individuals had hardly crossed the Russian border at Sebezh on July 1 when new difficulties began to crystallize. One of the most immediate involved Philip D. Cornies, *VBHH* vice-chairman and close associate of Janz, who was scheduled to accompany the first emigrant train on June 22. Janz had conferred with Cornies in Kharkov upon his return from Moscow on June 20. Cornies had come to the Ukrainian capital to seek aid against local administrative caprice and reprisals still evident in many of the Mennonite settlements and to find some solution for the problem of compulsory military training for Mennonite young men who, though exempted by law, were forced to take up arms by local authorities.

Responding to an appeal by Janz and Cornies, the Kharkov regime issued a sternly worded memorandum to local officials in the south. It excused young Mennonites from basic military training and ordered the release of all those arrested. Cornies did not wait for the formal document but returned to the colonies to assist the emigrants.[1] Upon arrival he was arrested and placed in strictest confinement by Melitopol *GPU* authorities. Because he was regarded as a political criminal, his whereabouts could be determined only with considerable difficulty.[2] In Kharkov, Janz at once submitted a petition to both the Foreign Commissariat and a special department of the *GPU* requesting his release. On July 10 he personally went to the *GPU* offices.[3] By July 15 Cornies had been released and was back at his post.[4]

Renewed Reluctance in Moscow

Janz remained in Kharkov only long enough to facilitate the departure of the first group. By July 1 he returned to Moscow to solve a technical problem. The officially sanctioned emigration lists had contained almost four thousand names. This number was substantially lowered by the preliminary medical inspection together with a list revision in the colonies. Janz now sought to maintain the original figure by drawing from the next list of emigrants not yet officially approved, hoping that such a course would serve a transitional purpose and aid in the ratification of new lists.

Moscow officials were reluctant to permit any further emigration. It was pointed out that the Central Executive Committee decree of September 22, 1922, involved only a limited movement. Froese asked permission for, and Klassen had spoken of, only 3,000 people. As these were presently leaving, the issue was closed. Janz, in view of Ukrainian autonomy, asked whether the CEC decree did not apply only to the Mennonites in the RSFSR. His request was not for exit permits. These had been granted in Kharkov by the Ukrainian government. He wanted only transit permits from the RSFSR office since the emigrants had to leave by Sebezh. The Moscow government in consultation with the *GPU* had promised to allow as many to cross Russian territory as possessed Kharkov issued permits.

"How many people were involved?"

"About twenty thousand," Janz affirmed.

Moscow authorities seemed taken aback by the figure. Janz was promised that a final decision on the issue would be made in two days.[5] He returned to Kharkov. One thing was becoming increasingly apparent. If Moscow decided to assert its authority, emigration might well be a thing of the past. On July 7 a Moscow dispatch reached Kharkov which informed Janz that for the present no further exodus was permitted.[6] The decision was not a final one, however. As long as Moscow remained undecided there was little to do but wait. The lack of any direct word from America made this a frustrating vigil. No new contract between the CPR and the CMBC seemed in the making. There was not even the assurance that a further movement out of Russia would take place if the currently hesitant emigration policy of the Soviet government should suddenly be replaced by a more favorable one.

What strategy did the new situation call for? Continued agitation in Moscow might exhaust the patience of already uninterested officials. The Kharkov government was more sympathetic and had no intention of terminating the emigration. Why not return to an earlier plan, the exodus via Odessa? There was only one plausible course of action. The colonists had to embark from Ukrainian territory as had originally been planned.[7] In the interim, the Mennonites in Canada should sign a contract for as many people as possible in order to ensure the future service of the CPR.

In Kharkov, Janz made every effort to renew the Mennonite exodus. Here he learned that while the CPR was still prepared to act, the CMBC considered any further emigration impossible in 1923. He sent an urgent appeal to the CPR office in Moscow[8] and similar dispatches to D. Toews in Canada and P. H. Unruh in the United States on October 22. On October 28 another urgent cable was sent to Toews, who replied that he was doing everything possible.[9] In early October, Janz contacted officials at Lechfeld about the possibility of accepting additional defectives. After carefully assessing their resources and clarifying some political questions, Lechfeld officials sent a hesitant though positive answer. This was of little help to the ailing refugees in the colonies since these were unable to pass the preliminary medical examinations. Potential medical rejects for Lechfeld were only those evacuated via the regular emigrant convoy. Any refugees who were obviously ill had no possibility of leaving.[10]

Despite these unfavorable circumstances, Janz spent the month of October in Moscow obtaining transit permission for lists four and five. They contained 1,333 and 3,541 names respectively. Except for the occasional setback caused by bureaucratic pedantry the talks came to a successful conclusion on November 30, when the final approval for the transport through the RSFSR was given.[11] Several basic problems still remained. Would the Canadian and American emigration committees be able to win the support of their constituencies? Was it possible for the CMBC to attach its signature to another contract? Might this be done in time to ensure an early departure date for the emigrants? What if the central government suddenly decided to halt the movement as such? Such an assumption was not unreasonable. In a recent interview with CEC member Smidovich, Froese and Klassen had detected a serious apprehensiveness about the renewal of the Mennonite emigration.[12] Perhaps this was shared by many of his associates.

The Medical Question

The emigrants permitted to leave Russia were divided into four groups. The first departed on June 22, the second on July 2, the third on July 13, and the last on July 24. By the third week of July it was apparent that the movement had run into serious difficulty. Word came to Janz that out of the first two groups 387 had been rejected for various medical reasons.[13] Somewhat later it was learned that the third group had contained 252 rejects.[14] In planning the evacuation the *VBHH* had counted on a maximum of about 200 medically unfit, particularly since special directives had been issued to the local emigration representatives in this regard. The situation was particularly depressing to Owen in Moscow. If almost one quarter of the emigrants were medically unfit, was there any purpose in authorizing the departure of the fourth group? From Lechfeld a telegram (July 20) arrived stressing that it was impossible for the *DMH* to care for so many emigrants.[15]

"What has happened?" emigration leaders asked themselves. "Are we all sick?" commented Janz after hearing of the 387 who had been set aside in the first two groups.[16] One thing was becoming clear. The warning against transporting defectives had not been taken seriously. Chortitza leader J. P. Klassen had been issued clear instructions. Apparently there was some difficulty in enforcing these regulations. A spirit of unconcern and selfishness prevailed among the emigrants. Why break up a family unit? Surely an ailing person would be allowed through once he had made the long journey.[17] Without a doubt the preliminary examination in Chortitza had been too lenient. By contrast the Latvian medical examination by Canadian doctors was possibly too severe, not taking into account the severe conditions under which the emigrants had been living. For the moment the future of the entire emigration movement hung in a balance. In Moscow, Owen could not with good conscience recommend the further transportation of such physically unsound people. Lechfeld, already hopelessly overcrowded, could not bear the strain of additional rejects. Should the departure of the fourth group be allowed? It was, after all, the last group to which the Moscow government had granted a transit visa. Any further emigration would probably be via Odessa.

Despite these obstacles it was decided to evacuate the last group. Philip D. Cornies was in charge of its organization. Painfully conscious of the experience of the earlier groups, Cornies applied the medical regulations very thoroughly. Since trachoma had been responsible for many of the rejections in Latvia, Cornies obtained the services of an eye specialist from the University of Kharkov. A thorough examination of 385 eligible Chortitza emigrants showed only eleven families fit for travel, a total of forty-one persons. In order to allow some of the rejects time for recovery the departure date was postponed. In the Nikolaipol group 350 out of 426 emigrants were found to be in good health. But after a second examination in Nikolaipol on July 29 only 226 out of the original 426 were acceptable. By this time adequate medical care had raised the number eligible in Chortitza to 138 and in Schönwiese to eighteen. The persons eligible for the fourth group were carefully listed on July 30. At seven o'clock that evening a fifteen-car emigrant train departed. Many families were separated at the last minute when acceptable members decided to leave their loved ones and seek their fortune in Canada. Cornies was bitterly blamed for enforcing such a severe medical examination.[18] But he had little choice. Existing circumstances did not allow additional rejects in Latvia. Unfortunately the procedure added to the despair of the destitute refugees in Chortitza and Nikolaipol who remained behind.

After the departure of the fourth group the Mennonite leaders continued to explore the possibility of further emigration. Particularly pressing was the question of the refugees who had been found medically unfit for the journey to Latvia. If an Odessa exodus could be arranged, and if the destination of the next group were Mexico, the unfortunate refugees might be included in this group. No new lists could be prepared, however, until the emigrants had a destination, an embarkation point, and a shipping company willing to transport them.[19] Even if Canada was not averse to the entry of more refugees, the severe medical examinations would make hundreds of them ineligible. Whether further Canadian immigration was possible or not, a country with more lenient entry requirements had to be found, either for a full-scale immigration or as a place of refuge for the medically unfit.

The most urgent problem still remaining after the departure of the fourth emigrant train was consequently related to the status of the medically unfit who had been forced to remain in the colonies. Most were totally destitute, having liquidated all their possessions. Technically they still belonged to the group on behalf of which the CMBC had signed the contract with the CPR. A satisfactory medical certificate entitled any one of them to emigrate. Many of them consequently placed themselves under a doctor's care. For some, however, poverty made this an impossibility. Simultaneously the prospects for spending another winter in the southern Ukraine were very dismal. The emigrants had to be evacuated either to Canada or, if disqualified, to Mexico.

Near the end of September, Janz left Kharkov for Moscow in order to discuss the planning of further emigration. Not only was there old business to complete, but the transport of the first

emigrants planning to leave from the Molotschna (3,641 individuals)
had to be discussed. Since there was still no word of a new contract
from Canada, the deliberations were largely confined to the problems
connected with the departure of the defectives. Little was really
accomplished, although Janz was given to understand that a fifth
echelon numbering 1,333 might be able to leave in November.[20]

In the south Cornies painstakingly prepared for the eventual
emigration of the defectives who had remained behind. A *VBHH*
council meeting in Schönwiese on October 3 had authorized another
inspection for the medically unfit. This was held in Nikolaipol on
October 18. The result was gratifying. One hundred and twelve
persons were declared physically fit for travel. Next day the process
was continued in Chortitza. Many of the emigrants because of poverty
or indifference had neglected to treat their trachoma, with the tragic
outcome that they had to spend another winter in Russia.[21]

In the end joy and sorrow were not so sharply differentiated. In
Moscow the CPR informed Janz that all further transport of emigrants
had been canceled until the coming spring. Cornies learned of the
development by telegram while the medical examination in Chortitza
was being terminated.[22] The emigrants responded by forming a committee to take charge of the material needs. Contact was also made
with the AMR representative in Alexandrovsk, who promised to do all
in his power to supply the distressed emigrants with foodstuffs. Some
time later the emigrants in the Ukraine drafted an official appeal
addressed to the Mennonites of America, which pictured their destitute
situation and requested continuing support from abroad in the matter
of emigration.[23]

A Day with the GPU

The departure of the first four emigrant trains naturally caused
a number of family separations. Medical factors were not alone responsible for this. Some parents left without their older sons because
they had been conscripted into the Red Army and were scattered
throughout Russia. Approximately twenty of these soldiers were
released by the Soviet high command in the summer of 1923 so that
they might join their emigrating parents. In order to avoid reenlist-
ment the young men were to leave Russia by December 1.[24] Most
were processed without too much difficulty. For several, complications
arising from the fact that they had married delayed their departure
past the December 1 deadline. For these men Janz petitioned the
Soviet high command. Its favorable response was sealed in an

envelope and given to Janz with the directive that he deliver it to the Commissariat of Foreign Affairs. Here the receptionist emptied the envelope of its contents, signed her name on the back, and returned it to Janz. Always reluctant to destroy any document, he slipped it into his briefcase. Unknown to him it was soon to be of critical importance.

It was December 22. An uneventful day had passed. Around eight o'clock in the evening Janz's hostess, Mrs. F. Isaak, summoned him to meet a caller. A man in a black leather jacket handed him an envelope. Was it perhaps from the *GPU*? The enclosed note confirmed Janz's premonition. "Comrade Janz. You are to appear at the *GPU* headquarters, Lubyanka 2, third floor, room 178 tomorrow at 10:30 p.m. You will be required to provide information on certain questions. In case of noncompliance you will be brought in by armed escort." The messenger gave no reason for the summons. Janz acknowledged its receipt with his signature. The motorcycle mounted messenger vanished. Tomorrow, December 23, he (Janz) would meet the *GPU*.[25] What could this mean—torture, imprisonment—but why? Had he not proceeded legally and openly? That night saw little sleep and much prayer.

What an innocent-sounding name *GPU, Gosudahztvennoe Politicheskoe Upravlenie* (State Political Administration)! Even the building on Lubyanka 2 had beauty. At the top of the front gable stood a large well-hewn statue of a hovering angel. Sometimes only a wall separated the sacred from the profane. An angel hovering over a labyrinth of death! Janz presented his summons to the guards, who acknowledged his entry by slightly tearing it. The reverse side of the summons was not yet endorsed. Only when it was, would Janz be free to leave again. Room 178 was not large. It contained several tables and a few chairs. Perhaps the purposes for which it was used did not require size or furniture. For Janz's interview one table and two chairs were necessary—one for Janz, the other for his inquisitor. From the onset it was obvious that he was highly experienced in obtaining the desired information from his victims.

"Who are you and where are you from?" Janz presented the necessary documents.

"What is the purpose of your trip to Moscow?" Janz chose not to mention the fact that he had come to seek the release of the Mennonite young men. He could nevertheless point out other reasons for his presence.

His inquisitor was not satisfied.

"Isn't your main purpose in Moscow to confer with Alvin J. Miller of the AMR and with him plot the emigration of the Mennonites to America?" Janz protested energetically. To no avail. The theme was repeatedly brought forward. Finally the impatient examiner shouted, "You lie! Take a piece of paper and record the facts!" He had already taken the liberty to list conspiracy with Miller as one of the facts of the case. Janz wrote, but only to deny this assumption. The inquisitor paced the floor, occasionally glancing at the paper. He finally grunted and with that snatched the paper from Janz. In the next moment he announced the topic he had probably wanted to discuss all along, the release of the Mennonite soldiers.

Janz proceeded to clear the slate. The entire list had been approved by some of the chief authorities in Moscow. All were sons of emigrating families. Their names had been presented to the general staff of the Red Army during the summer (1923) and approved for release. This release had been honored by the Revolutionary Military Council which granted exit passes to these young men.

"How do you know all this?"

"I personally carried the sealed letter from the Revolutionary Military Council to the Foreign Commissariat."

"Have you any proof of this?"

"Yes, the receptionist took the document out of the envelope, signed her name on it, and returned it to me."

"Show me the envelope!"

Janz began to search for the envelope in his briefcase. Though of considerable size, it was nowhere to be seen.

"I can't locate it," said Janz.

"Show me that envelope!" the examiner insisted. Janz carefully sorted the papers. There it was!

His inquisitor took the envelope as well as all the other papers contained in his briefcase into an adjoining room. When he returned, he gave all the papers back to Janz. He spoke with a most pleasant manner. "Everything is in order. Continue in your work. You are free."

The *VBHH* chairman was puzzled. What was the reason for this sudden change of attitude? Perhaps it was his turn to be aggressive. He addressed the *GPU* official:

"You have made a long and severe inquiry about the emigration; now I must also ask you a question."

"Very well."

"Please, what is your name?"

"Solovyov."

"Well, Comrade Solovyov, since you have examined me so critically, tell me openly and directly—does the central government not wish that I send the poor Mennonites to America?"

"You have done everything upon a legal basis, everything is in good order, and I can only tell you to continue in this manner."

"This is not enough. I would like to hear the opinion of the government from you. Is it perhaps better if I let the matter rest in order to avoid unpleasantness?"

"I cannot tell you more than what I have already said. Your business is in order and you may continue your work. Good-bye!"

Solovyov certified Janz's entry permit and left. Confused, Janz made his way to the exit. In what had he become entangled? At first Solovyov played the inquisitor, then the gentleman. Apparently the release of the Mennonite soldiers was a touchy issue. The guard at the door took Janz's entry permit. He was free once more.

Individual Emigration

Not long after Janz's interview with the *GPU*, a much more pleasant encounter took place. He was invited to dinner by CPR representative A. R. Owen in one of the best restaurants in Moscow. Also in attendance was Owen's assistant, N. F. Peshkov, his interpreter, as well as two Russian officials. Quite naturally the conversation revolved about the recent exodus of the Mennonite emigrants. Janz sensed that the occasion offered possibilities for the stalemated emigration movement. He informed the group that some of the emigrants possessing adequate financial resources desired to leave Russia independently of the group movement. Such a course of action had the sanction of the central government. Neither the *VBHH* nor the *AMLV* could do anything for these people. Perhaps the CPR could make arrangements with the Canadian government to receive these people. The proposal aroused a good deal of interest. All present expressed surprise at the fact that there were still colonists with sufficient means to finance their own way. Janz reaffirmed that this indeed was the case.[26]

No easy solution existed for this new problem. It was not simply a matter of transporting people from the steppes of Russia to the plains of Canada. The Canadian government would have to authorize entry while the CMBC had to secure adequate settlement sites. Both operations were bureaucratic procedures which took considerable time. Fortunately for the emigration movement the matter was not intractable. By mid-February 1924, all the technicalities connected with individual emigration had been cleared with Soviet authorities. A *VBHH* certificate confirming that a given family was registered in the officially ratified emigrant lists enabled it to obtain the necessary exit documents. The rigid Canadian medical requirements were fully applicable. Financially the arrangement had some drawbacks. Whereas the group emigrant paid five gold rubles per family permit, the individual emigrant was required to pay twenty-two gold rubles for every person over the age of sixteen because individual exit permits were required. Furthermore, all young men born between 1897 and 1903 who were fit for military service could not join their families if these decided to emigrate individually.[27] Except for these additions the individual differed little from the group emigration.

It was obvious that such an emigration venture required a reasonable economic solvency. Inflation had wiped out all savings. Only by selling their personal belongings, implements, livestock, and farm buildings could the people hope to gain sufficient funds for the journey to Canada. The land could not be sold since it belonged to the state. General poverty and a widespread distrust of Soviet economic policies hindered the success of an auction sale. Even those who still had much to sell were barely able to pay the expenses of emigration. "They may manage to go abroad with their limited means," Janz wrote, "perhaps a shilling might even remain in their pockets, but this will not buy a farm over there."[28]

The emergence of individual emigration as a legitimate alternative to group exodus proved indispensable to the future of the movement. After 1923 it became the only legal method of leaving Russia. As the framework of this type of emigration crystallized, it also became apparent that it was not dependent upon a sound economic status nor did it exclude those who were destitute. The landless and refugee elements of the Mennonite population were granted full credit or half-credit by the CMBC during and after 1924. Three emigrant categories consequently developed: cash, credit, and half-credit. The ultimate importance of the Owen-Janz dinner in Moscow can hardly be overestimated. It contributed to the initiation of a new strategy in the emigration which eventually enabled thousands to leave Russia.

Individual emigration was accompanied by critical domestic difficulties. To whom might the emigrating Mennonites sell their property? Most of their fellows, eager to leave themselves, had little interest in acquiring additional property. Since the social, cultural, economic, and religious structure of the village was usually based on an all-Mennonite population, widespread sales to Russians could bring about a loss of local self-government and eventual assimilation. The issue came into sharp focus when the residents of Tiegerweide began negotiating the sale of the entire village with Doukhobor settlers returning to Russia from Canada. Almost simultaneously the residents of the village of Steinfeld in the Grünfeld district investigated the possibility of such a transaction with neighboring Russians. Since Steinfeld was located on the periphery of the Mennonite settlement, the matter was not so crucial. Following the transactions the families of both villages hoped to emigrate by paying their own way. The *VBHH* refused to issue authorization of sale certificates to the villagers, as such a course of action might encourage a massive panic selling. The number of prospective emigrants would then far exceed the established norms. If such a situation came to the attention of authorities, a complete embargo on all further emigration was certain.[29]

CHAPTER ELEVEN

Misunderstandings

A Split in the Ranks

The *VBHH* Council which authorized the appointment of P. H. Unruh as a representative of the Russian Mennonites abroad had no misgivings about its course of action. It was simply a move designed to alleviate the threat of separate emigrant action in the Ukraine while simultaneously facilitating the venture in America. It symbolized no intention of malice and did not reflect upon the competence or incompetence of the regular members of the Study Commission. The documents relating to the episode suggest no calculated effort to oust any particular individual. Originally the *VBHH* appointment came as an emergency response to a critical situation.[1] The unhappy repercussions resulting from it came from a chain of misinterpretation, circumstance, and inadequate information.

The *VBHH* Council failed to realize that although the Study Commission had been elected by a Mennonite constituency, its mandate did not originally come from the *VBHH*. The inconsistency of appointing an American to serve on a Russian committee was likewise overlooked. The Council was not aware of conditions in America nor the role which Unruh played in American Mennonitism. It also forgot the difficulties under which some of the members of the Study Commission were working. When A. A. Friesen came to Canada the summer of 1921, he entered an atmosphere laden with party strife. Through persistent labor the obstacles preventing a Russian Mennonite entry into Canada were cleared away. Because of his identification with the movement Friesen found himself the object of widespread hostility. When the emigration was about to commence in August 1922, new impediments emerged—the cholera epidemic; the political eruption in the Dardanelles; the barring of Canadian doctors from entering Russia. In America this lack of action encouraged emigration opponents to launch a new campaign against the venture. It was particularly directed against the three chief leaders in Canada, D. Toews, G. Ens, and A. A. Friesen. In Canada constituency confidence in Friesen was subtly undermined by insinuations critical of his religious orthodoxy. Friesen was, to be sure, not of the creed-reciting type. Heretic hunters consequently found it easy to create suspicion. In America still another dimension made its influence felt, namely, the rather sharp conflict between Mennonite church leaders and church-related colleges. The religious outlook of many younger professors was in question. In this struggle P. H. Unruh took up the banner of orthodoxy. While in the United States, A. A. Friesen, a chemist by training, accepted a temporary teaching position at Bluffton College, Bluffton, Ohio. Influenced by adverse propaganda, some associated this move with religious liberalism.

In Russia, P. H. Unruh was appointed as a *VBHH* representative in April 1923, just before the actual emigration from Russia commenced. However, the *VBHH* failed to define the exact scope of Unruh's power or the nature of his working relationship with the Study Commission. Unruh was free to cooperate with them or ignore them. B. H. Unruh immediately expressed his concern over this fundamental fallacy when he learned of the appointment. A. A. Friesen unsuccessfully requested a clearer delineation of Unruh's mandate. The *VBHH* felt confident that the terms of the working relationship would evolve naturally. B. H. Unruh managed to meet with the new appointee when the latter passed through Berlin on his way to America. In the brief encounter B. H. Unruh sought to introduce P. H. Unruh to the work of the Study Commission, particularly the anticipated Canadian immigration. Though interested in the Canadian venture, P. H. Unruh advocated Mexico as a settlement site, but nevertheless expressed a willingness to cooperate.[2]

When P. H. Unruh returned to America, tension soon marked his relationship with Friesen. An incursion into A. A. Friesen's sphere of influence was inevitable. Mutual promises of cooperation by letter did not better the situation. Unruh played an overaggressive role at Friesen's expense. A character and personality clash was probably at the root of the intensifying conflict. Then, too, since each man held a rather different view of the emigration problem as such, their opinions as to the best course of procedure clashed. It was impossible for two men of such varying temperament and backgrounds to represent one cause to one constituency. Particularly frustrating for Friesen was Unruh's hesitancy to commit himself to an all-out emigration from Russia.[3] The discord between the two never came to an open rupture, however.

For A. A. Friesen, the appointment of a new confidence man abroad only signified a lack of trust in the representative elected earlier. His requests for a clarification of the situation by the *VBHH* remained unanswered. Even the pleas of associates who respected and valued his contribution were ignored.[4] When an acceptable explanation finally did come, Friesen felt it was too late to withdraw his resignation. The many attacks of a personal nature by opponents of the emigration had also led Friesen to question whether he should continue to hold his post on the Study Commission. Only later did it become clear that many of the attacks had been directed not against Friesen personally but against the cause he represented.[5]

Near the end of September 1923, Friesen handed in his resignation as a member of the Study Commission. Repercussions in Germany were almost immediate. Should the breach between Friesen and P. H. Unruh become irreparable, declared B. H. Unruh, it would be necessary for A. J. Fast and himself to clarify their position on the issue. In the meantime he hoped that P. H. Unruh would feel duty bound to cooperate more closely.[6] B. H. Unruh made every effort to heal the breach. When he received Friesen's letter of resignation he refused to forward it to the *VBHH* executive in the hope that Friesen might reconsider. By this time the American emigration committees had also been informed that the *VBHH* considered both A. A. Friesen and P. H. Unruh their *bona fide* representatives, and expected them to cooperate with one another and the American committees.[7] This clarification did not alter Friesen's intention to resign. Since he had meanwhile been appointed manager of the CMBC in Rosthern, and because most of the groundwork for the emigration was completed, Friesen felt his resignation would not seriously impair the emigration cause. Furthermore, his personal contribution to the welfare of the constituency was not an end. When Friesen heard of B. H. Unruh's delaying action, he chided him for the censorship he was establishing in Germany.[8]

Friesen's resignation remained a tense issue during the late fall and early winter of 1923. Janz once more tried to clarify the issue through a special letter addressed to Friesen in mid-December. Friesen responded by reaffirming his resignation, reiterating what to him was the main reason for his action. He had left his post because he detected a lack of confidence in his services on the part of the constituency in Russia.[9] There was moreover little need for his services in America at the present time.[10] When B. H. Unruh and A. J. Fast heard of Friesen's irrevocable withdrawal from the Study Commission, both men announced that they were resigning from the mandate originally granted them.[11] Only if Friesen could be persuaded to resume his post would they reconsider their resignation. Both men, however, expressed their willingness to remain at their posts until replacements could be found.

In Canada the misunderstanding between the *VBHH* and A. A. Friesen was augmented by the frequently false information supplied by public opinion. Particularly crucial in this regard were the utterances of newly arrived emigrants some of whom because of adverse experience or outright prejudice were extremely critical of the *VBHH* chairman Janz. Basing their information on rumor, these felt it necessary to inform Friesen that Janz was personally antagonistic toward him. Friesen found the situation extremely confusing since in his letters Janz appeared open and friendly. Another dimension unnecessarily exploited by the talebearers related to denominational misunderstandings prevalent among the new immigrants. Since Janz belonged to the Mennonite Brethren and Friesen to the General Conference Mennonites, these busybodies immediately assumed that any problems between the two men arose from this source. Letters often took as long as two months to get from Rosthern to Russia. The clarification of a given issue might therefore take one third of a year. During such an interval many false impressions matured.

B. H. Unruh was extremely eager to clarify the misunderstandings. For him the basic issues were not too complex. The *VBHH* had been eager to facilitate the emigration, and Friesen was apparently not too successful in his work. Perhaps an American could be used to supplement his efforts. It was further apparent that emigrant pressure had forced Janz's hand. By appointing P. H. Unruh the *VBHH* had not only found an American to represent their cause but had been spared the expense of maintaining him abroad. Inadequate and unclear communications had produced a rift, and B. H. Unruh appealed to Janz and Friesen to clarify their differences for the sake of the suffering brethren. "Here it is not a question of Rückenau or Lichtenau," Unruh wrote, "only nameless suffering—let us help. . . ."[12]

Unruh's appeal was not without success. Even before receiving it Janz had commissioned one of the emigrants, H. B. Janz from

Halbstadt, to mediate with Friesen on his behalf. H. B. Janz was able to clarify some of the misconceptions which had arisen from unfounded rumors. It was obvious, however, that the personal relationship between B. B. Janz and Friesen had been marred. Friesen felt that in view of past developments he could not represent the *VBHH* as long as Janz was chairman.[13] From the report he received from H. B. Janz, the *VBHH* chairman saw that the entire issue had become a personal matter which had to be personally settled. Janz's response denoted a noble character. Existing conditions might never allow a personal encounter. The misunderstanding had to be clarified at once. Janz wrote to Friesen:

> Today we live and are; today I want to clear the slate with you!
> . . . I will not spare myself, but rather I want to be in favor of what is true and good—even if this means humiliation.[14]

The issue was resolved. Great men had been humble enough to settle their misunderstandings. Happily, the split in the ranks never interfered with the progress of the overall emigration movement.

A Lack of Information

As the Russian Mennonites became more and more interested in emigration possibilities, the scope of the original movement naturally enlarged. Negotiations previously limited to the *VBHH* in Kharkov were now also carried on by accredited representatives of the RSFSR Mennonites in Moscow. In the spring of 1923 the preliminary steps for the creation of the *AMLV* had been completed, though the organization was not yet officially recognized. As a result there were two separate agencies at two different locations active in the planned Mennonite exodus. Both organizations were naturally desirous of being fully informed of developments abroad. In a country where all mail from abroad ran the risk of censorship and moved very slowly the problem of keeping both groups informed was a difficult one. Only one sure communication channel existed—the diplomatic courier service of the German legation in Kharkov. All confidential material from either Russia or Germany was sure to reach its destination when dispatched via this route.

By the late fall of 1922 both the *AMLV* and *VBHH* executive as well as the Study Commission members abroad were experiencing considerable difficulty in getting information to and from Russia. It was not only that letters sent by regular mail system failed to arrive in Russia. In the case of all concerned the lack of financial resources prevented the maintenance of a secretarial staff to duplicate a rather voluminous correspondence. Since the Moscow representatives could not utilize the diplomatic mail, Unruh in Germany was extremely hesitant to forward the more confidential reports to that address. In December 1922, he wrote to Janz, "I do not want to send any more correspondence to Moscow until the information question is clarified."[15] Instead, Unruh suggested that the mail be sent to Kharkov via the trustworthy channel, then sent to *VBHH* headquarters in Tiege to be forwarded to Moscow.

AMLV members felt slighted. Were they not located in the heart of Russia? Was it not here that the political and economic pulse of the nation was best ascertained? Neither Kharkov nor Tiege had an adequate staff for the duplication of all the correspondence. Even if it were available, considerable time might be lost through the use of the mail system. Internal mail was not always sure of arrival. The negotiations taking place in Moscow, the *AMLV* executive argued, were just as important as those in Kharkov, particularly since the Ukrainian Mennonites might have to deal with Moscow before the 1923 emigration became a reality. Both organizations must be furnished with all the reports from their common representatives abroad. If the problem on hand related to Moscow, a copy of the correspondence would also be sent to Kharkov. If the reverse was true, a copy would be sent directly to Moscow.[16]

Under normal circumstances this was correct business procedure. Unruh in Karlsruhe and Janz in Kharkov, however, realized that the situation in Russia was far from normal. On March 8, 1923, Unruh responded rather outspokenly to the *AMLV* demand for greater recognition. A unification on the part of the Russian and Ukrainian Mennonites on the matter of information distribution was long overdue. He had always been a supporter of regional autonomy, but in this matter he insisted on centralization. A cause as important as the emigration could not bear the strain of diverse local interests. Moscow and Kharkov must unify their efforts.[17] The *AMLV* executive reaction betrayed hurt feelings. They replied that their demand was simply for adequate information; until now it had been consciously bypassed. Hence the *AMLV* was frequently uninformed of the negotiations abroad, although it should have the right of equal participation with Kharkov. They urged Unruh to recognize this by simultaneous correspondence with both groups.[18]

Human nature was probably at the root of the communications problem. The *VBHH* enjoyed a definite seniority with regard to the emigration movement. Mennonite leaders abroad, perhaps conditioned

by Janz's letters of appeal during 1921 and 1922, continually associated the *VBHH* with the emigration movement. When the RSFSR
Mennonite constituency gave birth to another emigration agency, the
latecomer was naturally regarded as of somewhat less significance.
Moreover, the actual exodus as it was to take place in 1923 came from
the south, not the north. By 1923 the position of Kharkov in the
technical implementation of the emigration movement had nevertheless
declined. An RSFSR transit meant the participation of the Moscow
government. The *AMLV* role now became of equal importance to that
played by the *VBHH*. Under such circumstances a demand for equal
treatment and respect was not unreasonable. Both Unruh and Friesen
were correct in pointing out that internal communication was an
internal issue. Some type of administrative centralization was essential.
VBHH leaders must work for the best solution under the existing
conditions. Since the Study Commission represented all Mennonites in
Russia, all were entitled to information. This was clearly impossible
for the delegates abroad. Also some information pertained only to
specific localities. A central information center and clearinghouse
would solve the problem. The *AMLV* and the *VBHH* must work for
some such solution. In view of sudden political changes that might
adversely affect the Mennonites in Russia, close cooperation and
unity were essential.[19]

The information center was never organized, nor was the communications problem satisfactorily solved. Legal and political factors
prevented the union of the two organizations. Though in the following
years there was close collaboration and exchange of information, some
tension occasionally arose. Both agencies, feeling duty-bound to represent the interests of their constituencies as well as possible, sometimes tended to seek their own advantage when limited emigration
quotas were contrasted with large numbers of people clamoring for
exodus.

CHAPTER TWELVE

Success and Frustration

The possibility of individual emigration from Russia gave a new sense of hope to the wealthier elements in all the Mennonite settlements during the first months of 1924. The earlier group emigration as sanctioned by the Kharkov government had purposely bypassed the landed colonist in the interest of utilizing him in facilitating economic reconstruction. The new development had some ironic aspects. Many destitute refugees who ought to have left were simply unable to do so. The situation bred unnecessary jealousy and misunderstanding. Simultaneously it appeared to suppress the widespread discontent and restlessness. The calm was both illusory and brief.

> The new possibility of individual emigration at one's own expense has shown that we were only dealing with an apparent calmness. People simply told themselves, "It is impossible." Now that something can be done there is a widespread stirring.[1]

A substantial harvest in the fall of 1923 did improve the overall economic picture, but it did not decrease the desire to emigrate. For the colonists this turn for the better was offset by increased infringements on their freedom of worship as well as the forcible enlistment of young men who objected to military service on the grounds of conscience. Many of the wealthier colonists were determined to leave Russia regardless of personal losses. By April 1924, the *VBHH* had issued 450 certificates to families planning to emigrate privately.[2]

Until late April no word about the signing of a new contract was heard from America. This delay was particularly frustrating, for without it there were no prospects for either the private or the group emigrants. As late as April 24 Janz still had no word of the contract signed between the CPR and the Board.[3] For the first four months of 1924 the *VBHH* executive was able to inform its constituency only that American action might be forthcoming. All the while it was painfully aware that Moscow and not Kharkov now figured predominantly in the emigration. In Moscow the prevailing opposition to the movement might result in its sudden termination. A widespread evacuation had to begin immediately. Repeatedly Janz's letters and telegrams spoke of the 10,000 emigrants that would have to leave in 1924. A somewhat drastic revision of that figure soon became necessary. One bright prospect had appeared. During his stay in Moscow between March 20 and 30, Janz obtained a preliminary authorization which allowed the doctors from the Canadian Immigration Department to enter Russia. It was now possible to avert another Lechfeld by conducting the final medical examination of the emigrants in the colonies.[4]

A Question of Preference

The perpetual economic and religious pressures connected with living in Russia continued to augment the desire to emigrate during the first months of 1924, even though there were no prospects for embarkation. The *VBHH* executive became very conscious of this pressure as the Kalinovo Congress scheduled for March 1 drew nearer. This unrest expressed itself rather specifically in agitation for a revision of the emigration lists ratified at the Osterwick Congress in the fall of 1922.[5] Simultaneously an intense struggle for preference encompassing all the Mennonites in the Soviet Union began to make itself felt.

A new chapter was written in the emigration story during the first months of 1924. The first paragraphs of the story had been completed much earlier. The Mennonites in the RSFSR shared the emigration interest of their brethren in the Ukraine from the very beginning and had actively participated in dispatching the Study Commission. They followed its work with avid interest.[6] Organizationally the northern Mennonites had been almost as active as their southern counterpart. Permission to leave the RSFSR had been granted to 350 families by the Central Executive Committee in Moscow as early as September 20, 1922. Because the *AMLV* was not officially registered, bureaucratic complications prevented setting the exodus in motion. When the Ukrainian emigration was forced to move through the RSFSR in 1923, *AMLV* leaders not only recognized its prior claim but cooperated closely with Janz in the Moscow negotiations. Colonists represented by the *AMLV* were nevertheless determined to participate in the emigration. Delegates attending the Alexandertal Congress expressed the wish that in the event of a renewed exodus, a percentage arrangement be instituted to ensure a fair division between the RSFSR and Ukranian Mennonites.[7]

Prospects for leaving Russia improved considerably during February 1924. On February 18 the All-Russian Central Executive Committee meeting in Moscow heard a petition from the *AMLV* requesting exit visas for 550 families intending to emigrate at their own expense. The CEC approved the venture and even exempted the families from customary exit fees. This new development forced an alteration in the basic structure of the emigration program. In practice the process had affected only the Ukrainian Mennonites up to this point. Now the settlements in the RSFSR were eligible to join in. The detailed program of the evacuation was not clarified, however. Administratively Moscow authorities did not envisage two separate movements. Intentionally disregarding Ukrainian autonomy the central government saw the emigration of the Russian Mennonites as an extension of the southern movement which began in 1923. As a result the newly sanctioned emigrants numbering about 4,000 had to be interwoven with the lists completed at the Osterwick Congress. *AMLV* leaders, mindful of the cooperation and aid they extended to *VBHH* officials in 1923, now felt justified in demanding an early embarkation date for the eligible emigrants in their constituency. Since the Kalinovo Congress of the *VBHH* (March 1-4, 1924) did not officially deal with the migration question, the preference issue was bypassed.[8] Unofficially the two *AMLV* observers in attendance, P. F. Froese and J. Reimer, insisted that a reappraisal of the current emigration schedule was imperative.[9]

AMLV concern with this problem became more crystallized when its administrative council met with the executive in Moscow, March 20-24. B. B. Janz was also in attendance. The *AMLV* members censured a *VBHH* council decision on March 3, which stipulated that Mennonite emigrants from the RSFSR might depart only after 10,000 Ukrainian Mennonites had embarked. They insisted on a radical revision of existing emigration lists because only some 5,000 were expected to depart in 1924. To accomplish this a committee was formed, composed of representatives from both organizations as well as the Crimea, where Mennonite colonists were also much in favor of emigration.[10] Such a course of action seemed entirely reasonable since material conditions in the south had partially improved whereas those in Siberia had worsened.[11]

The *VBHH* Council considered the *AMLV* proposal when it met in Orloff on May 8 and 9.[12] The *AMLV* had specifically suggested an emigration allotment of the following proportions: sixty emigrants from the Ukraine for every thirty-five from the RSFSR and five from the Crimea. After deliberating over the problem the *VBHH* Council came to the conclusion that the Osterwick ratified lists must be kept intact. Most of the prospective emigrants were destitute victims of the Makhno era and could not hope for a future in the Ukraine. The *VBHH* did not thereby assert that the status of Ukrainian refugees was necessarily worse than that in the RSFSR or the Crimea. The question was rather one of strategy. Tampering with the present lists might well intensify government impatience and possibly invite interference.

In the end a compromise plan was adopted. Many of the refugees would be medically unfit for evacuation. As the selection took place in the colonies, vacated places might easily be filled by non-Ukrainian Mennonites before they left. It was also suggested that every effort be made to encourage materially able emigrants to leave privately and thereby create additional vacancies. The vacancies created by the severe medical inspection were to be reserved for the refugees from Terek, who were still awaiting evacuation.[13]

Regression and Progress

May Day had come to Kharkov. For days the two major newspapers, *Communist* (the party organ) and *Visti* (the popular Ukrainian language publication), had publicized the event, when the workers and peasants would celebrate their deliverance from capitalism. Colorful military parades for the benefit of the public marked the occasion. Most of the chiefs of state were in attendance. Numerous speeches endorsed the Bolshevik government as the sole agency bringing salvation and healing to the world. In a special ceremony the armed forces swore their loyalty to the Revolution. Their might would extend the new order throughout the world.

This glorification of militarism was witnessed by at least one unsympathetic spectator. For him the May Day festivities were not just pageantry but a painful reminder of the turbulent spirit which had swept his native land. Pacifist Janz could not help thinking of the Mennonite young men who shared his convictions. The Revolution prevented them from living according to the dictates of their conscience. Even worse, they were forced to become instruments of the Revolution. Only one escape from this tyranny existed—emigration. As yet, however, no word had come from America. Deeply depressed he returned to his lodgings. Even a pleasant spring shower could not refresh his sad spirit.[14]

A lengthy telegram from the RUSCAPA, the Russian-Canadian-American-Passenger-Agency supervising the technical aspects of the emigration in Moscow, greeted Janz when he entered his quarters. He could hardly believe its content. The contract had been signed! The Canadian government was prepared to receive 5,000 refugees on credit as well as a number of individual colonists paying their own way. Hummel and Drury, the physicians of the Canadian Immigration Department, were on their way to Russia. The medical examinations would be held in the colonies. Large CPR ships, capable of carrying 1,000 passengers each, were being dispatched to Libau. The Americans had done their part. The responsibility for initiating the movement now lay in Russia.[15]

Technical preparations for the evacuation were begun at once. The people constituting the first two groups came largely from the Halbstadt area. Their departure had been approved by both Kharkov and Moscow. Though the basic procedure was simple, its execution was not. All families who passed their medical inspection were issued certificates by the *VBHH* office in Orloff. These certificates were then taken to the *GPU* passport department in Moscow for final processing. J. J. Thiessen, a teacher from Tiegenhagen, was requested to take the first list containing about 1,250 names plus the necessary certificates to Moscow. Subsequently he headed several other transports to the Latvian border. Thiessen made immediate contact with Nikita F. Peshkov, Owen's official translator and member of RUSCAPA. The next encounter was not so pleasant. At the offices of the Moscow *GPU*, Thiessen introduced himself to the chairman of the passport department. He was given a harsh reception. Waiting until Thiessen had explained that he sought approval of the emigration list he shouted, "So you come from Janz. For three years I have not crossed myself, but if I could ever free myself of Janz, I would cross myself three times." Glancing at the list he requested Thiessen to return tomorrow. Nevertheless on the following day the list was sanctioned without incident.[16]

While in Moscow Thiessen, in consultation with Peshkov, tried to obtain a letter of protection for the emigrant train from the Foreign Commissariat in order to avoid the delays which had afflicted the 1923 transports. The woman authorized to deal with this problem proved most accommodating. Well disposed toward the

Mennonites because of favorable Red Cross contacts with them during World War I, she not only obtained a letter of protection for Thiessen, but dispatched a telegram ordering all officials at the railway terminals between Lichtenau and Moscow to facilitate the movement of the emigrant train to the utmost. Satisfied that all was in good order Thiessen returned to Lichtenau.[17] Meanwhile B. B. Janz, also in Moscow at this time, prepared to return to Kharkov. There was a last consultation with Peshkov. Taking leave of Janz the Russian official observed, "I am somewhat concerned about this new movement. Although everything is well ordered, I sense that difficulties will arise. I feel one should go into the cathedral and set up a very large candle for the great God."[18] At the moment Janz did not share his conviction.

Returning to Kharkov the *VBHH* chairman sought to complete the routine technicalities connected with the emigration. When he informed his friend in the German legation, Consul Herman von Hey, of his good fortune, Hey responded, "But, Mr. Janz, it is not desirable to carry out a mass emigration. The colonies must remain because they are of great importance!"[19] Somewhat discouraged Janz took his leave. Why were the colonies so important? They were on the verge of complete ruin. The colonists had no future in Russia. Didn't von Hey realize this? Unknown to Janz at the time, politics once again took precedence over humanitarianism. His friend Herman von Hey became a traitor to the emigration cause. He personally went to the chairman of the Ukrainian Council of People's Commissars, V. Y. Chubar, to seek an injunction against the mass emigration.[20]

Preparations for the departure were meanwhile completed in the Molotschna. The first train was scheduled to leave Lichtenau on June 23, 1924.[21] The documentary work required a great deal of time. Since photographs were not entirely essential, however, and because local officials were not allowed to interfere in the proceedings, the administrative work related to the first group progressed smoothly.

When Janz returned to Kharkov, unexpected difficulties set in. Peshkov's premonitions had been correct. The 1924 emigrants had not even begun their exodus when the entire operation was threatened with extinction. Janz wrote, "Government circles in Moscow as in Kharkov are very apprehensive about the mass exodus of the Mennonites. They express surprise, inquire, send out commissions to investigate, withdraw provisions for a free departure."[22]

The general situation which Janz described in this later letter related to three main problems. Since February, officials in the province of Donetz had refused to issue exit permits to seventy-nine Mennonite refugees despite the fact that Ekaterinoslav authorities continued to do so. The second problem took the form of two telegrams from the RUSCAPA in Moscow informing Janz that central authorities refused to honor the permits of the first emigrant group. The third was closely related. The supplementary emigrant lists, containing replacements for those medically disqualified in the regular lists, needed final ratification. Problems one and three were submitted to a special commission of the Ukrainian Council of People's Commissars, which was scheduled to meet on June 14. The second problem had to be solved in Moscow.

By now Janz had become well aware of the hostility in Kharkov toward the emigration movement. Fearful of the outcome of the June 14 meeting he sought to ascertain the prevailing climate of opinion. Attempts to obtain an interview with CPC chairman Chubar were unsuccessful. On June 12 he managed to confer with a representative of the People's Commissariat of Internal Affairs. The meeting convinced Janz that the prospects for further emigration were not bright. The Mennonites must be patient, he was told. Russia could accommodate them as well as America. Considerable district autonomy, greater religious freedom, and economic betterment lay in the immediate future. The government wanted to keep the colonists and was well disposed toward them. In Canada they probably faced much hardship. The object of all this conciliatory talk was obvious. The Mennonite exodus, once sanctioned as an emergency measure designed to alleviate the famine, was no longer desirable.[23]

The results of the June 14 meeting confirmed Janz's apprehensions. Though the commission ordered Donetz authorities to grant the permits in question, it refused to approve the supplementary lists containing about 453 names. These were returned to Janz with the explanation that in the future no group emigration according to lists would be allowed.[24] The future appeared extraordinarily bleak.

The two urgent dispatches from the RUSCAPA had reached Janz prior to the CPC commission meeting in Kharkov. Moscow authorities refused to honor the exit permits of the first group of 1924 emigrants without a reconfirmation of these by Kharkov. Janz could not leave the Ukrainian capital. What was to be done? It was reasonable to assume that Moscow obstinacy might influence the CPC commission's decisions on June 14. The increasingly less autonomous Kharkov regime would possibly not act without a directive from Moscow. Janz decided on a daring course of action. He sent a lengthy telegram simultaneously to Central Executive Committee member Smidovich and the *GPU* passport department. Since such an audacious approach might well invite retaliation from Moscow authorities, two days of anxious waiting followed. Finally the answer arrived. The first group could embark! Janz commented, "My small quarters became a hallowed place of worship, such as the largest candle in the greatest cathedral could not have supplied."[25]

In Lichtenau the hour of final farewell approached. The departure of the first group in 1924 was probably one of the most dramatic and best remembered in the entire history of the emigration.

The evening shadows lengthened, the sun was about to set. We loved the soil of our homeland. Now it was time to bid adieu and to leave one's hearth, village, customs, relatives, and friends. People took leave of one another. Even the strong wept, some sobbed. Perhaps not all were aware of the significance of this day, but a deep seriousness was written on all faces. Parting is painful. Some of the people were going, the others staying behind. The bell sounded once, then again. Everyone knew that only a few minutes remained. The mass of people became more restless. All those emigrating had to board the train. Here a firm handshake, there the last embrace, tears flow. Yes, parting is painful. The third bell, the train begins to move. "Good-bye. Come after us." "Reunion in eternity," shouted one emigrant. . . . Gradually those remaining behind fade into the distance. . . .[26]

The train sped to Alexandrovsk. There was a brief pause at Orel, then on to the Latvian border via Smolensk, finally reaching the border. Here the technical formalities connected with the border crossing were completed under the direction of echelon leader J. J. Thiessen. Finally the processing was finished. Slowly the train crossed over into Latvia. Thiessen remained behind. In the course of the summer he accompanied two additional trains to the Latvian border and remained in close contact with the events taking place in Moscow.

In Kharkov Janz made preparations to leave for Moscow before the departure of the first group. One more visit was necessary to the Kharkov offices of the *GPU*. What was their attitude toward recent developments? Was any support to be expected from this agency? The answers to these questions were supplied by more questions. Why did the *VBHH* promote the emigration in Moscow to the exclusion of the Ukrainian regime? When Janz tried to clarify the issue, the subject was changed. Why did the Canadian doctors come into the colonies? Was a massive evacuation of which the *GPU* knew nothing being planned? Why were all the sick and consequently useless people being left behind? Though Janz presented documentary proof that the entire operation was government sanctioned, the *GPU* remained dissatisfied. It appeared that from now on the emigration was a Moscow concern.[27]

Certain that the departure of the first group had not guaranteed an unhindered evacuation, Janz hurried to Moscow. The entire operation was in serious jeopardy. Decisive action was desperately needed. There were still friends in Moscow. One of these was Manzev, onetime head of the Ukrainian *GPU* and former Commissar of Internal Affairs in Kharkov. Janz had worked closely with Manzev in the registration of the *VBHH* charter. When he was transferred to Moscow, Janz had the good fortune to be present at his farewell. In response to a compliment on his work Manzev had invited Janz to notify him if ever a grave problem arose. It was now time to claim this promise.

The *VBHH* chairman contacted Manzev several days after his arrival in Moscow. His support of the emigration had an electrifying effect on the *GPU* passport department. List two was approved without any hesitation.[28] The second group was composed of emigrants from Halbstadt, Chortitza, and Memrik. The Halbstadt group departed from Lichtenau, then was joined by the Chortitza emigrants at Alexandrovsk and by those from Memrik at Sinelnikovo. This group, again led by J. J. Thiessen, contained about 1,220 emigrants.[29] The ratification of list three was meanwhile complicated by the arrival of a Kharkov memorandum protesting the emigration. In the hope of obtaining official approval for the third emigration list, Janz visited another friend, Smidovich, who promised to present the issue to the next meeting of the Council of People's Commissars. Further inquiry as to the stoppage of the third group in the Moscow *GPU* offices proved useless. Janz was told only that Kharkov must reconfirm its approval of the emigration before Moscow would act. Only one month earlier (May 18 and 19) he had been assured that all the technicalities connected with the emigration movement had been completed. Janz was reminded of a recent conversation with Cornelius Unruh, a lawyer of Ekaterinoslav. "I know the Reds better than you, Janz. They will promise you this and that, pull you back and forth, but when the moment for action comes nothing will happen."[30]

B. B. Janz bids farewell to several emigrants at the Lichtenau Terminal on July 13, 1924.

The delegates attending the last General Mennonite Conference held in Moscow, January 13-18, 1925.

Emigrants embarking at Lichtenau, Molotschna, on July 13, 1924.

List Three

The suspension of all further group emigration naturally brought a severe crisis for the Gnadenfeld refugees. All the preparations for an imminent departure had been made. Then came the news that an exodus according to the ratified lists was no longer possible. Many refugees were bitterly disappointed and harshly criticized the *VBHH* leadership. Why the delay in sanctioning list three? Why was it not processed together with the first two lists? Was this not simply an administrative oversight?

The story of list three was intertwined with a host of uncertainties. When the first two lists were processed in the fall of 1923, the *VBHH* executive had no idea how small or how large a number of refugees might be accommodated in the new contract, if a contract was to be had at all. There were other circumstances which dictated a cautious advance. Since the visas granted by Kharkov were valid for two months, a reconfirmation of these for all three lists had to be reckoned with. This made it almost certain that no movement of emigrants could take place until spring. Then, too, Kharkov still thought only in terms of a limited exodus. The first two lists sanctioned in the fall of 1923 contained 4,974 names. Whether Canada was willing to accept even that number was uncertain. To add list three with its 2,162 names in the fall of 1923 might have alarmed the Ukrainian government and resulted in the cancellation of the entire movement. At the earliest all groups concerned might leave in the spring of 1924. Why not reconfirm two lists in the fall and the third early in 1924? This would minimize a growing suspicion in Kharkov that a mass exodus was in the making. Unfortunately, Janz was unable to bring his plan to a successful conclusion.

In the 1923 emigration, the Moscow government became involved only insofar as the *GPU* passport department supplied the necessary transit visas. For the 1924 emigration a special decree of the Central Executive Committee was necessary. Every group departure had to be separately approved. When the Gnadenfeld list was dispatched to the Moscow Commissariat of Internal Affairs for delivery to the *GPU* in May, government authorities were confident that the list had already been approved by the CEC earlier in the year. Unfortunately officials confused the Gnadenfeld list with the *AMLV* petition for the evacuation of about 4,000 refugees sanctioned by the CEC on February 18, 1924. The *VBHH* was thereupon informed that list three had been sanctioned. It in turn advised the emigrants to prepare for embarkation. *VBHH* leaders learned of the error a short time later and immediately proceeded to correct it by an appeal to the CEC. It was too late. The Kharkov memorandum protesting further group emigration had already been received in Moscow. The central government refused to act unless Kharkov endorsed the Gnadenfeld list first.

Meanwhile the unfortunate Gnadenfeld refugees found themselves in difficult straits. Most crucial from the standpoint of the refugees remaining in the area for a lengthy period of time was the housing shortage. Five families frequently lived in accommodations originally designed for one. What was once intended to be temporary shelter became permanent residence. All had to share a common kitchen, dining room, and bake oven. Barns and machine sheds likewise became home for many refugee families. Under such circumstances sanitation was a perpetual problem. Such essentials as soap and bedding were almost nonexistent. In such crowded conditions illness became prevalent. As Gnadenfeld lay in a virtually treeless district, heating material for the winter was difficult to find. A successful though limited harvest in the fall had not substantially improved prospects. Cattle had to be slaughtered for lack of feed. A badly undernourished population faced further deprivation. There would be little milk or butter available for the coming winter. The natural produce tax, assessed when the crop outlook was still good, promised to absorb most of the grain harvested. Vegetable gardens had been almost totally ruined by the drought. With the coming of winter the refugees had to depend on outside help for survival. No new clothing was available. Most of the children faced the winter without sufficient protection from its cold. Fathers who hoped to provide their families with some security could not find employment. Men traveled as far as 250 versts to find work and considered themselves fortunate if they found employment for several days.[31] The suspension of all further group emigration now added a final tragic touch to these bleak circumstances—that of complete hopelessness.[32]

Little could be done for the Gnadenfeld refugees. The Ukrainian government remained firm in its decision. The large-scale group movement which it had so generously sanctioned in 1922 was at an end—irrevocably so! Emigration was possible only through individual applications via the regularly constituted channels. In this way it was easy to keep the desirable and evacuate the unwanted. For a time it seemed that the Gnadenfeld refugees might find help in Moscow.[33] Toward the end of August, Janz made a special trip to the capital

The so-called "Red Gate" leading from Soviet Russia into Latvia. Many emigrants crossed the Russian border at this point.

The emigrants arrive in Riga.

city on their behalf, hoping that it might be possible to sanction list three despite objections from Kharkov. Two weeks of sustained effort produced no result. The Ukrainian suspension of group emigration was honored. Formally officials gave the excuse that the previously sanctioned list was outdated and must be reconfirmed by Kharkov.[34] Two more attempts were made to effect the departure of the Gnadenfeld group during September and early October. The first was a direct appeal to the Kharkov government for a reconfirmation of list three. The second was large-scale individual application for exit permits to the customary authorities in Ekaterinoslav by the Gnadenfeld refugees. This procedure symbolized a realization of the fact that group emigration had terminated. In the end it proved to be the best course, for the Kharkov regime persisted in refusing to sanction list three.[35]

CHAPTER THIRTEEN

The Intensifying Crisis

While the *VBHH* executive was making desperate efforts to obtain government sanction of list three, developments in Canada contributed to the tragedy that had come to surround the 1924 emigration. The Canadian Mennonite Board of Colonization, meeting in Winnipeg during July, decided to reduce its immigration contract for 1924 to 3,000 persons. Colonel Dennis of the CPR ordered all further movement for credit passengers to cease on July 27, when the third group (approximately 195 persons) crossed the border at Sebezh. An additional 1,000 cash immigrants would be processed by the CMBC provided they reached Sebezh by August 10. P. F. Froese learned of the situation in Moscow on July 25.[1] Janz had been informed somewhat earlier.

The rapid termination of the emigration came as a grave shock to both *AMLV* and *VBHH* leaders. Hundreds of emigrants had liquidated their holdings in preparation for embarkation. Now destitute, they faced the prospect of spending another winter in Russia. Several telegrams of protest were of no avail. The news was a particular blow to Janz, for there was still some hope that list three might be ratified.[2] Addressing all the Colonization Committees in America he wrote:

> The percentage of the distressed and needy is particularly high in this list [Gnadenfeld]. Their departure is a crying necessity. And now the transport is stopped. We do not know the reasons. Either the brethren in Canada have become disunited and so annulled the contract or the political issues have arisen, which make further transport impossible. We will continue to suffer. Allow us to continue to hope.[3]

Only later did the Russian Mennonite leaders learn that a poor harvest and the consequent lack of funds in Canada had forced the reduction of the contract.

This reduction of the contract by the Board in America seriously jeopardized the evacuation plans in the RSFSR. Lists from three areas, the Kuban, Millerovo, and Neu-Samara, had been compiled and submitted to the *GPU* in the various provinces. They contained 1,284 names.[4] Medical examinations for the first group had begun when the disastrous news from America arrived. *AMLV* leaders were bitterly disappointed. Dissatisfaction with *VBHH* planning was openly expressed. Why had not Janz informed the *AMLV* of the Gnadenfeld dilemma? RSFSR emigrants could easily have been substituted for the Gnadenfeld refugees not able to leave with the third group in July if news of the difficulty had reached Moscow on time.[5] The matter was not that simple. The status of list three was in flux until the day the third group was scheduled to depart, even though its ultimate rejection remained uncertain until the end of August. As a result it was impossible to inform the *AMLV* of possible vacancies early enough to allow the substitution of RSFSR emigrants.

Renewed Hope

Colonel Dennis's order to halt embarkation proceedings was closely observed. The last credit passengers crossed into Latvia on July 27. They were followed by a small group of cash emigrants on August 10. The sense of finality was overwhelming. The CPR doctors stopped their examinations and departed for London on August 8. The technical representatives of RUSCAPA in the colonies departed six days later.[6]

In desperation Janz sent one more telegram to Rosthern. Would they accept 1,600 cash emigrants who had their permits and had been medically cleared?[7] The answer from Colonel Dennis came via RUSCAPA during the night of August 20. Janz could hardly believe its content. He had received more than he had requested. The CPR was willing to transport an additional 1,000 credit passengers as well as an undetermined number of emigrants able to finance their own way. Drs. Drury and Hummel were returning to the colonies. RUSCAPA was dispatching two men to the Molotschna and the Caucasus. If another large echelon could be gathered, transportation was available before winter.[8]

The Kharkov injunction against all further group emigration made it difficult to collect the required number of emigrants before winter, especially since the processing of individual passes was extremely slow. Then too the strict medical standards enforced by Canadian authorities made many who held exit permits ineligible. In view of these obstacles it was necessary to create some sort of reserve in order to fully utilize the generous offer of the CPR. Janz knew of only one alternative—the evacuation of medical rejects whose unfitness was temporary and could be remedied. Legally a part of earlier emigration lists, these were qualified for transport to Latvia. Thereupon they might be sent to some detention camp for recovery purposes.

Where could such a transient camp be found? Lechfeld was no longer satisfactory. Some emigrants had been detained here for well over a year with no prospects for their evacuation. The *DMH* was becoming extremely reluctant to continue the program.[9] Funds for a new detention camp were not available. Janz appealed to both B. H. Unruh and the Dutch Emigration Committee in Rotterdam.[10] Was it possible to arrange the necessary facilities in Rotterdam? Despite Dutch willingness to participate, technical difficulties prevented the establishment of a transient camp in Holland.[11] The *DMH* finally decided to reopen Lechfeld, but under certain conditions. The emigrants would not be supported by the German relief agency. Their stay in Lechfeld must be privately financed. All emigrants coming to Lechfeld had to possess certificates from Drs. Hummel and Drury stipulating that their illness was of a temporary nature and that entry to Canada was guaranteed pending full recovery.[12] The German Immigration Department was extremely cooperative in the undertaking by authorizing German officials in Moscow and Kharkov to issue German transit visas to the Russian emigrants requiring them.[13]

In the RSFSR and the Ukraine the preparations for the renewal of the emigration continued as rapidly as possible. While medical and permit difficulties hampered these efforts, they were not the only factors preventing a rapid fulfillment of the quota. By the late summer of 1924 a radical currency reform by the Soviet government had been more or less completed.[14] As a result of high exchange rates money was extremely scarce and private emigration became more problematical. The funds which prospective emigrants hoped to obtain from their farm produce never became available because of the poor harvest. Furthermore, some emigrants were still determined to go to Mexico.[15] All these obstacles made it impossible to fill the 1,300 places available by October 25. Happily the embarkation date was extended to mid-November.

By the end of August it was clearly apparent that the Gnadenfeld refugees could not leave except on an individual basis. Emigrant groups were accordingly constructed on the basis of individual pass holders. Meanwhile the fifth echelon of about 440 departed from the Molotschna on August 31.[16] Between September 19 and 22, the first echelon from the RSFSR containing just 300 persons from the Kuban crossed into Latvia.[17]

Despite this exodus, approximately 600 of the original 1,300 places still remained void.[18] In order to ensure an equitable distribution a special meeting between *AMLV* and *VBHH* representatives was held in Orloff on September 25. The *VBHH* felt certain that it could fill only about 250 of the available places. The remaining 350 were consequently at the disposal of the *AMLV*. Both organizations soon raised their original estimates. In the RSFSR alone approximately 450 emigrants were anticipated. A similar increase appeared certain in the Ukraine. On October 10 Janz informed RUSCAPA that about 340 emigrants might be expected from the Ukraine. P. F. Froese, working in conjunction with N. Peshkov of the RUSCAPA, decided to cable Rosthern for 200 additional places. Peshkov insisted on signing B. B. Janz's name to the cablegram. The request was granted. Though Janz was somewhat taken aback by this irregular procedure, it in no way affected the close working relationship between north and south.[19] Two more groups from the RSFSR embarked during October. The first was comprised of refugees from Millerovo and Ufa, while those in the second came largely from Samara.[20]

The Last Sixty

Another Ukrainian emigrant group was scheduled to depart from the Lichtenau terminal on October 25. Approximately 300 people were to leave the Molotschna for Moscow where they would join other emigrants from the RSFSR for passage to Sebezh and Libau. Because of technical difficulties RUSCAPA generously extended the departure date from October 25 to November 14. Carefully laid plans met with tragic reversal. By Sunday, November 9, only seventeen of the 300 applications had received their passes. Though these had been promised by provincial officials in Ekaterinoslav, an administrative shuffle in the exit permit department, involving the arrest of one of its members, prevented this. For a time Janz feared that the action was in retaliation for the generosity of the department in its processing of Mennonite exit permits. Nothing could be done to change the situation. On November 10 only seventeen were able to board the train for Moscow.[21]

Janz's fears proved to be premature. Within a few days an additional sixty people received their permits. Two urgent cablegrams pleading for another extension of the sailing date were dispatched to Rosthern on November 19 and 20. On November 26 RUSCAPA sent word that this was possible provided the emigrants reached Moscow by November 30. The order for embarkation was immediately given by the *VBHH* administration in Orloff, but technical difficulties delayed its implementation. The use of passenger rather than freight cars had been discussed somewhat earlier but echelon leader Jacob Janzen, painfully aware of the limited finances of the emigrants, decided on the use of freight cars. By the time these were readied for emigrant use the November 30 deadline was nearing. A delayed departure as well as the slowness of the freight train brought the emigrants to Kharkov during the night of November 30.[22] The ship was scheduled to leave Libau on December 5. Unless the emigrants reached Moscow by the next morning it was impossible for them to reach their destination.

Janz, warned of the crisis by RUSCAPA, managed to reserve sufficient space for the emigrants on the last express train leaving Kharkov for Moscow on December 1. In Moscow the arrival of the train was anxiously awaited since the emigrants had to transfer from the Kursk to the Windau railway terminal approximately two miles distant. When the emigrants finally arrived, only two hours remained before the departure of the train for Sebezh. A hectic transfer of passengers and baggage ensued. No one was left behind. On December 2 a laconic dispatch from Jacob Janzen reached the *VBHH* chairman in Kharkov—"Traversed Sebezh." Another hurdle had been crossed! Or had it? A telegram from the RUSCAPA arrived the next day in Kharkov saying that the emigrants had been detained in Sebezh pending a guarantee that the increased fare for their use of the passenger train would be paid. Lest they miss their ship Janz, on his own authority, informed Owen that the Board in Rosthern would accept the responsibility.[23] The train resumed its journey to Libau. A short time later sixty thankful emigrants boarded the CPR steamer.

Revision and Reversal

For the emigration movement the year 1924 was a curious mixture of disappointment and success. After four long months of patient waiting a contract was finally signed. The movement of emigrants had scarcely begun when the Kharkov regime decreed an end to group emigration. When the groups sanctioned prior to this had been evacuated and individual emigration was about to commence in July, the Board in Canada reduced its contract. One month later it was again extended to include 1,300 credit emigrants and an unlimited number of private ones. Before long the departure deadline (October 25) threatened to jeopardize the exodus. It was then generously extended to November 14. Again a crisis developed and again a concession was granted. The ship carrying the last emigrants for the year left on December 5. Despite this sequence of crises, about 5,048 emigrants managed to leave Russia during 1924. Of these, 3,894 emigrated on credit while the remaining 1,154 were cash passengers.

From the standpoint of the time and effort needed to accomplish the emigration thus far the results were meager. Comparatively few people out of the large constituency actively concerned with the exodus were able to depart. On the other hand, the very fact that some did depart was a success, for emigration on credit was simply nonexistent elsewhere in Russia at this time. The movement was of particular ideological significance for the Mennonite refugees in both the Ukraine and the RSFSR. Not only did it provide a potential alternative to their plight but also convinced them that they were not forgotten by their American brethren. Referring to the generosity of the churches abroad Janz commented, "It has preserved the courage and hope of a better future for us and has kept us from simply disintegrating."[24]

The attitude of the Kharkov government toward the emigration underwent substantial metamorphosis during 1924. Its position degenerated from a willing endorsement of the movement in 1922-23 to a calculated opposition in 1924. In the course of 1924 the Ukrainian Central Executive Committee adopted a number of resolutions with regard to the Ukrainian Mennonites. Most of these had been recommended by a special commission appointed by the CEC to investigate conditions in the colonies and to ascertain the causes for the Mennonite migration.[25] The findings of the commission presented a surprisingly accurate picture. Three basic issues agitated the colonists: (1) Administrative confusion on the local level; (2) the uncertainty of the land question; and (3) religious interference by local authorities. Considerable tact was essential in dealing with the Mennonite settlers. The principle of class struggle could not be applied because of certain religious-ethical principles to which the

Mennonites adhered. Only well-qualified German communists could effectively handle the situation. Several recommendations of the commission were specifically accepted by the CEC.[26]

(1) The *VBHH* was permitted to continue functioning. Under no circumstances was it to concern itself with legal matters. An investigation was to be launched to determine which members of the executive had done so.

(2) No emigration lists would henceforth be ratified. Exit permits were only individually available to those who had liquidated all their property.

(3) The CEC declared itself incapable of acting on the religious question. In essence this constituted a negative answer to Mennonite appeals for religious freedom and toleration.

The government intention with regard to the *VBHH* was obvious. It must be robbed of its independence and its aggressive leadership curbed by the threat of investigation. This was no empty threat. By the fall of 1924 Janz found himself under sharpest surveillance. All letters sent by the regular mail system were censored. Some of his colleagues feared he would be imprisoned.[27] Unguarded reporting of news from Russia in such American Mennonite publications as *Der Herold, Der Christliche Bundesbote, Vorwaerts,* and *Die Mennonitische Rundschau* added to the hazard. Since some of these periodical copies reached Russia, Janz repeatedly urged their editors to exercise censorship in regard to information about the Russian Mennonites.

The Worsening Prospects

The *VBHH* found itself in a particularly crucial position during 1924. A poor harvest combined with a growing hostility on the part of the Kharkov regime crippled its operations. By reducing individual income the crop failure not only curbed individual emigration, but contributed to a general lack of economic progress that proved rather detrimental to the prestige of the *Verband*. An even more demoralizing factor, however, was the continuous government interference in the economic and political life of the Mennonite colonies. Adverse pressure existed in a number of areas. Perhaps the most depressing related to the high natural produce tax, often levied before harvest, and frequently not in accord with the actual yield, which was usually lower than anticipated. Farm income was on the decrease. During the summer and fall of 1924 prices for agricultural products dropped sharply, a peculiar situation in an economy where demand far exceeded supply.[28] Why such a decline?

The Thirteenth Party Conference, meeting in Moscow from January 16 to 18, 1924, had decreed government control of both wholesale and retail prices. By fall the implementation of this decree was evident throughout Russia and the Ukraine. Prices paid for agricultural goods were low but the cost of the means of production, government controlled, was abnormally high. In the Molotschna the price of seed grain rose from just under one ruble per pud in the fall of 1924 to two rubles per pud in December. Not unrelated to the government price control was the reevaluation of the ruble inaugurated early in the year. A high exchange rate left colonists with little actual cash.[29] Credit for farm operations was impossible to obtain from government sources. The *VBHH* treasury suffered severely, for 60-70 percent of the membership dues were unpaid. Most of its members had been robbed of their initiative by the unstable agricultural policies. The spirit of optimism engendered by a good harvest in 1923 was virtually nullified by the events of the succeeding year. Then, too, government promises of enlarged land holdings were not kept.

Added to these economic problems were administrative and social ones. District government in the Mennonite regions was in the hands of non-Mennonite party members, who repeatedly discriminated against the colonists. The Mennonites were still able to elect their own nonparty representatives to the village soviet, but even here agitators were busy organizing Committees of the Poor for the purpose of gaining control over these bodies. In addition to this curtailment of local autonomy there was also the threat of forced russification. Despite various appeals, the land taken from the Mennonites and redistributed to Russians was not restored to them. Russian villages frequently sprang up among those of the Mennonites.[30] Since most of the Mennonites did not belong to the party, local officials regarded them as second-class citizens. Illegal land grabbing at Mennonite expense was frequent. To avoid the threat of further russification the *VBHH* had prohibitied its members from selling to Russian buyers. One notable exception, that of Tiegenhagen, had been permitted. Viewing this as a precedent many of the other colonists demand similar privileges. For most there was only one purpose in selling—to obtain sufficient funds for emigration. The *VBHH* executive insisted on a long-range perspective. What would be the consequence of such integration for those who stayed behind? Unrestricted intermingling would produce only one—assimilation and russification.

By and large the emigration question and related concerns received greater toleration in the RSFSR. The February 18 decree of the CEC had granted 550 families permission to emigrate. Since the Mennonites constituted a much smaller minority in the RSFSR than in the Ukraine, authorities were not too gravely concerned about the loss of a part of this population. While some technical difficulties hindered the evacuation of the first emigrant group from the Kuban, subsequent movements were uneventful. No particular pressure was exerted upon the *AMLV*. B. Bartels, chairman of the German Section of the Commissariat of Nationalities, was rather well disposed toward the organization, conceiving of it as a cooperative organization active in the task of socialist reconstruction. A bit intolerant of the emigration, he nevertheless concurred with *AMLV* leaders in recognizing it as a strategy basic to effective reconstruction. Two trends in local agricultural policy nevertheless appeared to threaten the future well-being of the *AMLV*. The first was a swing to the left in the local economic structure. Private trading was coming to a halt and many small businesses had gone bankrupt. The term "cooperative" became more and more popular in characterizing the newly emerging economic system. The second trend was an intensified effort to achieve a Bolshevik control over the village soviets. If unchecked, such action had a direct bearing upon *AMLV* autonomy and its ability to promote the emigration movement.[31]

Near the end of November a special congress of the German Sections of the Commissariats of Nationalities in the various republics brought additional clarification as to the actual status of both the *AMLV* and the *VBHH*. *AMLV* representatives in Moscow attended the opening ceremonies. All subsequent meetings were closed to the public. From Bartels P. F. Froese learned that the Mennonite organizations had been discussed and approved for continued existence by a 66 percent majority. Significantly all the opposition had come from Ukrainian representatives. Did this mean that the *VBHH* would be liquidated? Bartels felt that direct administrative suspension was not threatening them. The *VBHH* might, however, be forced into liquidation by the creation of independent agricultural organizations within the territory. The handwriting was upon the wall. A systematic undermining of the *VBHH* was underway. Eventually the same would be true of the *AMLV*.[32]

Some preventive action had already been inaugurated. The Crimean *Verband*, aware of its precarious position, officially joined the

AMLV during the summer of 1924. Few bureaucratic difficulties were encountered since the Crimea belonged to the RSFSR. This was not true of a possible union of the *AMLV* and the *VBHH*. Such a move, though frequently discussed and most desirable, crossed republican boundaries. In their functions both unions were concerned with local economic affairs and under the jurisdiction of respective government departments in either Moscow or Kharkov. Any attempt at unification might result in confusion on the part of the supervising organizations.[33] The Ukrainian government, increasingly critical of *VBHH* autonomy, certainly opposed union, and might even use such proceedings as an excuse to terminate its existence. Moscow, though more favorably disposed toward the idea, would probably honor the position adopted by Kharkov. In view of these political problems a joint session of the *AMLV* and *VBHH* executives, meeting in Moscow on December 19, 1924, decided to maintain the status quo. No formal efforts at union were to be made.[34]

CHAPTER FOURTEEN

The Beginning of the End

The Numbers Game

On June 27, 1925, the CMBC met with Colonel Dennis in Saskatoon. To how many immigrants might the CPR grant credit? Dennis informed the Board that the CPR was willing to transport 2,500 people provided two conditions were met. First, the Board must give assurance of its continued existence, even in the event that some of its members died. Second, the Board was to pay $100,000 of its debt to the CPR very shortly. When assured that these conditions would be met, Dennis promised to recommend the commencement of the 1925 movement.[1]

Immediately after the meeting a telegram was dispatched to Kharkov advising Janz of the new developments.[2] In a covering letter the CMBC chairman stressed that only those who really needed help should be allowed to make use of the credit provisions. Such counsel was rooted in some rather unhappy cases. Several of the immigrants, professing extreme poverty, had used the credit of the Board in coming to Canada. Once safe in the new country it became evident that they possessed considerable resources. Instead of settling their debt with the Board, however, their funds were applied to the purchase of farms and machinery. A few openly refused to acknowledge their outstanding accounts. Though few in number, these people placed the entire movement in jeopardy by breeding mistrust and dislike toward the newcomers.[3]

By July 10 the terms of removal for the 2,500 were completed. If the CMBC paid $40,000 in cash and if the Board provided a written guarantee promising to pay an additional $40,000 by the end of August, the movement would begin at once. The Board's reply promised an immediate payment of $15,000, the remaining $65,000 to be paid in full by the end of August. The offer was accepted by the CPR.[4]

RUSCAPA now received orders from America to dispatch one echelon numbering 400 from the RSFSR and a second numbering 1,100 from the Ukraine. It was stipulated that the southern emigrants must be of the Gnadenfeld refugees if at all possible. The first group of 400 was to embark on August 8, the second on August 22. For the prospective emigrants the departure dates were impossibly early. Since no one knew of the availability of credit until the beginning of May, many of the Gnadenfeld refugees had not made application for exit permits. The individual processing of 1,100 people proved time-consuming. It appeared highly uncertain that the second echelon would obtain the necessary documents by August 22. A further 1,000 Gnadenfeld refugees had no prospects whatever for departure. In the north an emigrant surplus of between 500 and 1,000 urgently needed a guarantee of credit.[5]

These difficulties were conveyed to the Board in Rosthern by cablegram on August 19 and 20. Janz requested an extension of the departure date to October 15. The Board hesitated to consent to such a lengthy extension. With winter approaching, quarters for the newcomers were increasingly difficult to find. Also an undetermined number of cash emigrants was expected. The sudden arrival of these together with a credit group might create innumerable problems. The embarkation date was consequently set for September 15.[6]

In late August word reached Moscow that Colonel Dennis had ordered the credit transport to terminate on September 5. A protest from Janz reached Rosthern on August 26. At the Board's insistence the CPR relented. The new embarkation date in the colonies was set for September 19. The ship carrying the emigrants would depart from Libau on October 7 and arrive in Canada on October 16.[7]

In the Ukraine the reason for the continual postponement lay with officials responsible for the exit permits. The first 300 permits for the Gnadenfeld echelon were issued only on September 14. The others were promised within a week. It was therefore obviously impossible for the transport to leave on September 19. In response to requests from both Owen in Moscow and Gnadenfeld emigrant representative K. Peters, Janz sent a dispatch to Toews and Dennis in Canada on September 12, petitioning for an extension of the embarkation date to October 3.[8]

The constant delay in facilitating the departure of the Gnadenfeld echelon was not only a matter of bureaucratic inefficiency. Government unfriendliness, which originally manifested itself in the suspension of group emigration, was now directed against the *VBHH* itself.

Throughout 1925, the Kharkov regime had entertained serious reservations with regard to the *VBHH*. There were those who advocated its outright liquidation. The entire position of the Ukrainian Mennonites with regard to the land question, emigration, religious freedom, and the *VBHH* received the attention of the Central Executive Committee. Fortunately for the Mennonites, the drastic measures suggested by the investigation commission were unacceptable to some of the CEC members. The issue was therefore tabled until the party congress in November. In all probability this active government concern with the Mennonites was responsible for the delay in the granting of exit permits.[9] By 1925 the communist press gave *VBHH* leaders increased cause for worry.

A highly critical article entitled "Hollanders" appeared in the official Kharkov party newspaper *Visti* on August 12, 1925. It accused the *VBHH* of not only working outside the economic structure of the state, but also continuously petitioning for privileges not available to the average Soviet citizen. This union of Dutchmen, the article argued, was destroying the Soviet Ukraine.[10] In previous years articles critical of the Mennonite exodus itself had appeared in the popular party newspaper *Communist*, as well as the special publication of the German Section of the Commissariat of the Interior, *Die Arbeit*.[11] All this contributed to a mounting apprehension about the future of the emigration movement.

To the relief of Janz and the other emigration officials in the Ukraine the Gnadenfeld embarkation progressed uneventfully. On September 19 the first half of the southern echelon, 635 persons, departed from Stulynevo near Waldheim under the leadership of K. Peters. The second half of the group, about 540 persons, left a few days later, led by W. Wiens.[12] One of the most frustrating problems facing the emigration movement was finally being solved. The extension of the departure date to October 3 enabled a number of small emigrant groups scattered throughout the Ukraine to leave. Approximately one hundred persons were able to leave Chortitza, one-third that number from both Olgafeld and Zagradovka. Many single families from various villages likewise managed to embark. There were still a few for whom October 3 came before their passes were available. By late November an additional one hundred passes had been approved. None of these people had any prospects of an existence in Russia. Their permits were valid for only three months. What was to be done? Once more Janz relied on the benevolence of his North American friends[13] to accept these people in mid-winter. "Do this once more," Janz pleaded. "Give these destitute people the beginning of a new life. The days will come when the consequences of your action will appear much more important than now."[14] Once again the Board saw fit to honor the request.

As 1925 drew to a close, the prospects for further emigration seemed extremely remote. No one in the *VBHH* knew precisely the extent of the anti-Mennonite feeling within the Ukrainian government. A number of threatening articles in the German newspapers of the Soviet press convinced Mennonite leaders that the liquidation of the *VBHH* was imminent. The situation was particularly worrisome for Janz. As the organization's leader he was somewhat protected from arrest or direct attack in the press by the public sentiment favorable to the existence of his organization. But by 1926 the *VBHH* had been systematically stripped of its power in both legal and emigration matters. Now it was about to be replaced in the agricultural field by locally organized and party-sponsored cooperatives. Janz observed, "Whatever may happen, it is certain that I will no longer remain at my post and that I personally will stand at the coffin of the precious union of all Mennonites at whose cradle I stood in 1921."[15] An episode in March 1926 seemed to confirm this conclusion.

A GPU *Hearing*

For B. B. Janz, March 5, 1926, was reminiscent of a day in December 1923. A young man in a leather jacket appeared at the door of his residence at Butovsky 4 in Kharkov. As in 1923 he had to acknowledge the receipt of a summons from the Kharkov *GPU*. It originated with Tolstov, head of the *GPU* department for Mennonite affairs. Janz was cordially received in Tolstov's office on March 6. Tolstov observed that he had wished to speak with Janz for some time. Janz suggested that the method chosen could have been less drastic. Tolstov's answer implied that the *GPU* had chosen the mildest procedure.

The examination began.[16] Why were the Mennonites still emigrating? Local conditions had improved immeasurably but the desire to emigrate remained as strong as ever. Most alarming was the fact that settlements which had never been interested in leaving Russia were now clamoring for exit permits. The Mennonites were a progressive agricultural element of great importance to Russia. Why did they want to leave?

"This is also surprising to me," Janz replied, "New York

[Russia], for example, is a very stable settlement. In view of a wide-spread wish to emigrate I asked its representatives what was going on. They replied that the compulsory resettlement of five former land-owners of the area had shattered the confidence of the colonists. If these must leave, when would it be their turn?"

"But they have a great deal of land." Tolstov retorted, "What are their other reasons?"

"There are the new school texts which contain anti-religious material. Then, too, a school commission has traveled through the villages and exerted excessive pressure on teachers and students. The thirteen-year-old head of the student collective was publicly scolded because he has as yet recruited no Young Pioneers."

"And further?"

"The land question, which needs no additional explanation."

Tolstov mentioned that the Fürstenland settlement as well as the Nepluyev villages near Nikopol had been hard hit during the imperi-alist war. "Now the situation has improved and now they want to emigrate. There is here some interested party, some guiding hand. According to the plan everything is organized."

"But we set up lists in 1922 which you ratified."

"How is the situation in Canada?"

"I do not know."

"We will not play hide-and-seek. I know everything. I have exact reports from America."

"I know nothing."

"How so?"

"Some time ago I informed the Board that the *VBHH* was no longer involved with the emigration. Now I am no longer fully informed."

Tolstov was unconvinced. "You certainly must be informed about the critical situation of the Board with regard to the payments. Then also I am interested how you personally view the movement. Should emigration take place or not?"

"That is a question that cannot easily be answered. If someone wishes to leave or stay, it is his personal decision. I accept no responsibility."

"Those are technical considerations which I understand. But what is your personal attitude to the matter?"

"My attitude is manifest in the Grigoryevka Congress resolution. The position of the *VBHH* is my position."

Tolstov again returned to the "interested parties" fostering the emigration. Various events were cited as evidence. Even Mennonite history entered the discussion. What of Janz's participation in the emigration movement? What of the certificates issued by the *VBHH?*

Janz replied, "I have informed the Mennonites that they will not be issued in the future. In the past they simply certified that the person in question was a Mennonite."

"I suspect they were more than that. I heard they were declarations of a political character. Such a document must have some importance!"

"The matter is very simple. I had to certify that the people involved were Mennonites. After all, RUSCAPA had received entry permits (Canadian) for Mennonites."

"Who will issue the permits in the future?"

"I do not know."

At that moment S. Karlson, head of the Kharkov *GPU,* entered the room. Two questions were put to Janz. What impression did the reorganization of the *VBHH* make upon the colonists? What would he, Janz, do in the future?

"I will not work any longer," Janz replied.

"What? No, you will work!" Thereupon Karlson left the room.

Tolstov had one more question with regard to a *VBHH* loan from abroad. What was the status of this matter?

Janz explained the issue as best he could and promised to provide the *GPU* with a written explanation of the affair. Tolstov finally closed the interview with the remark that Janz seemed to have considerable capacity for work.

A second hearing was held on March 10. Janz pointed to another reason for the emigration, namely, the question of military service. If this was not regulated, many more would leave. Tolstov insisted that the Soviet Union had a law capable of accommodating conscientious objectors.

"The law is adequate if all Soviet agencies operated with the respectability of the military and *GPU,*" explained Janz. "The People's Courts, however, are a great obstacle for the Mennonites."

"But it would be very hard to create a new law for the Mennonites."

"It might be well if a *GPU* circular, insisting the law be carefully observed, were sent to the People's Courts," Janz urged.

Tolstov abruptly changed the subject. Janz sensed that Tolstov had intended to ask the question for some time. "What connections do you have with the German consulate? We know that you had much to do with von Hey. What was your business?"

"During the time of the famine we sought help from the German Red Cross. Then too we sought to import German tractors and other machinery."

"Was the German Red Cross in the colonies to any great extent?"

"No, only in Zagradovka."

"Have delegates from the German Red Cross visited you? Has an American Relief Administration man been to see you?"

Was Tolstov seriously seeking to uncover counterrevolutionary activity? Or was he simply intimidating the *VBHH*? Janz explained that only the staff of the American Mennonite Relief had visited the colonies.

"Why does the German consulate and Germany have such a great interest in the German colonies?"

"We (the Mennonites) are Soviet citizens. Germany is probably interested in the colonies as centers of German culture."

"What nationality are the Mennonites?"

"Here you are touching upon a difficult question. If one asserts we Mennonites are Germans, it is probably a historical inaccuracy. At the same time you cannot call them Dutch." Janz related the beginnings of the *VBHH*, particularly stressing Manzev's role in the naming of the organization. At that time the nationality question was settled in favor of the Dutch.

With this the hearing was ended. Janz had learned two reasons for the government's great interest in the emigration: it was probably interested in keeping its most progressive farmers in Russia. Then too, the Mennonite press in America had attracted the attention of the Kharkov regime by its uncomplimentary articles about conditions in Russia.

Dr. Drury and the 1926 Emigration

Despite the *GPU's* interest in the emigration, the preparations for the 1926 movement continued. On April 19, 1926, the chief CPR medical inspector, Dr. Drury, arrived in Moscow. The processing of the emigrants was about to begin. The Board had extended credit to 1,800 persons thus far in the new year. The RSFSR was allowed 800 of these, even though it was not quite in accord with the four to six ratio agreed upon earlier. Unfortunately Drury's arrival had been delayed for well over a month. A sense of urgency was consequently discernible in both the north and the south. Each area was anxious to have its candidates for emigration examined as rapidly as possible.

A special meeting designed to outline Drury's itinerary was held on April 20, barely two hours after Janz had arrived from the Ukraine. The atmosphere was somewhat tense. The *AMLV* had already selected two representatives from Siberia to accompany Drury on his northern itinerary. The first stop was Slavgorod. One and a half months were required to complete the circuit. The *AMLV* based its priority claim on the fact that the 400 Slavgorod as well as the 300 Orenburg emigrants had not yet begun spring planting. If medically fit for travel, they would be spared this expense. It was also pointed out that most of the trachoma cases in these two centers had been under medical treatment throughout the winter. Legally, all the necessary steps for emigration had been completed.[17]

For his part Janz insisted that the south could not wait for six weeks. Many settlers had taken no initiative in farming operations simply because they expected to leave very shortly. Particularly critical was the situation of four villages in the Fürstenland district where the colonists had sold their farms in February and March 1926. They had been granted them a high priority, but technical difficulties had prevented their departure. Their passes were now readily obtainable. By June 1 they must leave their farms. Moreover, they were scheduled to embark for Canada by August 8, 1926. For these reasons a northern monopoly on the services of Dr. Drury was simply unthinkable.[18]

The deliberations continued on the afternoon of April 20. Though most of the RUSCAPA members were inclined toward the southern viewpoint, the issue of priority was not resolved. At an evening session both sides reiterated their positions. Neither was willing to compromise. Negotiations were resumed the next day under the chairmanship of A. R. Owen, who finally outlined an acceptable compromise. Drury would make a partial medical examination in both the north and the south in the next two weeks. His itinerary included Slavgorod, Omsk, a part of the Ukraine, and Orenburg. In this way a representative echelon might be readied for departure.

The internal problems related to the emigration had hardly been resolved when external ones arose. District authorities in Slavgorod refused to honor Drury's diplomatic visa. There was no alternative but to move on to Omsk. Here too authorities raised objections, but Drury was nevertheless able to proceed with his work. A surprisingly large number of people announced their intention to emigrate, despite the fact that the Omsk district was one of the most promising for Mennonite agriculture. By mid-May Drury left for the south. In the Halbstadt district examinations were carried on in Orloff and Petershagen while in the Gnadenfeld area the villages of Alexandertal and Landskrone served as centers. In general the eligibility rate as concerned the medical examination was much higher than in previous years. Trachoma was on the decline. Drury spent three weeks in the Ukraine and then returned to Siberia.[19]

Leave-taking

The Kharkov Congress (February 17-19, 1926) of the *VBHH* symbolized a final milestone in the Mennonite emigration from Russia. Its proceedings witnessed several significant developments. One of these resulted from the very fact that it was held in Kharkov. Pressure from government authorities had forced the *VBHH* to transfer its central administration from Orloff to Kharkov, and at the same time to make a fundamental revision in the structure and purpose of the *VBHH*. Earlier government action had forbidden it to act in legal and emigration matters and limited its activities solely to agriculture. The reorganization was officially launched by the Ukrainian Central Executive Committee on September 8, 1925.[20] The revision was essentially intended to destroy the autonomy of the *VBHH* and to make the agency directly dependent on the state and the party. In essence it became one of many government-sponsored cooperatives. Nonparticipation meant the loss of official credit and support. Referring to possible noncompliance on the part of the *VBHH*, a representative of the German section of the Ukrainian Communist Party declared: "If the Congress adopts a resolution in this sense, the German Section will make direct contact with the farmers regardless of the *VBHH* administration or the Congress." Though the Kharkov Congress censured the German Section for its arrogance and intimidation, it complied with its demand.[21]

One other event at the Congress substantiated the view that it was indeed the end of an era, namely, the resignation of B. B. Janz as the *VBHH* chairman. While his administration had seen an active pursuit of agricultural interests, his name was invariably linked to two words—relief and emigration. Janz had been the great proponent of *VBHH* autonomy in every possible field, and had continually fought for the preservation of the Mennonites as a distinctive national minority. Willing to cooperate with government officials in economic matters, he nevertheless staunchly opposed any attempt to rob the

The last congress of the VBHH in Kharkov, February 17-20, 1926. Among the delegates seen are the following in the second row from the front: J. I. Defager, chairman of the Zagradovka district; Gerhard Funk, chairman of the Chortitza district; Peter F. Froese, chairman of "Allrussischer Mennonitischer Landwirtschaftlicher Verein," Moscow; Philip D. Cornies, vice-chairman of VBHH; Peter I. Dyck, chairman of Ekaterinoslav district; B. B. Janz, chairman of VBHH; Comrade Lobanov, chairman of the Ukrainian Commissariat for National Minorities; J. J. Thiessen, chairman of the February congress; Comrade Buzenko, secretary of the Ukrainian Central Executive Committee; Hermann F. Dyck, second chairman of the congress; H. Sawatzky, third chairman of the congress; Comrade Zelarius; Comrade Gebhard, representative of the German Section of the Commissariat of Nationalities; Comrade Drobot; Hans Thielman.

Mennonites of their cultural and religious heritage. At the same time he was keenly aware that he was fighting a losing battle. Thus privately and unofficially he had always been the great advocate of emigration from Russia. Deeply convinced that the Mennonites had no future in the land of their birth, he had tirelessly explored even the remotest possibilitiy in the hope of leading his people from the land which he frequently compared with Egypt of old. Janz's resignation signified the beginning of the end of the Mennonite emigration from Soviet Russia.

Janz officially laid down his duties as chairman of the *VBHH* on March 11, 1926.[22] He was succeeded by H. F. Dyck, a teacher at the Halbstadt School of Agriculture. Before resigning Janz was careful to ensure the continuation of the emigration movement by carefully informing interested people that the *VBHH* would no longer issue its certificates. All old certificates issued before March 11 remained valid, however. Special arrangements were made with the RUSCAPA whereby Owen and Drury issued similar certificates valid after that date. Janz also made preparations of a more personal nature. Well aware that he had no future in Russia as the retired leader of the *VBHH* he had made application for an exit permit on March 9, 1926. By mid-April Kharkov authorities assured him it would be granted. The promise was kept on April 29.[23] His family was promised a permit toward the end of May or the beginning of June in Melitopol.

On May 14 Janz took his leave at the *Kommission für Kirchenangelegenheiten* (Commission for Church Affairs) meeting in Margenau. Ten days later he made his farewell address in the Mennonite Brethren Church in Tiege, Molotschna. On May 24, 1926, Janz delivered his last public address in Russia.[24] In his opening remarks he observed that as a group the Mennonites had during the last years proceeded openly and legally. The emigration was a deliberate government-sanctioned movement, not a mass flight. He soon changed the subject. Most of the people listening to Janz were staying in Russia. Did he have something to say to them? For Janz there was only one thing which could sustain the Mennonites through any adversity—an inner spiritual vitality. The economic decline of the colonies was not the greatest loss. It had in fact restored the much greater treasure of personal religion.

> In 1914 a new period began in the history of our people. Mothers, fathers, and teachers—all have acknowledged one thing. All of us were struck down; some were led into prison. But

B. B. Janz in 1963.

thanks to God the Mennonite can pray in the last great crisis. Where others curse and rant and damn their fate, the Mennonite prays. The past years have shown this.

Janz pointed to the material abundance that had characterized the pre-1914 era. There had been large wheat reserves.

But this is no longer true. Previously barns were torn down and larger ones built; today they are torn down and smaller ones built. But this is not the greatest misfortune. A question: Have we not been happier and more blessed with the small barns and the small wheat piles? Be content with what there is. . . . God was able to use a wealthy Mennonite society less effectively than a poor one. A certain deportment is essential. It is not serious that we are all poor. The results will be beneficial. The greatest misfortune is to lose your hold on God. Our churches have cooperated as best they could. Prior to 1914 a difference existed between them. During the time of troubles we were all unified—one calamity, one God; despite various teachings— unified! Between 1914 and 1922 a decline; from 1922 till now a rise. And during the most difficult time, down in the valley, individually—how they folded their hands—they were unified. A common searching after the Way of Life. That was lovely.

He had taken his leave. There was one last visit to familiar Kharkov. How frequently this locale had meant disappointment, anxiety, and fear. There was still fear. Did the *GPU* know of his intent to leave Russia? Would he be allowed to leave Kharkov? Arrangements for the departure were carefully made. Special agents purchased the railway tickets for Janz, carried his baggage into a train compartment, and aided him in boarding the train without being recognized. The train carrying Janz left Kharkov on May 3. Only a few hours after his departure the Kharkov *GPU* began an unsuccessful search for Janz. His journey, though filled with anxiety, was unhindered. On June 4 the emigration leader crossed into Latvia at Sebezh, and he himself also attained the freedom he had won for so many. Officially the emigration movement was now at an end. In actual fact, however, it did not terminate in 1926. A number of emigrants still managed to leave Russia during 1927 and 1928. These, however, came only on the strength of the organizational structure which successfully secured the exodus of thousands between 1923 and 1926. The emigration after 1926 experienced the calculated termination of the movement by government authorities.

These years marked the beginning of the end for the group as a separate cultural and religious body in the Soviet Union. Discerning leaders already sensed this trend in 1925 and 1926. The lack of religious toleration was increasingly evident. The last General Mennonite Conference *(Allgemeine Mennonitische Bundeskonferenz)* met in Moscow during January 1925. A petition for greater religious freedom directed to the Central Executive Committee was rejected by that powerful government organ. The Conference periodical, *Unser Blatt,* only begun in October 1925, ceased publication as early as 1928. By 1927 the treatment of religious leaders was consistently severe. Arrest and exile became alarmingly common. Exemption from military service was largely nonexistent after 1926. Economic and political pressures were also intensified. The government-sponsored reorganization of the *VBHH* virtually destroyed its effectiveness by the late fall of 1925. In the RSFSR the *AMLV* was suspended in 1928. Parallel to these developments was the systematic restriction of emigration. Complex bureaucratic processes or outright refusal awaited most Mennonite applications for exodus after 1926. Only 511 Mennonite immigrants entered Canada in 1928.

The curtailment of religious, political, and economic activity went hand in hand with the termination of the New Economic Policy and the inauguration of the First Five Year Plan in 1928. Preparatory work for the introduction of this ambitious scheme to industrialize and collectivize Russia all but destroyed economic initiative and independence by the end of 1927. The unreasonable objectives of the Plan as well as its exploitation of human resources drove some of the despairing colonists to radical action. In the fall of 1929 some of the Mennonite colonists, together with a number of their Lutheran and Catholic counterparts, responded to conditions by an attempt at flight.

The trek was initiated when it was learned that some of the settlers had obtained exit permits by a direct and personal appeal to Moscow officials. Colonists soon poured into Moscow's suburbs by the thousands in a desperate effort to obtain permission to emigrate. Before long the episode made international headlines. Living under the worst possible conditions for months, these refugees persisted in their efforts to leave Russia. Since worldwide attention was focused upon these unfortunate people the Soviet government tried to remove this source of embarrassment as quickly as possible. As a result the episode ended in tragedy for many of the colonists. Forceful deportation not only separated many families, but resulted also in the death of a large number of children from exposure, disease, and mistreatment. Others, aided by both the diplomatic action of the German government and the determined efforts of the CMBC, succeeded in

The delegates attending the last General Mennonite Conference held in Moscow, January 13-18, 1925.

The Canadian Pacific **S.S. Melita** and **Minnedosa** used by some of the emigrants.

Atlantic Park Hostel.

escaping. The Moscow flight was not emigration in the earlier sense of the term. Though motivated by many of the same factors, the flight was much more a gamble based on the assumption that prevailing conditions justified the risks involved. It lacked the legally sanctioned organizational structure responsible for the earlier migration, even though theoretically individual emigration was still possible. In actual fact such an application for exodus might well invite dire personal consequences, and in many cases it did just that.[25]

Unknown to the Moscow refugees an escape of smaller proportions was going on in the Far East. Here individuals and small groups crossed over into the countries bordering Russia. Already in the fall of 1928 Mennonites began crossing into China, Afghanistan, Persia, and Turkey. Harbin in Manchuria soon became the most important refugee center in the Far East. One of the most dramatic group escapes took place in December 1930, when 217 Mennonites crossed the Amur into China despite the sub-zero temperatures and deep snow. By 1933 well over a thousand refugees from Russia were living in Harbin, and more than half of these were Mennonites.[26] The rescue and resettlement of these displaced people was a gradual process. While there were exceptions, the refugees were generally barred from entering Canada and the United States and eventually settled in Paraguay and Brazil.

There were other tragic aspects of the emigration drama whose final acts unfolded only after 1926. These were usually associated with two names, Lechfeld and Atlantic Park. Normally the emigrants who were cleared at Lechfeld were sent to Atlantic Park near Southampton for final processing. The Park, a former United States Air Force base, had been purchased by the Canadian Pacific Railway, and the Cunard and White Star lines, for use as an emigrant detention center. Here further disappointment often awaited the already disappointed. Emigrants in transit often were the victims of unfair medical inspections, bureaucratic caprice, and outright discrimination. Families were frequently separated for months and even for years if one member was medically unfit. In some individual cases long-cherished hopes of a better future were forever shattered.[27] Eventually even this chapter of the emigration story came to an end. Almost unobtrusively the lengthy drama which saw the Mennonite brotherhood in one of its most critical yet finest hours faded into history.

Epilogue

The emigration from Russia during the 1920's represents the largest organized movement undertaken by Mennonites during the first half of the twentieth century. For most of the settlers the desire to leave Russia was rooted in the prevailing social, economic, and religious conditions. From this standpoint the exodus symbolized massive protest against Soviet economic and social practices. This sentiment was based upon two controversial issues. The first rested upon the assumption that economic reconstruction was impossible in the immediate future. The Mennonite colonist witnessed the destruction of the old agricultural pattern and felt that he was not offered a reasonably stable alternative solution which satisfied his traditional interest in the land. Eventually the Mennonites would have been willing to modify their method of land tenure had not a second major issue, freedom of conscience, confronted them. In the end such questions as freedom of worship, the religious instruction of children, and freedom of conscience with regard to bearing arms, were not affirmatively answered by the Soviet government.

The lack of a positive government response in these two areas led many of the Mennonites to believe that its policies in relation to minorities were as discriminatory as those of prerevolutionary Russia. In actuality most of the better-informed members of the Kharkov and Moscow governments were rather well disposed toward the Mennonites, and looked upon the settlements as vital links in the reconstruction of Soviet agriculture. This viewpoint made the Kharkov regime extremely reluctant to sanction a wide-scale emigration. The government consistently viewed the movement as an emergency measure calculated to aid in alleviating the catastrophes which had befallen the Ukraine. It was simply a means of removing the refugees and the landless who were of no value to agricultural reconstruction. Both Mennonite emigration agencies, the *VBHH* in the

Ukraine and the *AMLV* in the RSFSR, followed this pattern of reasoning in their dealings with central authorities. Consequently, with overall economic improvement the government became more and more reluctant to allow this drain of manpower. Nevertheless the authorities did little to assure the colonists of a stable future in Russia. It was simply expected that the removal of surplus population would terminate the general restlessness in the Mennonite colonies. The reverse was true. The desire to emigrate intensified as the prospects for actual exodus narrowed. Officials responded to the continuing interest in emigration by restricting the activities of the agencies in charge of it, by closer surveillance of its leaders, and by outright press attacks.

As seen by the Mennonite constituency itself the emigration movement ran an often confusing course. While most of the colonists took a very active interest in the evacuation as such, their commitment to the movement was based on blind faith rather than on factual information. In the early stages of the movement a precise knowledge of future prospects was simply out of the question, for the colonists generally and for the *VBHH* in particular. The years 1921 and 1922 had no practicable alternatives. Emigration leaders had great difficulty in planning. Many of their plans were made without any concrete communications from abroad. In its early operational philosophy the *VBHH* lacking adequate information, revealed a feverish sense of daring that often bordered on frustration and despair. The constituency, even less informed, was correspondingly more restless, particularly when concrete results were not in sight.

The responsibility for establishing a basic ideological and operational basis for the Mennonite exodus ultimately rested upon the *VBHH* leadership. This organization had to convince the government that emigration was in the interest of a more productive Ukraine. Furthermore, it had to prepare the technical base for such a movement in Russia and establish extensive contacts abroad to convince the American constituency of its necessity. This demanded men unfalteringly committed to emigration as the only possible solution to the problems facing Russian Mennonitism. In this respect *VBHH* chairman, B. B. Janz, more than any other one individual became the sustaining force behind the emigration. Janz was uncompromisingly dedicated to exodus from Russia, regardless of any political, religious, or economic changes which might be initiated. This conviction grew as his interaction with the Bolshevik regime in Kharkov and Moscow became more involved. His letters abroad continuously asserted that the

Mennonites had no future in Russia. To the fulfillment of this aim he devoted long hours of clerical labor, bore the often uncharitable criticism of the constituency, and exposed himself to official interviews which at times threatened his personal safety. Particularly significant were his written appeals to the American Mennonites in which he pleaded first for bread, then for deliverance. Persistently he demanded action, either by describing the material catastrophe which had devastated the colonies or by appealing to a humanitarian and Christian conscience. Always sensitive to the sufferings of his people he did not even stop in the face of intimidation. In some letters he held the Americans collectively responsible for what might happen to the Mennonites in Russia if they did not act. Occasionally he crossed swords with his own colleagues in both the *VBHH* and the Study Commission, particularly when some of them overstressed reconstruction. For him reconstruction was only a possible survival tactic for those who had to stay. Between 1921 and 1923 some contemporaries viewed his inflexible dedication to emigration as an unnecessary gamble. Subsequent history proved that his foreboding premonitions were correct. By 1926 many who had chided him earlier now shared his point of view, for by that time the entire constituency was making a desperate bid for survival.

From the standpoint of the Russian Mennonites the emigration was both a success and a failure. The two concepts were often diffused. The successful legal departure of well over 20,000 people from Russia was naturally a diplomatic triumph. This was especially true of the group emigration in 1923, which constituted one of the few mass movements of its kind ever sanctioned by the Soviet government. The initial scope of the group emigration was equally amazing. During 1922 political and legal obstacles for the group evacuation of perhaps 20,000 people were cleared away. This astounding success was hampered by the inability of the American constituency to initiate a rapid removal operation. As a result of this procrastination, unavoidable though it may have been, thousands lost the opportunity to leave Russia in 1922 and early 1923. By the fall of 1923, government disapproval of the emigration was making itself increasingly felt. The reversion to individual emigration enabled authorities to control it, both as to the number and the kind of people leaving Russia. In a sense 1922 was the crucial year for the entire movement. The flexibility and freedom of movement granted the Ukrainian Mennonites during this period through the *VBHH* was unprecedented. Selection and processing for group emigration was almost entirely controlled by the *Verband*. Whether this generosity would have continued in the event of a mass exodus during 1922 cannot be determined. When such a possibility did emerge in 1923, the Kharkov regime decisively counteracted it.

During the period of active emigration, success was constantly overshadowed by the threat of failure. There was no possibility for implementing the organizational emigration structure so painfully constructed in 1922. The next year, when the actual evacuation was finally initiated, bureaucratic opposition soon terminated the proceedings. The renewal of the operation in 1924 came only after problems in Canada, Germany, the RSFSR, and the Ukraine had been solved. By the end of the year a systematic restriction of the freedoms granted the *VBHH* was discernible. Within a relatively short time this pressure was also felt by the *AMLV*. Problems accumulated so rapidly that one was hardly solved when it was replaced by another, even more complex. Inadequate credit from abroad, inflation in Russia, the genius of Soviet bureaucracy, the Latvian medical examination, Lechfeld—the total investment of time and effort appeared to bring very meager returns. Somehow the movement of over 4,000 persons in 1924 appeared small in relation to the intense efforts needed to expedite the emigration. The 1925 exodus began in late summer. Only the first echelon managed to leave on schedule. Departure dates for subsequent groups were continuously postponed, either for lack of necessary documentation, foreign credit, or government cooperation. Most of the problems encountered during 1926 were of a similar nature. The character of the movement remained unchanged until the very end. Legally and administratively the emigration was only sustained by the persistent efforts of its leaders. These faced the unending task of inventing supportive designs for a structure that was constantly threatened with collapse.

Symbolically the emigration represented but one aspect of the social and economic breakdown of Russian Mennonitism. Most of the emigrants were fleeing from a land they felt had no future for them. The farms which had sustained them as a distinct minority for over a century were gone. For many this appeared to be the death knell of their way of life. No satisfactory alternatives existed. In the final analysis, however, the majority of the Mennonites were willing to sacrifice their old economic and social structure in response to the demands of the new order. This flexibility was proved by the conditions under which many of them entered Canada. The progressive loss of religious freedom, however, was regarded as an evil omen which eventually meant the destruction of faith. Though emigration symbolized the loss of time-hallowed ethnic-cultural patterns, it simultaneously revealed the essence of Russian Mennonitism. In its basic dimension it .did not consist of a historic faith hopelessly interwoven in an economic-cultural web. Instead, faith emerged as the highest personal good, worthy of all sacrifice. For those who remained in Russia this insight was implanted by force and violence. The breakup of past patterns left no alternative but a personal faith, unsupported by community and historic ties. A religious purging of a similar nature faced those who came to Canada. The process was not a direct or violent one but eventually just as effective. Here the more peaceable, subtle, and protracted forces of assimilation, by their very persistence, eventually ensured a severe struggle for a faith unrelated to ethnic tradition. For the Mennonites who stayed in Russia, and for those who left to find a new life in another country, a common problem remained. Religious faith had to be adapted to new forms.

Footnotes

CHAPTER ONE

1. The word "province" is used instead of the Russian term *Gubernia* which has essentially the same meaning. In addition to this major administrative division there was also the *uezd* or district. This in turn was subdivided into the *volost*, which might be comparable to a township in the North American sense. It usually comprised a number of villages. The Halbstadt and Gnadenfeld volosts, for example, each contained 30 villages.

2. H. Goerz, *Die Molotschnaer Ansiedlung* (Steinbach, Man., 1950). On the alternative service see also D. P. Heidebrecht and G. J. Peters, *"Onsi Tjedils' Ersatzdienst der Mennoniten in Russland unter den Romanows* (Yarrow, B.C., 1966).

3. J. W. Ewert, "Aus dem Leben der Chortitzer Mennoniten-Gemeinden während der Kriegs- und Revolutionszeit," *Die Mennonitische Rundschau*, Vol. 43, No. 20 (May 19, 1920), p. 13.

4. *Ibid.*, No. 21 (May 26, 1920), pp. 10, 11.

5. See *Die Mennoniten-Gemeinden in Russland während der Kriegs-und Revolutionsjahre 1914 bis 1920* (Heilbronn a. Neckar, 1921).

6. JA (I,d), J. G. Dyck to B. B. Janz. Leamington, Ont., Sept. 15, 1956.

7. JA(I,d), A. A. Wiens, "Anfang des mennonitischen Selbstschutzes."

8. JA(I,d), H. Goossen, "Unsere grosse Vaterlandsliebe und Treue zum Kaisertrone ershält einen Schlag und wird schwer geprüft," p. 3.

9. JA(I,c), Protokoll der Allgemeinen Mennonitischen Bundeskonferenz im Bethause zu Lichtenau am 30. Juni 1. und 2. Juli 1918, pp. 3-11.

10. *Ibid.*, pp. 12-18.

11. For further details see P. Arshinov, *Geschichte der machnowschen Bewegung, 1918-22* (Berlin, n.d.).

12. T. Block, "Der Selbstschutz der Kolonisten Tauriens (1919 und 1920)," *Die Mennonitische Rundschau*, Vol. 44, No. 39 (Sept. 28, 1921), p. 13.

13. JA(I,d), J. P. Epp, "Die Entstehung des Selbstschutzes," pp. 6-9.

14. *Ibid.*, p. 4; see also JA(I,d), "Beifügung zur Frage Selbstutchutz."

15. JA(I,d), J. P. Epp, *op. cit.*, pp. 12-15.

16. J. H. Willms, "Politisches Geschehen an der Molotschna von Februar 1917 an" (ms. in the possession of the author), pp. 4, 5; G. Lohrenz, "Nonresistance Tested," *Mennonite Life*, XVII (April 1962), pp. 66-68.

17. "Wie die Kolonisten aus der Molotschna nach der Krim flüchteten," *Die Mennonitische Rundschau*, Vol. 43, No. 29 (July 21, 1920), pp. 7, 10.

18. JA(I,d), H. Goossen, *op. cit.*, pp. 6, 7.

19. Mennoniten Gemeinden, *op. cit.*, pp. 75-79.

20. JA(I,d), J. P. Epp, *op. cit.*, pp. 14, 15.

CHAPTER TWO

1. Heinrich Warkentin, "Zur Zeit des Bürgerkrieges in der Altkolonie," *Die Mennonitische Rundschau*, Vol. 44, No. 31 (Aug. 3, 1921), pp. 13, 14; No. 32 (Aug. 10, 1921), pp. 7, 10.

2. JA(I,d), B. B. Janz to "Mein lieber Freund." Abbotsford, B.C., June 20, 1963; JA(I,d), B. B. Janz to Bergmann. Coaldale, Alta., Sept. 25, 1960.

3. JA(I,d), B. B. Janz, "Wir haben gesündigt," pp. 1, 2; G. G. Hiebert, "Die südrussischen Mennoniten in der Kriegs- und Revolutionszeit," *Die Mennonitische Rundschau*, Vol. 43, No. 29 (July 21, 1920), pp. 6, 7.

4. JA(I,d), "Etliche Hauptmomente von dem Mordtag in Altonau im Oktober 1919."

5. JA(I,d), B. B. Janz, *op. cit.*, pp. 3, 4.

6. See A. Kroeker, *Bilder aus Sowjet-Russland* (Striegau in Schlesien, 1930), pp. 43-

49. Toward the end of October the Makhno forces had overrun and devastated the village of Eichenfeld-Dubovka. Over 80 persons were murdered. See Heinrich Toews, *Eichenfeld-Dubowka. Ein Tatsachenbericht aus der Tragödie des Deutschtums in der Ukraine* (Karlsruhe i. B., n.d.), pp. 24-41. For an eyewitness account of the character and nature of the Makhnovzi depredations, see D. A. Quiring, "Die Schreckenszeit in dem Dorfe Eichenfeld, Süd-Russland im Oktober 1919," *Die Mennonitische Rundschau*, Vol. 49, Nos. 34-42 (Aug. 25 to Oct. 20).

7. Gerhard Lohrenz, *Sagradowka, Die Geschichte einer mennonitischen Ansiedlung im Süden Russlands* (Winnipeg, Man., 1946), pp. 94-98. See also D. Neufeld, *Mennonitentum in der Ukraine. Schicksalsgeschichte Sagradowkas* (Emden, 1922), pp. 27-39.

8. H. Warkentin, *op. cit.*, No. 33 (Aug. 17, 1921), pp. 11, 12.

9. A. Lepp, "Das schreckliche Elend in der Alten Kolonie," *Die Mennonitische Rundschau*, Vol. 43, No. 45 (Nov. 10, 1920), pp. 5-7. In the village of Rosenthal typhus struck 1,183 out of the 1,346 inhabitants; in Chortitza 662 out of a total population of 676. T. O. Hylkema, *Die Mennoniten-Gemeinden in Russland während der Kriegs- und Revolutionsjahre 1914 bis 1920* (Heilbronn a. Neckar, 1921), p. 92.

10. FA, "Schematischer Ueberblick über den wirtschaftlichen Niedergang der mennonitischen Kolonien des Chortitzer Gebiets," p. 1.

11. *Ibid.*, p. 2.

12. Peter Wall and Peter J. Braun, "Die Mennoniten in Russland während des Bürgerkrieges (1917-1920)," *Die Mennonitische Rundschau*, Vol. 43, No. 46 (Nov. 17, 1920), p. 7.

13. For a description of the situation in Chortitza see "Die Hungersnot in der alten Chortitzer Kolonie nach der Missernte im Jahre 1921," *Die Mennonitische Rundschau*, Vol. 49, No. 39 (Sept. 29, 1926), p. 7.

14. "Kurze Leidensgeschichte der Ljwowschen Tereker Ansiedlung," *Die Mennonitische Rundschau*, Vol. 43, No. 39 (Sept. 29, 1920), pp. 12, 13.

15. *Ibid.*, Nos. 40-43 (Oct. 6, 1920, to Oct. 27, 1920).

16. For further details see J. H. Brucks and H. Hooge, *Neu-Samara am Tock* (Clearbrook, B.C., 1964), pp. 102-13; Peter P. Dyck, *Orenburg am Ural. Die Geschichte einer mennonitischen Ansiedlung in Russland* (Yarrow, B.C., 1951).

17. C. F. Klassen to Alvin J. Miller. Orenburg, Dec. 16, 1921. Published in *Die Mennonitische Rundschau*, Vol. 45, No. 9 (Mar. 1, 1922), p. 22.

18. *Die Kubaner Ansiedlung* (Steinbach, Man., 1953), pp. 60-62.

19. H. Goerz, *Die mennonitischen Siedlungen des Krim* (Winnipeg, Man., 1957), pp. 62-66.

20. See M. B. Fast, *Geschichtlicher Bericht wie die Mennoniten Nordamerikas ihren armen Glaubensgenossen in Russland geholfen haben* (Reedley, Calif., 1919).

21. For an eyewitness account see FA, P. F. Froese, *Durch die mennonitischen Dörfer in Sibirien.* Moscow, August 1924.

CHAPTER THREE

1. For an account of Miller's journey, O. O. Miller, *Personal Diary Covering His Trip into the Mennonite Communities of South Russia, October 6-20, 1920* (ms. in Bethel College Historical Library). See also FA, B. B. Janz to the Mennonitische Hilfsorganisation, July 25, 1921, p. 1. Published in *Die Mennonitische Rundschau*, Vol. 44, No. 43 (Oct. 26, 1921), pp. 7, 9, 10. B. B. Janz had requested that his letter not be published. The editors of the Mennonite periodicals in America, eager for news from Russia and ignorant of the danger in which they placed Janz, did not comply. For the early history of the MCC see John D. Unruh, *In the Name of Christ. A History of the Mennonite Central Committee and Its Service 1920-1951* (Scottdale, Pa., 1952), pp. 11-25.

2. JA(I,c), "Die Wehrlosigkeit der Mennoniten in Russland nach dem ersten Weltkriege," p. 7.

3. JA(I,c), "Die Gründung des Verbandes in Alexanderwohl," pp. 1, 2.

4. *Ibid.*, pp. 3, 4.

5. *Ibid.*, pp. 4, 5; JA(I,c), "Die Wehrlosigkeit der Mennoniten in Russland nach dem ersten Weltkriege," p. 8.

6. In the final analysis the creation of the *Verband* was a necessary survival tactic employed by the Mennonites in the Ukraine. See FA, Jacob Janz, "Zur Entstehung des Verbandes der Bürger holländischer Herkunft in der Ukraine." Tiege, June 6, 1922.

7. JA(I,c), "Die Gründung des Verbandes in Alexanderwohl," pp. 6, 7.

8. FA, Protokoll der allgemeinen Versammlung der Bevollmächtigten des mennonitischen Verbandes in Südrussland aus dem Saporoger Gouvernement am 3. & 4. Januar 1922 in Margenau.

9. For a good description of the operations of the Gnadenfeld chapter of the *VMSR* see Jacob Neufeld, "Erinnerungen eines Beteiligten des Verbandes der Bürger Holländischer Herkunft in der Ukraine" (ms. in Bethel College Historical Library, Newton, Kan.).

10 JA, Memoirs, "Die Reise nach Moskau," pp. 1-3.

11. *Ibid.*, pp. 7, 8; JA, Memoirs, "Audienz bei Tow. Litwinow."

12. JA, Memoirs, "Die Reise nach Moskau," p. 8.

13. JA, Memoirs, "Die Rückreise von Moskau."

14. P. C. Hiebert (ed.) and O. O. Miller (ed.), *Feeding the Hungry. Russia Famine 1919-1925* (Scottdale, Pa., 1929), pp. 111-15.

15. For a general account of Quaker relief activity in Russia see Richenda C. Scott, *Quakers in Russia* (London, 1964).

16. Hiebert and Miller, *op. cit.*, pp. 116-23.

17. *Ibid.*, pp. 135-46; FA, B. B. Janz to the "Mennonitische Hilfsorganisation." Kharkov, July 25, 1921, p. 13.

18. Hiebert and Miller, *op. cit.*, p. 146.

19. For a copy of the contract see *Ibid.*, pp. 446-52. For a good summary of the general nature and extent of Miller's work see A. J. Miller, "The Beginning of American Mennonite Relief Work," *Mennonite Life*, XVII (April 1962), pp. 71-75; A. J. Miller, "Relief Work in Revolutionary Russia," *Mennonite Life*, XVII (July 1962), pp. 126-31; A. J. Miller, "Clothing the Naked," *Mennonite Life*, XVIII (July 1963), pp. 118-21.

20. On Nov. 15, 1917, the Soviet Commissar of Nationalities, Joseph Stalin, issued the famous "Declaration of the Rights of the Peoples of Russia" which asserted the right of minorities in the Soviet Union to secede from the Russian Socialist Federative Soviet Republic. In short order a number of areas including Finland, the Baltic states, White Russia, and the Ukraine proclaimed their independence. While sympathetic to the RSFSR the Ukrainian state insisted on a recognition of its national honor and independent status. The independence movement in the Ukraine was somewhat complex. A Ukrainian People's Republic was established after the fall of the Provisional Government in Petrograd. The new republic was recognized by the Soviets but ousted by the Red Army in February 1918. This Soviet puppet government was in turn overthrown by the advancing German Army, and a rightist government headed by Paul Skoropadsky was inaugurated. When Denikin's White Army overran the area. Skoropadsky's government was deposed. With Denikins retreat in the fall of 1919 the Red Army again restored Soviet authority in the Ukraine. The Russian-sponsored government in the Ukraine was nevertheless granted considerable autonomy in domestic affairs, perhaps as a necessary concession to the prevailing spirit of nationalism.

21. JA, Memoirs, "Zweite Reise nach Moscow," p. 1.

22. *Ibid.*, p. 2.

23. Hiebert and Miller, *op. cit.*, pp. 157-62. Miller took advantage of his interview to inquire as to the whereabouts of the American Clayton Kratz, who had been arrested in Halbstadt and had not been heard of since. Rakovsky promised to look into the matter.

24. *Ibid.*

25. FA, B. B. Janz to B. H. Unruh. Kharkov, Nov. 20, 1921.

26. JA, Memoirs, "Zweite Reise nach Moscow."

CHAPTER FOUR

1. FA, B. B. Janz to the *Stdk.* Nov. 26, 1921.

2. FA, Bittgesuch an das All-Ukrainische Zentrale Executiv Komitee. Dec. 17, 1921.

3. H. H. Kornelsen, "Wie kleine Begebenheiten und Ereignisse mitwirkten, dass es anno 1923 zu einer grossen Auswanderung der Mennoniten kam" (ms. in the possession of the author), pp. 7-10.

4. *Ibid.*, pp. 11-14; JA, Memoirs, "Wieder das Statut," pp. 1-5.

5. *Ibid.*, p. 7.

6. FA, B. B. Janz to B. H. Unruh. Kharkov, Feb. 18, 1922.

7. JA, Memoirs, "Wieder das Statut," p. 8.

8. FA, "Who Are the Mennonites?" *Communist*. Kharkov, July 22, 1922.

9. FA, Protokoll der allgemeinen Versammlung der Bevollmächtigten des mennonitischen Verbandes in Südrussland aus dem Saporoger Gouvernement am 3. & 4. Januar 1922 in Margenau, pp. 1, 2.

10. *Ibid.*, p. 4.

11. FA, Protokoll der Ratssitzung am 10. Januar 1922 in der Kanzlei des Verbandes in Tiege, pp. 1, 2.

12. FA, B. B. Janz to the *Stdk.* and others. Kharkov, Feb. 28, 1922. See also H. S. Bender, "A Russian Mennonite Document of 1922," *Mennonite Quarterly Review*, XXVIII (April 1953), pp. 143-47.

13. FA, B. B. Janz to B. H. Unruh. Kharkov, Mar. 12, 1922, p. 3. Janz was deeply convinced that emigration was the only solution. "Es wird draussen in einem freien stillen nicht hungernden Lande leichter sein eine Ansiedlung durchzumachen, als in einem rein ausgezogenen total ruinierten, hoffnungslos hungernden Lande sich wieder aufzubauen." *Ibid.*, p. 4. See also FA, B. B. Janz to B. H. Unruh. Kharkov, Feb. 27, 1922, p. 2.

14. FA, B. B. Janz to B. H. Unruh. Kharkov, Mar. 15, 1922.

15. JA, Memoirs, "Wieder das Statut," p. 1.

16. *Ibid.*, p. 2.

17. FA, B. B. Janz to B. H. Unruh, Apr. 7, 1922, p. 4.

18. FA, B. B. Janz to B. H. Unruh. Kharkov, Apr. 27, 1922.

19. JA, Memoirs, "Wieder das Statut," pp. 9, 10.

20. FA, B. B. Janz to B. H. Unruh. Kharkov, Apr. 27, 1922.

21. JA, Memoirs, "Wieder das Statut," p. 11. Manzev's hesitation was not unreasonable. For him the difference between the Mennonites and the German colonists in South Russia was somewhat nebulous even though he was aware of some distinctions. In view of the Commissar's busy schedule it was not possible for Janz to explain fully the social, economic, administrative, educational, and religious differences between the two. JA, Memoirs, "Das Statut," pp. 1-3.

22. FA, B. B. Janz to B. H. Unruh. Kharkov, Apr. 27, 1922, p. 4.

23. JA, Memoirs, "Das Statut," p. 5.

24. FA, Statuten des Verbandes der Bürger Holländischer Herkunft in der Ukraine.

25. FA, A. A. Friesen to B. B. Janz. Rosthern, June 16, 1922, pp. 2, 3.

26. FA, B. H. Unruh to B. B. Janz. Aug. 28, 1922, p. 10.

27. For a general description of the overall situation see FA, W. P. Neufeld and J. D. Jantzen, "Die Mennonitischen Flüchtlinge in Batum"; FA, "Batum Mennonite Refugees to the *Stdk.*" Batum, June 19, 1922; FA, "Batum Mennonite Refugees to the *Stdk.*" Batum, Aug. 19, 1922; FA, P. M. Janzen to the Mennonite Relief Agencies. Batum, Oct. 20, 1922; FA, A. Fröse, "Ein Blick in das Leben der Mennoniten-Flüchtlinge in Batum, Georgien." This report was also published in *Die Mennonitische Rundschau*, Vol. 46, No. 5 (Jan. 31, 1923), pp. 4, 5.

28. V. Smucker, "Hilfswerk-Notizen," *Die Mennonitische Rundschau*, Vol. 46, No. 3 (Jan. 17, 1923), p. 1.

CHAPTER FIVE

1. FA, H. Enz, J. Klassen, and others, "Denkschrift zur Frage über die Auswanderung der russländischen Mennoniten." Chortitza, July 1922, p. 1.

2. FA, P. B., "Einige Gedanken zur Auswanderungsfrage." June 21, 1922, p. 1.

3. *Ibid.*, p. 3. There were some who argued that assimilation and oppression were an inevitable experience for the Mennonites regardless of the country to which they migrated. Consequently it was better to face this struggle in Russia, where the Mennonites were historically better entrenched. FA, J. Janzen, "Meine principielle Stellung zur Auswanderungsfrage." Tiege, June 22, 1922.

4. H. Enz, J. Klassen, and others, *op. cit.*, pp. 2, 3.

5. FA, H. Janz, "Warum ich auswandere." Halbstadt, June 21, 1922, p. 2.

6. FA, K. Wiens, "Zur Auswanderungsfrage der Mennoniten." Neu-Halbstadt, June 20, 1922, p. 4.

7. FA, B. B. Janz to the *Stdk.* and others. Kharkov, Feb. 28, 1922. See also H. S. Bender, "A Russian Mennonite Document of 1922," *Mennonite Quarterly Review*, XXVIII (April 1953), pp. 143-47.

8. "Der Congress der Bürger holländischer Herkunft in der Ukraine, Grigorjewka

vom 25.-28. Februar, 1925," *Der Bote*, Vol. 2, No. 23 (June 10, 1925), pp. 5, 6.

9. See the reports of the Commission for Church Affairs in *Der Bote*, Vol. 2, Nos. 26 (July 1, 1925); 30 (July 29, 1925); 41 (Oct. 14, 1925); 52 (Dec. 30, 1925); Vol. 3, No. 13 (Mar. 31, 1926); Vol. 4, No. 18 (May 4, 1927).

10. J. W. Ewert, "Etwas über die Einwanderungs- und Kolonisationssache der russländischen Mennoniten," *Die Mennonitische Rundschau*, Vol. 46, No. 39 (Sept. 26, 1923), pp. 6, 7.

11. C. F. Klassen, "Die Lage der russischen Gemeinden seit 1920," *Bericht über die Mennonitische Welt-Hilfs-Konferenz vom 13. August bis 3. September 1930 in Danzig*, pp. 49-58.

12. D. Toews, "Die Auswanderung aus Russland bis Herbst 1928," *Bericht über die Mennonitische Welt-Hilfs-Konferenz vom 31. August bis 3. September 1930 in Danzig*, pp. 73-79.

13. B. H. Unruh, "Die Massenflucht der deutschen Bauern aus der Sowjetunion, ihre Gründe, ihre Auswirkungen in Russland und ihre Folgen für das Hilfswerk im Ausland," *Bericht über die Mennonitische Welt-Hilfs-Konferenz vom 31. August bis 3. September 1930 in Danzig*, pp. 79-88.

14. FA, B. B. Janz to the *Stdk.* Kharkov, Mar. 1, 1922, pp. 1, 2.

15. *Ibid.*, p. 4

16. FA, B. B. Janz to the *Stdk.* Kharkov, Mar. 7, 1922, p. 1.

17. FA, B. B. Janz to B. H. Unruh, Kharkov, Mar. 12, 1922, p. 4.

18. FA, B. B. Janz to the *Stdk.* Kharkov, Apr. 27, 1922, pp. 5, 6.

19. FA, B. B. Janz to the *Stdk.* Kharkov, Apr. 7, 1922, p. 5.

20. JA, Memoirs, "Die Reise nach Moskau," p. 8.

21. FA, Protokoll der allgemeinen Versammlung der Bevollmächtigten des mennonitischen Verbandes in Südrussland aus dem Saporoger Gouvernement am 3. u. 4. Januar, 1922 in Margenau, p. 3.

22. FA, B. B. Janz to the *Stdk.* Kharkov, Mar. 7, 1922, p. 4; FA, B. B. Janz to the *Stdk.* Kharkov, Apr. 7, 1922, p. 5; FA, B. B. Janz to the *Stdk.* Kharkov, Apr. 27, 1922, p. 8.

23. FA, Protokoll der General-Versammlung der Vertreter d. VBHH in der Ukraine. Abgehalten in Landskrone am 29. 30. und 31. Mai 1922.

24. FA, B. B. Janz to the *Stdk.* July 25 to Aug. 4, 1922, p. 5.

25. FA, B. B. Janz to the "Verwaltung des VBHH in der Ukraine Tiege Ohrloff." Moscow, Nov. 9, 1922, pp. 2, 3; FA, B. B. Janz to B. H. Unruh. Moscow, Nov. 7, 1922, p. 4.

26. FA, Excerpt from Minutes No. 41 of the Presidium of the Federal Committee for Lands, Nov. 22, 1922; FA, Federal Committee for Lands of the Presidium of the All-Russian Central Committee to the People's Commissariat of Agriculture of the USSR. Nov. 24, 1922.

27. FA, B. B. Janz to the American Emigration Committees, Kharkov, Feb. 14, 1924, p. 1. The Canadian Mennonite Board of Colonization spoke in terms of credit, half-credit, and cash emigrants. After 1923 all of these were private emigrants in the sense that group emigration was no longer possible.

28. FA, B. B. Janz to the *Stdk.* Moscow, Dec. 17, 1922, pp. 1-6.

29. A more detailed treatment of the problem is found in B. H. Unruh, "Der Kampf der russischen Gemeinden um die Wehrlosigkeit," *Der Bote*, Vol. 2, Nos. 35-37 (Sept. 2, 1925, to Sept. 16, 1925).

30. FA, P. Neufeld to J. Rempel. Chortitza, Nov. 5, 1924.

31. *Die Mennonitische Rundschau*, Vol. 53, No. 12 (Mar. 19, 1930), p. 6.

CHAPTER SIX

1. FA, B. B. Janz to the *Stdk.* Kharkov, Mar. 1, 1922, pp. 1, 2.

2. P. F. Froese, traveling through the Chortitza and Molotschna settlements with Mr. Miller between Feb. 21 and Mar. 7, 1922, estimated that 99 percent of the settlers were ready to emigrate. FA, P. F. Froese to B. H. Unruh. Moscow, Mar. 29, 1922.

3. FA, B. B. Janz to the *Stdk.* Kharkov, Feb. 25, 1922, pp. 1, 2.

4. FA, B. B. Janz to the *Stdk.* Kharkov, Mar. 1, 1922, p. 5.

5. FA, B. B. Janz to B. H. Unruh. Kharkov, Mar. 15, 1922, p. 3.

6. FA, B. B. Janz to B. H. Unruh. Kharkov, Mar. 12, 1922, p. 2.

7. FA, B. B. Janz to the *Stdk.* Kharkov, Mar. 16, 1922, p. 2.
8. FA, B. B. Janz to the *Stdk.* Mar. 31, 1922, p. 8.
9. *Ibid.*
10. FA, B. B. Janz to the *Stdk.* Kharkov, Apr. 27, 1922, p. 5. The compiling of lists had already begun prior to Apr. 24. Many of the local officials who were required to ratify them refused to do so. In the Molotschna, local authorities threatened to send the Mennonites to the dungeon rather than a foreign land. FA, B. B. Janz to the *Stdk.* May 5, 1922.
11. FA, B. B. Janz to AMR. Apr. 30, 1922. Printed in *Die Mennonitische Rundschau,* Vol. 45, No. 28 (July 12, 1922), p. 13.
12. FA, B. B. Janz to the *Stdk.* May 5, 1922, p. 2.
13. FA, B. B. Janz to the *Stdk.* May 7, 1922, pp. 1, 2.
14. FA, B. H. Unruh to B. B. Janz. Karlsruhe, Apr. 10, 1922, pp. 3, 4.
15. FA, B. B. Janz to the *Stdk.* Kharkov, May 10, 1922, pp. 2, 3.
16. *Ibid.*, p. 4.
17. FA, B. B. Janz to A. A. Friesen. May 27, 1922, p. 1.
18. FA, B. B. Janz to the *Stdk.* Alexandrovsk, May 16, 1922, pp. 1, 2. Also FA, B. B. Janz to A. A. Friesen. Alexandrovsk, May 16, 1922.
19. FA, Protokoll der General-Versammlung der Vertreter mennonitischer Dorfsgemeinden und Gruppen im Süden Russlands. Abgehalten in Landskrone am 29., 30. und 31. Mai 1922, pp. 4, 5.
20. FA, Landskrone Konferenz an das Kommittee für russisch-mennonitische Emigration nach Canada, May 29-31, 1922.
21. FA, B. B. Janz to the *Stdk.* July 13, 1922.
22. FA, B. B. Janz to the *Stdk.* July 25, 1922.
23. FA, "Who Are the Mennonites?" *Communist,* Kharkov, July 22, 1922.
24. BA, B. B. Janz to the CMBC. Aug. 4, 1922, p. 2.
25. FA, B. B. Janz to A. A. Friesen. Aug. 28, 1922, pp. 3-7.
26. FA, Protokoll der Sitzung des Rates und der Verwaltung des VBHH zu Tiege am 14. August 1922.
27. BA, B. B. Janz to the CMBC. Aug. 4, 1922, pp. 10, 11.
28. FA, Statistical Chart of the Halbstadt Volost Committee of the AMR. Aug. 18, 1922. By July 1, 1922, 15,279 out of a total population of 18,185 were starving. Only 7,454 of the hungry could be fed by the AMR. Between Apr. 1 and Aug. 15 the deaths from starvation increased from 127 to 317.
29. FA, B. B. Janz to A. A. Friesen. Kharkov, Sept. 9, 1922.
30. FA, B. B. Janz to B. H. Unruh. Kharkov, Sept. 4, 1922, p. 3.
31. FA, B. B. Janz to the *Stdk.* Kharkov, Sept. 13, 1922, p. 2.
32. FA, B. B. Janz to the *Stdk.* Kharkov, Sept. 11, 1922.
33. FA, B. B. Janz to the CPR. Sept. 19, 1922.
34. FA, Protokoll der allgemeinen Delegiertenversammlung des Verbandes der Bürger Holländischer Herkunft in der Ukraine zu Osterwick am 22. und 23. September 1922.
35. BA, D. Toews to B. B. Janz. Rosthern, Sept. 29, 1922.
36. FA, B. H. Unruh to P. F. Froese and C. F. Klassen. Berlin-Lichterfelde, Oct. 2, 1922.
37. FA, A. A. Friesen to B. B. Janz. Rosthern, Sept. 12, 1922.
38. FA, P. F. Froese to the *Stdk.* Moscow, Sept. 24, 1922, pp. 2, 3.
39. FA, P. F. Froese to the *Stdk.* Moscow, Oct. 1, 1922, pp. 1, 2.
40. *Ibid.*
41. FA, B. B. Janz to the *Stdk.* Alexandrovsk, Oct. 9, 1922, p. 2.
42. *Ibid.* See also BA, B. B. Janz to D. Toews. Moscow, Oct. 23, 1922.

CHAPTER SEVEN

1. FA, P. F. Froese to the *Stdk.* Moscow, Oct. 15, 1922.
2. FA, B. B. Janz to the *Stdk.* Moscow, Oct. 24-29, 1922, p. 4.
3. *Ibid.*, pp. 5, 6.
4. BA, B. B. Janz to D. Toews, Moscow, Oct. 23, 1922, pp. 3, 4.
5. FA, B. B. Janz to the Stdk. Moscow, Nov. 6, 1922.

6. FA, B. B. Janz to the *Stdk.* Moscow, Oct. 24-29, 1922, pp. 6-8 .

7. FA, B. B. Janz to the "Rayonverwaltung Chortitza" and others. Moscow, Nov. 7, 1922. Since land was state-owned, only the movable and personal property of the colonists could be sold. At an executive committee meeting of the *VBHH* somewhat later it was decided to appoint a special commission responsible for the long-term liquidation of the emigrants' property. FA, Protokoll der Ratssitzung des VBHH am 15. und 16. November 1922 in Schönwiese, pp. 1, 2.

8. FA, B. B. Janz to the Executive of the *VBHH* in Tiege-Orloff. Moscow, Nov. 9, 1922, pp. 1, 2.

9. FA, B. B. Janz to the *Stdk.* Moscow, Nov. 19, 1922.

10. FA, B. B. Janz to the *Stdk.* Moscow, Nov. 26, 1922, pp. 9, 10.

11. *Ibid.*, p. 1.

12. *Ibid.*, p. 2.

13. FA, B. B. Janz to the *Stdk.* Moscow, Dec. 11, 1922, p. 8.

14. FA, B. B. Janz to the *Stdk.* Moscow, Dec. 16, 1922, p. 8.

15. *Ibid.*, pp. 8-10.

16. FA, B. B. Janz to the *Stdk.* Moscow, Dec. 28, 1922, p. 4.

17. In view of these developments, Philip D. Cornies, active in the southern colonies during December, drafted a memorandum in which he urged the entire constituency to unity and cooperation. "Is it not apparent," he wrote, "that the general welfare also encompasses my welfare?" FA, Ph. Cornies, "Eine Notwendige Klarstellung."

18. FA, B. B. Janz to the MCA. Kharkov, Jan. 22, 1923, p. 5.

19. FA, P. F. Froese and C. F. Klassen to the *Stdk.* Moscow, Jan. 20, 1923, p. 2. Though Litvinov was not entirely opposed to the petition, the problem was referred to the Anglo-American Department of the Interior Commissariat where it was categorically rejected.

20. FA, B. B. Janz to the MCA. Kharkov, Jan. 22, 1923, p. 2.

21. See F. H. Epp, *Mennonite Exodus* (Altona, Man., 1962), pp. 119-35.

22. FA, J. P. Klassen to W. P. Neufeld. Rosenthal, Jan. 5, 1923. While in Moscow during December, Klassen had conferred with William P. Neufeld from Reedley, Calif., who had given the impression that he would aid the emigrants in any way he could. Not long after the Chortitza meeting, Klassen wrote to Neufeld requesting his assistance in investigating the possibility of emigration to Mexico. On Feb. 5, 1923, another meeting was held by the Chortitza emigrants at which two delegates were selected and commissioned to explore any country suitable for settlement. FA, J. P. Klassen to W. P. Neufeld. Rosenthal, Feb. 1, 1923.

23. FA, "Aeusserung und Bitte einer Gruppe von Flüchtlingen-Emigranten der Gnadenfelder Wollost."

24. FA, B. B. Janz to the MCA. Kharkov, Jan. 22, 1923, pp. 10, 11.

25. BA, B. B. Janz "an die leitenden Brüder der Konferenzen und Organisationen der Mennoniten in Amerika." Moscow, Dec. 31, 1922, and Jan. 1, 1923.

26. FA, B. H. Unruh to B. B. Janz. Jan. 11, 1923, p. 1. In his correspondence with Janz, B. H. Unruh repeatedly emphasized that the revolution had moved as far to the left as possible. On occasion he chided Janz for his extremely pessimistic views regarding the future of the Russian Mennonites. Unruh concurred with the political notions of his day which by 1923 held that the worst aspects of the revolution were over, particularly as concerned the peasantry. The New Economic Policy seemed particularly good evidence for this view. In the end, the Stalinist era proved Janz had taken the most realistic position. During 1922 and 1923, however, his position was certainly not shared by all the Mennonites in Russia. Janz's close friend and consultant, Philip D. Cornies, insisted that Canada gave too few guarantees and that it was not a light affair to leave the home of one's forefathers.

27. FA, B. B. Janz "an die leitenden Brüder der Konferenzen und Organisationen der Mennoniten in Amerika." Moscow, Dec. 21, 1922, and Jan. 1, 1923, p. 7.

28. *Ibid.*, pp. 5, 6.

29. "Wo findet die Seele die Heimat die Ruh? Nein! *Hier* ist sie nicht." *Ibid.*, p. 7.

30. JA, P. F. Froese, "Wie entstand der Allrussische Mennonitische Landwirtschaftliche Verein?" p. 2.

31. *Ibid.*, pp. 5, 6.

32. FA, C. F. Klassen, F. Isaak, and P. F. Froese, "Bericht über die Entstehung des Allrussischen Mennonitischen Landwirtschaftlichen Verbandes." May 21, 1923, p. 2.

33. *Ibid.*

34. *Ibid.*, pp. 2, 3.

35. JA, P. F. Froese, *op. cit.*, pp. 8, 9.

36. FA, Protokoll der ersten Vertreterversammlung des Allrussischen Mennonitischen Landwirtschaftlichen Vereins zu Alexandertal Gouvernement Samara, am 10. Oktober 1923.

CHAPTER EIGHT

1. For a more detailed description see F. H. Epp, *Mennonite Exodus* (Altona, Man., 1962), pp. 51 ff.

2. See *Die Mennoniten-Gemeinden in Russland während der Kriegs- und Revolutionsjahre 1914 bis 1920* (Heilbronn a. Neckar, 1921). Officially the book was published anonymously. In actual fact it was the work of T. O. H. Hylkema and B. H. Unruh.

3. FA, B. H. Unruh to B. B. Janz, Feb. 15, 1922, pp. 1, 2.

4. *Ibid.*, p. 7.

5. Regius Professor of Civil Law at Oxford from 1880 to 1893, Bryce was perhaps best known for *The American Commonwealth*, published in 1888, and *The Holy Roman Empire*, which appeared in 1866. Several of his more prominent government positions included the office of undersecretary for foreign affairs (1886); president of the board of trade (1894-95); chief secretary for Ireland (1905-7). He died in 1922.

6. The rather voluminous work reports filed by B. H. Unruh between 1921 and 1924 all testify of the broad base upon which Unruh and Fast operated. Since much of the work was exploratory in nature, the results achieved were often unspectacular.

7. FA, B. H. Unruh to B. B. Janz. Feb. 15, 1922, p. 12.

8. FA, B. H. Unruh to B. B. Janz. Apr. 10, 1922, pp. 2, 3.

9. One of these areas was Poland. Because of unsettled domestic conditions no agreement concerning the refugee problem could be signed with the Polish government As a result, a number of Mennonite refugees from Russia were deported shortly after they arrived in Poland. FA, B. H. Unruh to B. B. Janz. May 3, 1922, p. 1. The *MFF* delegated Victor Günther of Danzig to investigate the situation. FA, B. H. Unruh to B. B. Janz. Feb. 21, 1922, pp. 17, 18.

10. FA, B. H. Unruh to B. B. Janz. May 3, 1922, p. 3.

11. FA, B. H. Unruh to B. B. Janz. Feb. 15, 1922, pp. 12-15.

12. FA, B. H. Unruh to B. B. Janz. Feb. 15, 1922, p. 13. See also FA, B. H. Unruh to A. A. Friesen May 3, 1921.

13. FA, B. H. Unruh to B. B. Janz. Feb. 15, 1922, p. 14.

14. FA, B. H. Unruh to B. B. Janz. Feb. 21, 1922, pp. 1, 2.

15. FA, J. Wiens to B. H. Unruh. July 4, 1921.

16. FA, B. H. Unruh to B. B. Janz. Feb. 21, 1922, pp. 1, 7.

17. BA, B. H. Unruh to B. B. Janz. Jan. 14, 1922, p. 1.

18. FA, B. B. Janz to the "Mennonitische Hilfsorganisation." July 25, 1921.

19. FA, B. B. Janz to B. H. Unruh and others. Kharkov, Nov. 20, 1921.

20. FA, B. H. Unruh to B. B. Janz. Feb. 21, 1922, pp. 11-13.

21. FA, B. H. Unruh, "Bericht über meine Verhandlungen mit dem Secretär der Doopsgezinden Commissie Ds. F. C. Fleischer, am 29. Dezember 1921 im Hospiz Schweizerhof, Frankfurt a. M." pp. 2-4.

22. *Ibid.*, pp. 4, 5.

23. FA, B. H. Unruh to A. A. Friesen. Karlsruhe, Feb. 18, 1922.

24. FA, B. H. Unruh to A. A. Friesen. Karlsruhe, July 3, 1922.

25. FA, B. H. Unruh to A. A. Friesen. Karlsruhe, June 19, 1922; FA, B. H. Unruh to A. A. Friesen. Karlsruhe, July 3, 1922.

26. FA, B. H. Unruh to A. A. Friesen. Karlsruhe, July 8, 1922.

27. FA, B. B. Janz to A. A. Friesen. May 27, 1922.

28. *Ibid.*

29. FA, B. B. Janz to A. A. Friesen. Aug. 28, 1922.

30. FA, Vertrag der Belieferung des VBHH in der Ukraine mit Saatgut für die Herbstbestellung 1922. Gestätigt zwischen der Handelsvertretung der Ukr. S.S.R. in Berlin und dem Direktor der holländischen Hilfsaktion. Aug. 21, 1922.

31. See FA, B. B. Janz to A. A. Friesen. Sept. 9, 1922; FA, B. B. Janz to the *Stdk.* Kharkov, Sept. 10, 1922; FA, B. B. Janz to the *Stdk.* Kharkov, Sept. 11, 1922.

32. FA, B. B. Janz to P. C. Hiebert. Sept. 19, 1922.

33. FA, Protokoll der allgemeinen Delegiertenversammlung des VBHH in der

Ukraine zu Osterwick am 22. und 23. September 1922.

34. FA, B. H. Unruh to B. B. Janz. Mar. 23, 1923, p. 9.
35. FA, B. H. Unruh to B. B. Janz. Jan. 11, 1923.
36. FA, B. H. Unruh to B. B. Janz. Mar. 23, 1923, pp. 5-7.
37. FA, B. B. Janz to the *Stdk. Mar.* 29, 1923.
38. FA, B. B. Janz to the *Stdk.* Apr. 16, 1923, pp. 4, 5.
39. FA, B. B. Janz to A. A. Friesen. July 13, 1923.

CHAPTER NINE

1. FA, B. B. Janz to the *Stdk.* Kharkov, Feb. 1, 1923, p. 2.
2. FA, B. B. Janz to the MCA and MECC. Kharkov, Feb. 4, 1923.
3. FA, B. B. Janz to A. Miller. Feb. 18, 1923.
4. FA, F. Isaak, C. F. Klassen, and P. F. Froese to the *Stdk.* Moscow, Feb. 20, 1923, pp. 1, 2.
5. *Ibid.*, pp. 3, 4.
6. FA, P. F. Froese and C. F. Klassen to B. B. Janz. Moscow, Feb. 14, 1923, p. 1.
7. *Ibid,* pp. 2, 3.
8. The Foreign Office informed Froese and Klassen that with the *GPU* sanction no further obstacle to an immediate emigration existed. FA, P. F. Froese and C. F. Klassen to the *Stdk.* Moscow, Mar. 4, 1923.
9. FA, B. B. Janz to B. H. Unruh. Feb. 24, 1923, p. 5.
10. FA, B. H. Unruh to B. B. Janz. Feb. 16, 1923.
11. FA, B. H. Unruh to B. B. Janz. Mar. 23, 1923.
12. Rev. B. B. Janz had learned of the Lechfeld negotiations by the end of February. One month later it was certain that the *DMH* would accept responsibility for the refugees. At first Janz was not too enthusiastic about this possibility because of the extra expenses involved. FA, B. B. Janz to the *Stdk.* Apr. 16, 1923, p. 9. B. H. Unruh insisted that this was the only plausible solution since no country would receive physically unfit people. FA, B. H. Unruh to B. B. Janz. May 4, 1923, pp. 4, 5. For additional information see FA, B. H. Unruh and A. J. Fast, "Arbeitsbericht," Apr. 18, 1923; also "Arbeitsbericht," May 4, 1923.
13. FA, B. B. Janz to the *Stdk.* Apr. 16, 1923, pp. 9, 10.
14. FA, Protokoll der Sitzung der Vertreter der Emigranten des Chortitzer Rayons in Rosental am 10. April, 1923.
15. FA, Protokoll der Ratssitzung des VBHH in der Ukraine abgehalten in Schönwiese am 26. und 27. April, 1923.
16. FA, B. B. Janz to the *Stdk.* May 24, 1923, p. 1.
17. FA, F. Isaak, P. F. Froese, and C. F. Klassen to the various settlements. Moscow, June 25, 1923, p. 4.
18. FA, B. B. Janz to the *Stdk.* Mar. 29, 1923, p. 4.
19. FA, B. B. Janz to the *Stdk.* Apr. 16, 1923, p. 8.
20. FA, F. Isaak, P. Froese, and C. F. Klassen to the various settlements. June 25, 1923.
21. FA, P. F. Froese to the *Stdk.* Moscow, June 7, 1923.
22. FA, F. Isaak and P. F. Froese to the *Stdk.* Moscow, June 27, 1923.
23. FA, B. B. Janz to the *Stdk.* Moscow, July 1-4, 1923, p. 2.
24. FA, B. B. Janz to the Stdk. July 30, 1923.

CHAPTER TEN

1. FA, B. B. Janz to the *Stdk.* Moscow, July 1-4, 1923, p. 6.
2. FA, H. Dück to B. B. Janz. June 30, 1923.
3. FA, B. B. Janz to the *Stdk.* Kharkov, July 9, 1923.
4. FA, B. B. Janz to P. Cornies. Kharkov, July 15, 1923; FA, P. Cornies to B. H. Unruh. Orloff, Aug. 7, 1923.
5. FA, B. B. Janz to the *Stdk.* Moscow, July 1-4, 1923, pp. 6, 7.
6. FA, B. B. Janz to the Administrative Offices of the VBHH (Orloff). Kharkov, July 8, 1923, pp. 1, 2.
7. FA, B. B. Janz to P. H. and D. Toews. Kharkov, July 9, 1923. Printed in *Die Mennonitische Rundschau*, Vol. 46, (No. 33). See also FA, B. B. Janz to A. A. Friesen. Kharkov, July 13, 1923.
8. FA, B. B. Janz to the CPR (Moscow). Kharkov, Oct. 19, 1923.
9. BA, Canadian National Telegram. Rosthern, Sask., Oct. 30, 1923.

10. FA, B. B. Janz to the "Rayon-Verwaltungen des VBHH in Chortitza, Nikolaipol und New York und deren Emigranten-Gruppen." Kharkov, Nov. 1923.

11. FA, B. B. Janz to the Emigration Committees in America and others. Kharkov, Dec. 22, 1923.

12. FA, P. F. Froese and C. F. Klassen, "Bericht über die Besprechung mit dem Mitgliede des Praesidiums ZIK Peter Smidowitch (12. Dezember, 1923)."

13. BA, B. B. Janz to the American Mennonite Committees for Colonization. July 23, 1923, p. 5.

14. FA, F. Isaak and P. F. Froese to the *Stdk.* Moscow, July 28, 1923.

15. *Ibid.*

16. BA, B. B. Janz to the American Mennonite Committees for Colonization. July 23, 1923, p. 5.

17. FA, B. B. Janz to the "Rayon-Verwaltungen des VBHH in Chortitza, Schönwiese usw." Kharkov, July 14, 1923.

18. FA, Ph. Cornies to B. B. Janz. Schönwiese, July 31, 1923; FA, Ph. Cornies to B. H. Unruh. Orloff, Aug. 7, 1923.

19. FA, B. B. Janz to the Central Offices of the VBHH in Orloff. Aug. 8, 1923.

20. FA, B. B. Janz to P. H. Unruh and A. A. Friesen. Moscow, Sept. 29, 1923.

21. FA, Ph. Cornies, "Arbeitsbericht in Sachen der Emigration. 18-24. Oktober."

22. FA, Ph. Cornies to B. B. Janz. Alexandrovsk, Oct. 20, 1923.

23. FA, "Hilferuf der mennonitischen Emigranten in der Ukraine an die mennonitischen Brüder in Amerika." Dec. 21, 1923.

24. FA, B. B. Janz to B. H. Unruh, Moscow, Dec. 18, 1923.

25. JA, Memoirs, B. B. Janz, "Soldaten und Kassenpassagiere," p. 1.

26. *Ibid.*, pp. 4, 5.

27. FA, "Regeln für private Ausreise von Mennoniten nach America."

28. FA, B. B. Janz to the American Emigration Committees and others. Kharkov, Feb. 14, 1924, p. 3.

29. *Ibid.*

CHAPTER ELEVEN

1. This was the position taken by the *VBHH* executive at the time of the appointment and also later. FA, B. B. Janz to B. H. Unruh. Dec. 16, 1923.

2. FA, B. H. Unruh, "Zur Orientierung." Karlsruhe, Feb. 6, 1924, p. 5.

3. BA, A. A. Friesen to B. B. Janz. Rosthern, Apr. 11, 1924.

4. BA, D. Toews to B. B. Janz. Rosthern, Sept. 22, 1923.

5. BA, A. A. Friesen to B. B. Janz. Rosthern, Apr. 11, 1924, p. 2.

6. FA, B. H. Unruh, "Zur Orientierung." Karlsruhe, Feb. 6, 1924, p. 7.

7. FA, B. B. Janz to the American Committees. Aug. 30, 1923, p. 1.

8. FA, A. A. Friesen to B. H. Unruh. Rosthern, Oct. 17, 1923.

9. JA, H. B. Janz to B. B. Janz. Herbert, Sask., Sept. 27, 1924.

10. BA, A. A. Friesen to B. B. Janz. Rosthern, Apr. 11, 1924.

11. FA, B. H. Unruh to the *AMLV* Executive. Karlsruhe, May 10, 1924; FA, A. J. Fast to the *AMLV* Executive. Berlin, May 12, 1924.

12. FA, B. H. Unruh to B. B. Janz and the *AMLV* Executive. Aug. 12, 1924.

13. JA, H. B. Janz to B. B. Janz. Herbert, Sask., Sept. 27, 1924.

14. BA, B. B. Janz to A. A. Friesen. Nov. 17, 1924.

15. FA, B. H. Unruh to B. B. Janz. Dec. 19, 1922.

16. FA, P. F. Froese and C. F. Klassen to B. H. Unruh. Moscow, Feb. 21, 1923.

17. FA, B. H. Unruh to P. F. Froese and C. F. Klassen. Karlsruhe, Mar. 8, 1923.

18. FA, P. F. Froese and C. F. Klassen to B. H. Unruh. Moscow, Mar. 28, 1923.

19. FA, A. A. Friesen to P. F. Froese and C. F. Klassen. Rosthern, Apr. 5, 1923; FA, A. A. Friesen to F. Isaak, P. F. Froese, and C. F. Klassen. Rosthern, Apr. 13, 1923.

CHAPTER TWELVE

1. FA, B. B. Janz to the American Emigration Committees. Kharkov, Feb. 14, 1924, p. 1.

2. FA, B. B. Janz to the Mennonite Colonization Association and the Mennonite Colonization Board. Kharkov, Apr. 6, 1924, p. 2.

3. The telegram informing Janz of the signing of the contract was dispatched from Rosthern only on May 2. BA, Telegram. D. Toews to B. B. Janz, May 2, 1924.

4. FA, B. B. Janz to the Mennonite Colonization Association and the Mennonite Colonization Board. Kharkov, Apr. 6, 1924, p. 2.

5. FA, B. B. Janz to the American Emigration Committees and others. Kharkov, Feb. 14, 1924, p. 4.

6. At its first congress the *AMLV* (meeting in Alexandertal, Samara, during October 1923) expressed its appreciation of the service of the *Studienkommission* by a special vote of thanks. FA, Protokoll der ersten Vertreterversammlung des Allrussischen Mennonitischen Landwirtschaftlichen Vereins zu Alexandertal, Gouvernement Samara, am 10. Oktober, 1923, p. 26.

7. FA, Anhang zum Protokoll der Ersten Vertreterversammlung des AMLV, am 16. Oktober, 1923, p. 4.

8. See FA, Protokoll der Vertreterversammlung des Verbandes der Bürger holländischer Herkunft in der Ukraine am 1. 3. u. 4. März 1924 in Marienort (Kalinowo) Donetz. Gouvernement Jusower Kreis.

9. FA, B. B. Janz to the American Emigration Committees. Kharkov, Apr. 6, 1924, p. 3.

10. FA, Protokoll der Gemeinsamen Sitzung des Rates und der Verwaltung des Allrussischen Mennonitischen Landwirtschaftlichen Vereins vom 20. bis zum 24. März 1924, in Moscow, p. 6.

11. FA, P. F. Froese, F. Isaak, and C. F. Klassen to the *VBHH* Executive. Moscow, Apr. 10, 1924.

12. FA, Resolution über die Zusammensetzung der für den nächsten Abschub in Betracht kommenden Gruppen. Abgefasst auf der Ratssitzung in Orloff am 8. und 9. Mai 1924.

13. FA, B. B. Janz to the Mennonite Colonization Board. Moscow, May 15, 1924.

14. JA, Memoirs, "Eine Mai-Feier im Sovietlande," p. 1.

15. *Ibid.*, p. 2.

16. J. J. Thiessen, "Vor 40 Jahren." Saskatoon, Sask., June 1964 (ms. in possession of J. J. Thiessen), pp. 1, 2.

17. *Ibid.*

18. *Ibid.*, p. 6.

19. *Ibid.*

20. Interview with B. B. Janz, August 1963. Also JA, Memoirs, "Eine Mai-Feier im Sovietlande," pp. 6, 7.

21. For an eyewitness account of the departure see "Eine Auswanderung aus Russland nach Canada," *Der Bote*, Vol. I, Nos. 33, 34 (Aug. 27, 1924 to Sept. 3, 1924).

22. FA, B. B. Janz to B. H. Unruh and A. A. Friesen. Moscow, June 27, 1924, p. 1.

23. *Ibid*, p. 2.

24. *Ibid.*

25. JA, Memoirs, "Eine Mai-Feier im Sovietlande," p. 8.

26. J. J. Thiessen, *op. cit.*, pp. 2, 3.

27. This was soon confirmed by a case in point. One day after Janz departed from Moscow, E. W. Suderman arrived in Kharkov from Tiege with 101 passes for the second echelon that needed the sanction of authorities. The approval was not given. FA, B. B. Janz to B. H. Unruh and A. A. Friesen. Moscow, June 27, 1924, pp. 3, 4.

28. *Ibid.*, p. 4; interview with B. B. Janz, Aug. 1963.

29. J. Sawatsky, "Der zweite Auswandererzug," *Der Bote*, Vol. I, No. 35 (Sept. 10, 1924), p. 3.

30. JA, Memoirs, "Eine Mai-Feier im Sovietlande," p. 9.

31. FA, A. Rempel and A. Bauer, "Bericht über die Lage der Flüchtlinge im Gnadenfelder Bezirk." July 22, 1924.

32. FA, B. B. Janz to D. Toews. Kharkov, Aug. 14, 1924, pp. 1, 2.

33. FA, B. B. Janz to D. Toews. Kharkov, Aug. 14, 1924, p. 2.

34. FA, B. B. Janz to D. Toews, Moscow, Aug. 31 to Sept. 5, 1924, pp. 4, 5.

35. BA, B. B. Janz to D. Toews. Orloff, Oct. 7, 1924.

CHAPTER THIRTEEN

1. FA, *AMLV* Executive to the Mennonite Representatives Abroad. Moscow, Aug. 9, 1924; also FA, *AMLV* Executive to the Mennonite Representatives Abroad. Moscow; July 1924.

2. JA, C. F. Klassen to B. H. Unruh and A. J. Fast. Moscow, July 27, 1924.

3. BA, B. B. Janz to the American Colonization Committees. Kharkov, July 19, 1924.

4. FA, *AMLV* Executive to the Mennonite Representatives Abroad. Moscow, July 1924.

5. JA, C. F. Klassen to B. H. Unruh and A. J. Fast. Moscow, July 27, 1924.

6. FA, B. B. Janz to D. Toews Kharkov, Aug. 14, 1924, p. 1.

7. *Ibid.*

8. FA, B. B. Janz to the Dutch Emigration Committee. Aug. 21, 1924.

9. FA, B. H. Unruh, "Arbeitsbericht." Nov. 22, 1924, pp. 1, 2.

10. FA, B. B. Janz to the Dutch Emigration Committee. Aug. 21, 1924.

11. FA, J. De Jong to B. H. Unruh. Rotterdam, Sept. 17, 1924.

12. FA, B. H. Unruh, "Arbeitsbericht." Nov. 22, 1924, pp. 5, 6.

13. *Ibid.* Also JA, B. H. Unruh to the German Ministry of the Interior. Berlin, Oct. 7, 1924.

14. See E. H. Carr, *The Interregnum 1923-1924* (London, 1954), pp. 131-35.

15. BA, B. B. Janz to D. Toews. Moscow, Aug. 31, 1924, p. 3.

16. *Ibid.*, p 2.

17. JA, *AMLV* Executive to D. Toews. Moscow, Nov. 1924.

18. FA, B. B. Janz to B. H. Unruh. Kharkov, Sept. 19, 1924.

19. On the issue see JA, B. B. Janz to *AMLV* Executive. Kharkov, Oct. 25, 1924; JA, *AMLV* Executive to B. B. Janz. Moscow, Oct. 27, 1924.

20. JA, *AMLV* Executive to D. Toews. Moscow, Nov. 1924.

21. B.A, B. B. Janz to D. Toews. Kharkov, Nov. 9, 1924.

22. FA, B. B. Janz to the Mennonite Colonization Board. Kharkov, Nov. 30, 1924.

23. BA, B. B. Janz to D. Toews. Moscow, Dec. 17, 1924.

24. FA, B. B. Janz to D. Toews. Kharkov, Aug. 8, 1924, p. 3.

25. In this case the *VBHH* was not given a copy of excerpts from the CEC meeting. The report of the investigating commission was, however, made available. In all probability most of its recommendations were accepted by the CEC. The report consequently provided a reasonable record of the government's attitude toward the Mennonites and the emigration question. FA, P. F. Froese to the Mennonite Representatives Abroad. Moscow, Nov. 12, 1924.

26. *Ibid.*

27. FA, Marginal notation by B. H. Unruh on B. B. Janz's letter to D. Toews. Oct. 31, 1924.

28. FA, B. B. Janz to the Mennonite Representatives Abroad. Moscow, Dec. 21, 1924, pp. 1, 2.

29. The old currency was redeemable between March 10 and May 10 at the rate of 50,000 Soviet rubles of the 1923 type for one gold ruble. The exchange rate for pre-1921 rubles was 50,000 million to one gold ruble.

30. JA, P. F. Froese and F. K. Thiessen, "Bericht," Dec. 19, 1924.

31. *Ibid.* For a good account see C. F. Klassen, "The Mennonites of Russia, 1917-1928," *Mennonite Quarterly Review*, No. 2 (April 1932), pp. 69-80.

32. JA, P. F. Froese to the Mennonite Representatives Abroad. Moscow, Dec. 30, 1924.

33. FA, P. F. Froese to the Mennonite Representatives Abroad. Moscow, Oct. 4, 1924.

34. JA, P. F. Froese and F. K. Thiessen, "Bericht." Dec. 19, 1924.

CHAPTER FOURTEEN

1. BA, D. Toews to B. B. Janz. Rosthern, June 30, 1925.

2. BA, Telegram. D. Toews to B. B. Janz. Rosthern, June 27, 1925.

3. See BA, D. Toews to B. B. Janz. Rosthern, Aug. 4 and 21, 1925.

4. BA, D. Toews to B. B. Janz. Rosthern, July 10, 1925.

5. BA, B. B. Janz to D. Toews. Kharkov, July 27, 1925.

6. BA, D. Toews to B. B. Janz. Rosthern, Aug. 21, 1925.

7. BA, D. Toews to B. B. Janz. Rosthern, Sept. 2, 1925.

8. BA, K. Peters to B. B. Janz. Ekaterinoslav, Sept. 11, 1925. Additional information contained in a marginal note by B. B. Janz.

9. BA, B. B. Janz to D. Toews. Kharkov, Sept. 17, 1925. See also FA, P. Froese to B. H. Unruh and A. J. Fast. Moscow, Oct. 10, 1925.

10. F. Mossenko, "Hollanders," *Visti*. Kharkov, Aug. 12, 1925. Similar sentiments were already expressed in FA, "A Good Lesson," *The Red Star*. Ekaterinoslav, Nov. 16, 1924.

11. See G. Petrovski, "Mennonites in the Ukraine," *Communist*. Kharkov, June 22, 1924; H. Unger, "Ein Paar Worte über die Emigration der Ukrainer Mennoniten nach Amerika," *Die Arbeit*, No. 20 (Sept. 15, 1923).

12. BA, B. B. Janz to D. Toews. Kharkov, Sept. 17, 1925.

13. BA, Telegram. B. B. Janz to D. Toews. Moscow, Nov. 24, 1925.

14. BA, B. B. Janz to D. Toews. Moscow, Nov. 24, 1925, p. 1.

15. *Ibid.*, p. 2.

16. The record of this interview has been preserved in both the Friesen and Janz archives under the title *Aktenvermerk*, June 16, 1926. It apparently represents B. H. Unruh's compilation of material received from B. B. Janz.

17. *Ibid.*, p. 1.

18. *Ibid.*, p. 2.

19. *Ibid.*, pp. 3, 4.

20. Printed in *Der Bote*, 1926, No. 19. See also "Aus einem Briefe aus Russland," *Die Mennonitische Rundschau*, Vol. 49 (No. 16), Apr. 21, 1926, p. 12.

21. JA, Protokoll des allukrainischen Kongresses des VBHH in der Ukraine vom 17.-20. Februar 1926 in Kharkov, pp. 18, 19.

22. BA, B. B. Janz to the Canadian Mennonite Board of Colonization. Moscow, Apr. 22, 1926, p. 1.

23. JA, "Zeit-Tafel für die Zeit des ersten Weltkrieges 1914 bis 1926," pp. 11, 12.

24. From original notes compiled by Jacob Hein of Tiege and published in A. A. Toews, *Mennonitische Maertyrer* (Winnipeg, 1954), II, pp. 484-87.

25. See B. H. Unruh, *Fügung und Führung im Mennonitischen Welthilfswerk 1920-1933* (Karlsruhe, 1966); *Vor den Toren Moskaus* (Clearbrook, B.C., 1961); H. L. Dyck, *Weimar Germany and Soviet Russia 1926-1933* (New York, 1966), pp. 162 ff.

26. A. Loewen and A. Friesen, *Die Flucht über den Amur* (Steinbach, Man., 1946); W. Quiring, *Russlanddeutsche suchen eine Heimat* (Karlsruhe, 1938).

27. "Ein Durcheinander vom Atlantic Park," *Der Bote*, Vol. 4, Nos. 15, 16 (Apr. 13 to Apr. 20, 1927); P. Reimer, "Die Lage der Zurürkgestellten in Southampton, England," *Die Mennonitische Rundschau*, Vol. 49, No. 45 (Nov. 10, 1926), p. 10; "Zu dem Aufsatz 'Atlantic Park,'" *Die Mennonitische Rundschau, Vol.* 50, No. 13 (Mar. 30, 1927), p. 4.

Appendix

The letters included in this collection were selected for the purpose of illustrating the inner character of the emigration movement. While originating from the pen of one man, *VBHH* chairman B. B. Janz, they in part portray the corporate experience of the Mennonite constituency in Russia between 1922 and 1925. The letters, chronologically arranged, reflect the tensions, anxieties, and hopes of those who participated in this dramatic exodus and graphically define some of the forces behind it. They represent only a very small segment of the massive emigration correspondence which has survived. In most cases the contents of the letters are selfevident. Occasionally an explanatory note has been added.

No. 1

Verband der Mennoniten
im Süden Russlands.   Kharkov
Februar, am letzten, 1922

> An die *Studienkommission der Mennoniten S. Russlands,* z. Z.
> im Auslande, Die Herren: A. A. Friesen, B. H. Unruh, C. H.
> Warkentin. An die *Algem. Commissie voor Buitenlandsche
> Nooden,* Holland.
> An die *American Mennonite Relief,* Scottdale, Pa.

BERICHT.

Es gibt Tage und Zeiten im Leben eines jeden Volkes, die wie Bergesgipfel über dem Niveau der übrigen Zeitläufe emporragen, und an die sich, einem Elmsfeuer gleich, das schicksalschwangere Wetterleuchten einer heraufbrechenden neuen Zeit heftet. Das sind die Kulminationspunkte in dem Werdegange von Generationen und Völkern, geschichtliche Brennpunkte, wo sich die Strahlenbündel der geistigen, seelischen und moralischen Kräfte eines Volkes in einem Augenblick treffen.

Auch die Geschichte unseres Volkes ist in den letzten Jahren reich an solchen Tagen gewesen; sie häuf en sich von Jahr zu Jahr, teils unabhängig von uns, teils aber auch gerade infolge eines kurzsichtigen Verhaltens unsererseits, und drängten zu e!ner letzten Entscheidung. Diese Entscheidung ist gefallen an jenem denkwürdigen 7. Februar 1922 in Ohrloff, sie ist getroffen worden im Namen der Mennonitenschaft von ihren gewählten Vertretern und Vertrauensmännern und hat infolgedessen die Bedeutung einer juridisch unanfechtbaren, historischen Begebenheit.

Ehe wir die verschlungenen Fäden der psychologischen und moralischen Motive aufrollen, welche die Entscheidung bedingten, ist es unseres Erachtens von Wichtigkeit, wenn Sie kurz über die chronologischen Ereignisse orientiert werden, die dieser Entscheidung vorangingen. Eigentlich müssten wir dann weit zurückgreifen und Momente berühren, die in die Zeit des grossen Krieges fallen. Doch sind die Ereignisse, die zum Teil von Ihnen (d.St.K.) selbst miterlebt und mitempfunden worden sind und jedenfalls unauslöschlich in Ihrem Gedächtnis verzeichnet stehen.

Der Krieg mit seiner Deutschenhetze, Liquidationsgesetz, Resolution in der Prischiber Kirche, Selbstschutz, Machnowschtschina, Umwälzungen jeglicher Art, etc., das sind die bitteren Wurzeln, die ihren bitteren Saft auch zu jener Entscheidung gegeben haben.

Dazu kommen dann die Ereignisse der letzten Jahre welche ihre Schlagschatten weit vorauf in die Zukunft geworfen haben.

1) Da war zuerst die fast unerträgliche Last der Einquartierung von Rotarmisten, welche am Anfange des Jahres 1921 einsetzte und mit kurzen Unterbrechungen bis zum heutigen Tage angehalten hat und heute schwerer denn je von der hungernden Bevölkerung empfunden wird.

2) Dann die Entwendung des Stimmrechts bei dem grössten Teil der Gesellschaft, wodurch dieselbe vom eigentlichen bürgerlichen Leben ausgeschlossen und zu rechtlosen Parias gemacht wurde.

3) Ferner von den örtlichen Behörden systematisch durchgeführter Niedergang des wirtschaftlichen Lebens, der sich besonders in dem fast gänzlichen Mangel an lebendigem Zug- und Arbeitsvieh bemerkbar macht. In manchen Dörfern sind beispielsweise kaum einzelne Gespanne brauchbarer Pferde aufzutreiben.

4) Die im Frühling 1921 mit aller Strenge vollzogene Getreideaufbringung war an und für sich schon schwer und hatte ausserdem noch eine Unmasse von Verhaftungen, Untersuchungen und Erpressungen im Gefolge.

5) Dazu kam dann die beispiellose Dürre, welche die Ernte fast total vernichtete und zum erstenmal das Schreckensgespenst des Hungers heraufrückte.

6) Die im Herbste einsetzende Eintreibung der Naturalsteuer spottet ob ihrer Unsinnigkeit jeglicher Beschreibung. Fast jedes Dorf sollte 1000-2000 Pud Getreide mehr zahlen, als die gesamte Ernte betrug, von Gemüse ganz abgesehen.

7) Auf diesem Wege spielten sich dann die wüstesten und unglaublichsten Fälle von Erpressungen und Drohungen jeglicher Art ab.

8) Auch das Verhalten unserer Landlosenkomitees, die sich aber fast ausschliesslich aus fremden Elementen rekrutierten, war ein starker Keil, der die Bevölkerung von der heimatlichen Scholle losmacht. Denn die Schikanen, welche in manchen Dörfern von diesem Institut ausgingen, sind für europäische Begriffe vom Recht der Persönlichkeit einfach unverständlich.

9) Nicht unerwähnt darf die Sorge ums tägliche Brot bleiben, welche immer dominierender hervortrat.

10) Endlich kam im November der letzte Wirbelsturm in Gestalt der "Tscheka" (ausserordentliche Kommission zur Bekämpfung der Konterevolution), der vielen das Leben gekostet hat. Manchmal, wenn man an all die Gefangenen zurückdenkt, so ist man versucht mit Hesekiel auszurufen: "Und ich allein war noch übrig."

Es hätte dieses letzten Aktes wahrlich nicht bedurft, um uns unserer Stellung zur Auswanderungsfrage klar zu werden; aber sicher ist, dass er dermassen die Wunde vertieft hat, dass eine vollkommene Heilung nicht mehr zu denken ist.

Das zustimmende Verhalten unseres Volkes zur Auswanderungsfrage kennzeichnet sich am besten durch folgende Steigerungsstufen:

Stufe 1. Bei ihr sprechen hauptsächlich wirtschaftliche Gründe mit. Naturalsteuer, wirtschaftlicher Ruin, Brotmangel, das sind die Motive der Auswanderungslust. Sollte aber hierin ein Wandel eintreten, so würde sich auch die Stimmung wandeln. Auf dieser Stufe steht die Bevölkerung der Krim und Sagradovka.

Stufe 2. Sozusagen der Komparativ. Zum wirtschaftlichen Massstab kommt hier der soziale und allgemeinmenschliche, welcher an die Zeitverhältnisse angelegt wird und zu einem negativen Ergebnis führt. So stehen die Kolonien an der Molotschna, die Alt-Kolonie, die Flüchtlinge aus den Reihen der Gutsbesitzer.

Stufe 3. Der Superlativ. Ausser und neben den oben angeführten kommen hier hauptsächlich ethische und sittlich-religiöse Momente in Betracht. Das sind die tiefer und weiter Schauenden aus allen Schichten und Orten unserer Gesellschaft, besonders in den Stammkolonien, die sich auf keine Kompromisse, auf keinen Wiederaufbau mehr einlassen können, weil sie erkannt haben, dass nicht blos die wirtschaftliche, sondern auch soziale und sittliche Grundlage dazu fehlt, welche allein massgebend für uns sein kann. Denn das System der kommunistischen Beeinflussung, welches gegenwärtig konsequent und mit Nichtachtung aller Prinzipien der Glaubensfreiheit durchgeführt wird, geht gegen unsere Ideale und kann deshalb von uns nicht akzeptiert werden. Deshalb kann unseres Bleibens hier nicht sein. Freilich, ein Teil der Gesellschaft wird bleiben und—qualitativ untergehen. Damit müssen wir rechnen. Doch wollen wir auch für sie versuchen, eine wirtschaftliche Basis zu schaffen, wovon die beigelegte Kopie der Eingabe Zeugnis ablegt. Mit dieser Eingabe haben wir auch für die anderen die entsprechende Losung ausgegeben. Möge Gott sie anerkennen. . . .

Mit brüderlichem Gruss (gez.) B. Janz, Ph. Cornies.

No. 2

Kharkoff 1/III/22

AN UNSERE STUDIENKOMMISSION IM AUSLANDE!

Liebe Brüder!

Möchte im Nachfolgenden aus der Fülle des Materials für Berichterstattung das Wesentlichste herausgreifen und Ihnen vortragen. Das wir vor allen Dingen konstatieren müssen, dass die allgemeine Lage nicht allein täglich, nein stündlich haltloser wird, und wir und alle unsere Lieben sich mitten drin befinden, in dem brausenden tosenden Meere, wo die Wellen tatsächlich über unserm Haupte zusammenschlagen, das ist sehr, sehr traurig! Und ein grosses Sterben bricht nun auch für uns Mennoniten an. Ich habe das nie erwarten können, erstlich dass wir so sehr des tägl. Brotes beraubt wären und dann, dass die so opferfreudige Hilfe, die dort das Aeusserste tut, um uns zu retten, so unerreichbar für uns bleibt. Denn bis morgen den 1. März hat noch niemand ein Stück Brot, von dem was uns längst versprochen, erreichen können. Hier in Kharkoff liegt es und ist nicht vom Fleck zu bewegen. In Russland sind einige wenige, die leben, viele vegetieren und der grosse hungernde Süden stirbt! Muss da bis zum Mai von dem Kadaver aber ein Gestank gen Himmel steigen! Brüder, der rasende Niedergang benimmt uns fast die Ueberlegung hier weiter zu arbeiten, abgesehen von dem Treibsand, auf dem man zu bauen hat! *Um jeden* Preis, möchte man sagen, hinaus!

Nun aber, wenn auch nicht ein Gosen ist, wenn die Vorteile des Bodens, des Klima, der Naturreichtümer auch nicht in ein Paradies zusammengedrängt sind; es geht einfach nicht mehr. Nur noch der Tod—an Leib, Seele und Geist ist da.

Unser Volk ist noch rettungsfähig und willig—lassen wir diese Gnadenzeit nicht vorübergehen. Und sollten die politischen Ereignisse sich auch überstürzen, das Oberste zu unterst kehren, unsere Leute haben den Entschluss gefasst—hinaus und werden ihm zum grössten Teile treu bleiben. . . .

Ich weise noch einmal darauf hin, dass, sobald die Erlaubnis zur Emigration erfolgt, die ganze Masse der Flüchtlinge in Aktion gerät, die sind stehenden Fusses fertig, aber auch Tausende andere, Tausende sind bereit die Familie an die Hand zu nehmen and zu gehen—leer wie Lot aus Sodom. Zu wenig gesagt, nein Zehntausende! Vom Vermögen retten redet kaum jemand.

No. 3

Kharkoff, d. 7. III. 22

AN DIE STUDIENKOMMISSION DER MENNONITEN DES SUEDEN RUSSLANDS IM AUSLANDE

Zu Händen des Herrn Lic. Theol. B. H. Unruh

Lieber Bruder Unruh,

Du kannst Dir kaum vorstellen mit welchem Enthusiasmus, mit welcher Freude, wir hier Deine resp. Eure Berichte empfangen, mit welchem Heisshunger daheim jede, auch die kleinste Nachricht, verschlungen wird, welch ein Legendenkreis sich um den kleinen Kern der Wahrheit in der Gesellschaft bildet. . . . Die ganze Lage ist noch nicht genug stabil, besonders in den untersten Instanzen. Ueberhaupt scheint die ganze Situation wieder mehr gespannt zu werden. Die Kluft zwischen Soll und Haben, zwischen Produktion und Verbrauch, zwischen Angebot und Nachfrage wird auf allen Gebieten täglich weiter und tiefer und treibt mit rasender Schnelligkeit in die dunkle Zukunft—in die Nacht, ins Bodenlose—zur Katastrophe. Welcher Art diese letztere nun sein könnte, entzieht sich ganz und gar unserer Beurteilung, denn es sind der Katastrophen und Krisen schon so viele und so schwere gekommen, dass etwa nur ein allgemeiner Untergang eine Ausnahme machen könnte.

Es geht zum Frühjahr. Die Vorräte im Lande sind herausgefischt oder von der Bevölkerung selbst verzehrt. Auch die nicht vom Hunger betroffenen Gebiete werden wohl kaum durchhalten bis zur Ernte, haben zum Teil ungenügend Saatgut. Wir wollen auch gewisse lokale Verhältnisse im kleinen Rahmen als besser stehen lassen. Die Teuerung ist jetzt rapid angewachsen, wenn das Tempo der letzten Wochen für die kommenden Monate bis zur Ernte eingehalten wird, so kann kein Mensch überdenken, was wir im Juni, Juli haben werden und ziehen wir die Konsequenz ruhig weiter—was infolge der Teuerung von 1921 auch im Juli des nächsten 1923 Jahres noch für eine Summe von ungestilltem Leid sein muss. . . .

Im ganzen bewundere ich die Führung der göttlichen Vorsehung. Das grosse Leid unserer Gemeinden hier, die Liebe zu den Brüdern schliesst die Brüder dort in aller Welt zusammen und eine starke Bruderhand streckt sich uns Versinkenden entgegen und der Pulsschlag echter Liebe durchflutet die Herzen von Meer zu Meer, von Pol zu Pol. Und jedenfalls fliesst durch den Zusammenschluss und die gemeinsame Hilfsaktion den Gemeinden selbst dort mancher Segen zu. Und was mag unser Vater im Himmel an ewigen Gütern für Herz und Gemüt in den Gemeinden dort und hier in Vorbereitung haben, dürfte nicht eine allgemeine Neubelebung, ein neuer Geistesfrühling durch die Gemeinden gehen? Sollten wir wirklich nur eine zeitweilige Begeisterung zwecks leiblicher Rettung zum Ziele aller Führung Gottes konstatieren, um dann womöglich das beste Stück Land auf dem Erdball zu belegen und bei den besten weitesten Privilegien die besten Farmer zu sein, um wieder— in ausgiebigster Weise dem Materialismus zu dienen? Da sei Gott vor! Die mit Tränen säen, werden mit Freuden ernten. Und auf diese Freudenernte rechne ich so bestimmt, als wir nun das Tränensäen bereits Jahre lang haben.

Zum andern ist mir der Gedanke gross geworden, wie der grosse Gott schon rechtzeitig die Studienkommission hinausgesandt und Vorsorge getroffen, da während es hier in den letzten Jahren systematisch zu Ende geht und man am Rande des Abgrundes angekommen, im Begriff hinabzustürzen, während man hier die ganze Zeit in voller Ungewissheit über das Ergehen der Studienkommission ist, während man im Geiste schon nicht nur dem Geiste, sondern auch dem Leibe das Grab gräbt—es schlägt also die Stunde des Verderbens: da kommt die erste reale, lebenswarme Botschaft in Person und legt Wege des Lebens dar: Was wollt Ihr? Hier ist die reale Grundlage für ein Endweder—Oder! Wo könnten wir hin, falls unsere Errettung nicht mit den Jahren schon vorbereitet wäre und nun im entscheidenden Moment mit fertigem Plane vortreten dürfte! Es ist grossartig.

Es is aber nur die erste Hälfte—die Realisierung, die zweite Hälfte steht noch aus und soll nun dran kommen. Welch grosse vielfach von uns unabhängige Faktoren kommen da in Betracht.

No. 4

Kharkoff, den 12. III. 22

Teurer Bruder Unruh

. . . Du hast recht, lieber Bruder Unruh, dass hier die schwersten Entscheidungen zu treffen sind! Dass man dann weiter vielfach solche Entscheidungen auf sein einzelnes Gewissen (wenn natürlich auch nicht ganz allein) nehmen muss, lässt einen bisweilen unendlich schwer tragen. Unsere grosse Gesellschaft, die Gemeinden bringen mir unbedingtes Vertrauen entgegen, aber eben darum möchte ich auch alles mit ihnen beraten und entscheiden. Das ist nun aber gar nicht möglich.

Die Lage zu Hause unendlich schwer: Hast wohl mal am Schmelz-ofen vor dem kleinen Beobachtungsfensterchen gestanden, wenns da drinnen siedet und brauset und zischt, wenn der riesige Ofen selbst in jeder Faser zittert—wenn da drinnen unter Feuers Hitze alles vergeht?— Es vergeht! . . . Uebrigens, meine Lieben, ist es klar, im ganzen Volk kann nur der grosse Gott monatelang unterhalten! Darum bitte ich im Namen meiner unglücklichen Leute: Mit Gottes Hilfe jede Faser angestrengt, um uns herauszureissen, das ist wirkliche volle, doppelte, dauernde Rettung! Ich wiederhole: Es wird draussen in einem freien stillen nicht hungernden Lande leichter sein, eine Ansiedlung durchzumachen, als in einem rein ausgesogenen total ruinierten, hoffnungslos hungernden Lande sich wieder aufzubauen. Dass ich heute diesen Jammer meines Volkes mit erleben muss, macht mich elend, alt und krank! Ich dachte damals, es gäbe nichts Schlimmeres als Blumenort! (bei jenem Massenmord.) . . .

Soll ich auch von mir schreiben? Nein, ich habe bei meinem Volke auszuharren, mit ihm weiter zu leiden, wie gross etwa auch die Gefahr für mich wäre. Mitarbeitern daheim gehts auch schwer. Sodann könntet Ihr vielleicht auf meinen Namen in Kharkoff, Butowsky Wjesd N 9 an der Belgorodskaja ein paar Lebensmittelpackete senden? Meine Lebensunter-haltung hier wird problematisch.

No. 5

März 15, 1922

An den Sekretär der südruss. Studienkommission der Menno-niten Herrn Lic. theol. B. H. Unruh.

Lieber Bruder Unruh!

Es geht eine schonungslose Liquidation jeder Art von Existenz vor sich! Und sie beginnt sich auch für die drohend zu machen, die die Geister riefen. Russland wird je länger desto mehr Staat des Schreckens, ein "Jammertal" im buchstäblichsten Sinne des Wortes—ein Grab! Der Gestank von den unbeerdigten Kadavern muss die kommende milde Frühjahrsluft verpesten. Darum möchte auch wohl jeder fliehen! . . .

Und wenn niemand gehen wollte, und wenn sie alle bleiben wollten wegen der—sagen wir hoffnungsvoll—wirtschaftlichen Perspektive in Russlands Zukunft, ich habe liebe Kinder, Buben und Mädel, ich gehe bestimmt, ich gehe immer—vor allem um der Kinder willen. Mich ge-lüstet nicht nach dem schnöden Lohn. Wir haben die Zukunft des Volkes zu retten! Der aufgerührte russische Sumpf wird noch Jahrzehnte stinken und zersetzend wirken, darum eile! rette deine—deiner Kinder Seele. Und Gott sei Dank! Wie freue ich mich, dass in unsern Volksschichten noch soviel gesunde Ueberlegung, sittlicher Gehalt—mit einem Wort—Glauben ist. . . . versprecht uns Zustände, welche Ihr wollt, in dem Kern unserer Volksseele ist der Entschluss unwiderruflich herangereift.

No. 6

7. April, 1922

An unsere im Auslande weilende Studienkommission der Mennoniten Süd-Russlands. Zu Händen des Sekretärs derselben, Herrn Lic. theol. B. H. Unruh

Lieber Bruder Unruh,

Der Wochenschluss drängt zu einer Berichterstattung. Das Aprilwetter trägt uns den Frühling ins Land. Wirklich auch in diesem Lande wollen milde Lüfte wehen, warme Sonnenstrahlen leuchten und wärmen; wir treten ins Freie, atmen tief auf, versuchen durch Umschau uns zu orientieren: Sind wir noch wir geblieben oder andere geworden? Die ganze Psychologie hat sich geändert, weil ringsherum alles alles anders geworden ist; alles Frohe, Sichere, Heimliche oder Heimatliche, jede Unterlage für Zufriedenheit, Arbeit, Fleiss, für Arbeitsmöglichkeit ist weg. Ich bin nicht mehr ich; oder meine Gegend, mein Dorf, die Wiese, der Garten, das Haus—alles mit den lebhaftesten Spuren fremder Prinzipien mit Maximen belegt, die mich in meinem Haus eines entsetzlichen Todes sterben lassen. Der Hungertod ist nur eine Form; das Zugrundegehen kleidet sich auch noch in andere Formen. Eines nehme ich bis auf den heutigen Tag nicht auf einem Gebiete wahr: nirgends Aprilwetter, nirgends Frühlingswehen, neue Lebensanfänge. Darum sind wir so fremd, haben keine Heimat mehr! . . .

Die Auswanderung ist gerade der Teil meiner öffentlichen Arbeit, woran die Bevölkerung das meiste—ein brennendes Interesse bekundet. Was die Landfrage betrifft, so fragt kaum ein Mensch darnach; da muss ich, in dessen Fach es eigentlich nicht schlägt, an die Zukunft der Kolonien denken. Denn jedenfalls werden die Mennoniten hier noch Land brauchen und wenn auch nur um bis zur Emigration nicht zu verhungern. Manche jedenfalls auch länger. Aber zur Zeit ist die Lage so kritisch, so hoffnungslos, so traurig, dass es keinen andern Lebensweg zu geben scheint, als auszuwandern. Ob man Augenblicksmensch für die Gegenwart oder denkender Mensch über die Gegenwart hinaus ist, ändert nicht viel an der Sache. Denn heute sterben in der Ukraine täglich hunderte Menschen, von den unsern einige und für den nächsten Winter wirds jedenfalls schwerer. 1) Das empfangene Saatgut wird meistens aufgegessen. 2) Das Arbeitsvieh ist meistens hin. 3) Es gibt keine frische Kleidung. 4) Weil kaum etwas gesät wird, gibts nicht Stroh als Heizmaterial für den Winter oder Futter für die Kuh. 5) Der Sturm vom 3. und 4. April hat der jungen Wintersaat enormen Schaden gemacht. Sollten schliesslich unsere Kolonien, wo wir mal die günstigste Werndung annehmen wollen, wirtschaftlich mit viel Saathirse und einigen Traktoren bedacht werden, dass sie zum Leben haben, dann—der Hunger rings umher, der seine Wellen schäumend in die Kolonien schlagen müsste. Weil aber alle Ansiedlungen bis auf einige Ausnahmen nicht Saatgut haben so weiss ich auch nicht wie diese durchkommen wollen. Das ist die reale Grundlage der Gegenwart. Soll ich noch die Zukunft beschreiben? Was etwa für staatliche Verhältnisse wir noch für die nächsten Jahre bei der günstigsten Evolution haben müssen—an den Orten? Ich verzichte darauf.

No. 7

Written shortly after the Kharkov Government authorized emigration to Paraguay for Mennonite refugees—April 24, 1922. On April 25 the VMSR Charter (VBHH) was registered. After a long and discouraging struggle Janz was filled with hope and a sense of urgency.

Kharkoff, den 27. April 1922

An die Studienkomission der Mennoniten Süd-Russlands im Auslande— Zu Händen des Sekretärs derselben, Herrn B. H. Unruh

. . . Dass hier nun unsere gesamte Bruderschaft im Auslande mit Leib und Seele dabei sein muss, ist mir schon klar. "Das Werk ist gross und weit und wir sind nicht zerstreuet von einander," . . . dürften wir vielleicht den Bibelvers Nehemia 4:13 für unsern Fall verändern. Nicht wahr, unsere Brüder sind nicht innerlich zerstreut von einander: sie sind ein Volk von Brüdern! Dann aber sagen wir buchstäblich mit dem folgenden Vers: "An welchem Ort ihr nun die Posaune tönen hört, dahin versammelt euch zu uns. Unser Gott wird für uns streiten." Und in Gottes Namen darf ich Euch verkündigen, Die Tür ist auf! Nun den Esel her, der dem Samariter zur Verfügung steht! Und diese Flüchtlinge sind buchstäblich unter die Mörder Gefallene. Um Gottes und der Menschen willen—rasch! Nun die Zeit aufbrauchen, denn es ist Gnadenzeit. Wie lange und wie weit es gehen wird, entzieht sich unserer Beurteilung. Heute!

No. 8

An die American Mennonite Relief
Scottdale, Pa. USA.

30. April 1922

Teure Brüder im Komitee!

Es ist mir Herzensbedürfnis vor meiner Abreise in den Süden, die in den nächsten Tagen erfolgen soll, noch mal von Kharkoff her direkt in Ihren Arbeits-und Bruderkreis zu treten, um vor den Vertretern der ganzen amerikanischen Mennoniten-Union Rechenschaft abzulegen über den Dienst für unsere Gemeinden in Kharkoff, über den augenblicklichen Stand der Dinge, sowie um die Sorgen für die Zukunft miteinander zu teilen.

Vor allen Dingen ist es mir eine grosse Freude, Ihre legitimen Vertreter, die Br. Hiebert und Krehbiel, im Süden im Kreise der Unsern zu wissen, mitten in dem tausendfachen Leid des so unglücklichen Russlands, umwogt und umbrandet von dem Jammer unseres Volkes. Gestatten Sie mir, im Namen der Gemeinden Ihnen einzeln warm die Hand zu drücken mit einem "Vergelts Gott" aus tiefstem Herzen! Das vergessen wir Ihnen nie! Es war ein grosser Moment für uns, als die ersten sechs Waggon Lebensmittel in Alexandrowsk bei Chortitza und gleich darauf drei von diesen Waggons in Halbstadt einfuhren. Im Laufe der Zeit ist nun immer nachgeschoben worden und nun sind schon Tausende bis in den Mai vom Hungertode gerettet worden. Das hat auf Geist und Seele und Leib eine entscheidende Wirkung; aber die grösste moralische

Bedeutung für die Gemeinden gewinnt der persönliche Zuspruch, das persönliche Eingehen in die Nöte, persönlich "Weinet mit den Weinenden." Dass Ihr vom Komitee für solchen Engeldienst ein paar Brüder gesandt habt, das wollte ich hiermit auf Euer Konto *gut* angeschrieben haben!

... Wenn Gott uns hier hat vor der Regierung Gnade finden lassen, dass wir Euch die längst ersehnte Botschaft melden dürfen. Die Tür ist geöffnet! Wir dürfen! Mit Erlaubnis von Gott und Menschen! Dann denke ich, spürt Ihrs, dass nun nur noch eine starke Bruderhand mit einem warmen treuen Herzen fehlt; dass unser Vater sie bei Euch sucht. Nachdem Gott mir Gnade gab für das Öffnen der Tür, ist mir als Aufgabe nur noch geblieben, Ihnen dort das zu sagen und dann später Ihnen die Leute einzuschiffen. Dass es ausserdem notwendig sein müsste, die Brüder drüben von der Notwendigkeit der Aktion zu überzeugen, kann mir kaum in den Sinn kommen: weiss ich doch, wie sie seit Jahr und Tag mit gelitten haben. Weiss ich doch, wie bewegt sie gesessen in jenen Tagen und den Mitteilungen der Zeugen menschlichen Elends Unruh, Friesen und Warkentin gelauscht und Vorsätze zur Rettung gefasst. Jetzt ist der Tag gekommen.

Jetzt ist der Tag des Heils! Wie sich ferner die Verhältnisse gestalten werden, bleibt der dunklen Zukunft vorbehalten. Weils nun geht, sollten die Emigranten in ein paar Monaten hinüber geschafft sein.

No. 9

5. Mai, 1922

An die Studienkommission der Mennoniten Süd-Russlands im Auslande an die Herren A. A. Friesen und K. H. Warkentin zur Zeit in Nord-Amerika.

Teure Mitarbeiter,

Wenn ich von Freude in der Arbeit sprechen soll, so würde ich nur eines zu nennen wissen trotz der nunmehr scheinbar erlangten guten Position im Centrum: Die Freude für die Gesellschaft, die demnächst zu Ihnen hinausdarf! Und ich muss sagen, durchweg solides Publikum. Sehen Sie, die Vertriebenen haben früher meistens in bessern Verhältnissen gelebt, sind mit produktiver Arbeit gut vertraut, haben einen Wirtschaftssinn und Wirtschaftserfahrung, sind von Intellekt . . . Man kann sich dort gratulieren zu dieser Kategorie. Zudem sind sie nun durch viel Trübsal gegangen, haben innerlich viel durchgemacht. Sie gehen aber, will ich meinen, innerlich nicht als Zerschlagene, Verzagte, Pessimisten—sondern als Geläuterte. . . .

Ihr
B. Janz

No. 10

27. Mai, 1922

A. A. Friesen, Leiter der Studienkommission

Der 19. Mai brachte Herrn Krehbiel und mich bis Halbstadt, und am folgenden Tage kam ich endlich daheim an. Damit war ich in das eigentliche grosse Notstandsgebiet getreten. Uebrigens kann das Elend im Chortitzer Rayon nicht kleiner sein. Hier wirkte es systematisch und dauernd auf mich ein. Die Wogen der Not umbranden mich. Auf Schritt und Tritt zuckt die Seele zusammen: T. Ewert-Waldheim, Mitglied des Rates, ein populärer tüchtiger Landwirt, der als neuer Delegat ins Ausland im Januar gewählt worden war, ist an Typhus gestorben; einer von vielen, die zum Teil an dieser oder jener epidemischen Krankheit, zum Teil direkt vor Hunger nicht ausgehalten haben. Da und dort hat der Tod seinen Kandidaten noch einmal eine Lebensfrist gewährt—wie lange? Ferner stellen die Aerzte für die nächsten warmen Monate noch ein Draufgehen einer Kategorie der Gesellschaft an Unterernährung fest. Die Gesellschaft bekundete die lebhafteste Freude des Wiedersehens mit ihrem längst erwarteten Vertreter, für mich war es durchgängig ein Stich ins Herz. Wie sahen die meisten Leute aus? Das Menetekel in Babylons Königspalast konnte nicht deutlicher ausgedrückt sein, als die Spuren tiefsten Elends in den Gesichtern unseres Volkes hier. Mit David, dem einstigen Flüchtling zu Sauls Zeiten, muss man konstatieren: "Wahrlich, es ist nur ein Schritt zwischen mir und dem Tode!"

Es ist ja Tatsache, dass die eingetretene Hilfe noch lange nicht in das entsprechende Verhältnis zur Not hat treten können, allein das, was bereits geleistet worden ist durch zehntausende von liebewarmen Herzen und Händen, liefert uns den schlagenden Beweis, welche prinzipielle Bedeutung man der Hilfe beimessen muss. Es ist augenscheinlich, dass in unseren Kolonien das Massensterben mit all den entsetzlichen Begleiterscheinungen, wie wir sie in weiterer und näherer Umgebung beobachten, wüten müsste, ausgenommen—vielleicht—den Kannibalismus.

Die Zukunft liegt vor uns schwarz wie die Nacht! Immer noch tasten wir nach der Basis für eine geregelte, gesicherte, ruhige Existenz. Die Landfrage und mit ihr verbunden die Besorgnis vor einem nationalen Konglomerat durch Zwischensiedlung von anderen Volksangehörigen, die Naturalsteuer sowie allerlei andere grosse Auflagen, die Soldatennot, die gänzlich unzureichende Aussaat, sowie das Verderben eines grossen Teiles derselben etc. etc. lassen unsere an Erfahrung so reichen Familienväter durchaus nicht zur Ruhe kommen.

Die *Ausdauer*, die *Zähigkeit* der mennonitischen Kolonisten zur Erreichung der von Ihnen gesteckten Ziele ist bekannt, sie kann auch geschichtlich vielfach nachgewiesen werden. Es muss Staunen erregen, wie man bei der Frühjahrsbestellung den Kampf ums Dasein geführt hat. Erstlich in der Beschaffung von Objekten zur Aussaat, indem man das so dringend Notwendige zum Munde absparte oder auch unentbehrliche Stücke an Kleidung oder Hausgeräten veräusserte. Dann in der Bestellung des Ackers, wo man alle möglichen, schier bis zur Verzweiflung oder an Tollheit und Wahnwitz grenzende Versuche und Anstrengungen gemacht hat, das edle Saatkorn in den Boden zu bringen. Versuche, die an die unkultivierten Naturvölker erinnern. Ihre Vertreter haben zum Teil Gelegenheit gehabt, solches zu beobachten. In dieser Richtung, hat man ein Examen bestanden. Die nun wieder folgende grosse Dürre, dann die Erdstürme des Winters und Frühlings haben bei allem Vorhergesagten die Hoffnung nicht aufkommen lassen. Alle Mann auf Deck war die Losung—ohne Zuversicht, ohne Hoffnung!—

No. 11

25. Juli 1922.

An die Studienkomission der Mennoniten Süd-Russlands im
Auslande Herrn A. A. Friesen
Herrn B. H. Unruh

Liebe Brüder!

. . . Es war einmal! Einmal hatten wir eine schöne, schöne Molotschna—unsere kleine edle Welt, voll Lust und Leben! Jedenfalls aber
auch mehr Sünde und Unrecht als man gemeiniglich glaubte! Sie
muss. . . ! Doch will ich unbedingt auch die Umgebung in ihrer Gesin-
nung und ihrer Stellung zu den Kolonien ausser acht lassen; die sind es
eben, die ihnen den Garaus machen. . . .

Wie muss es nun weiter? Es gähnt vor uns ein dunkles, nacht-
schwarzes Etwas—Abgrund—Chaos—oder was mans nennen soll. Ach
könnten wir noch ein Jahr weiter voraus sehen—wenigstens ein paar
Monate, vielleicht ists auch so trübe nicht—

No. 12

9. September 1922

Herr A. A. Friesen, den Vertreter des Mennonitischen Verbandes in Amerika.

. . . Die Hungersnot ist gross. Daher ist die Frage der Uebersiedlung
der Flüchtlinge eine brennende. Es sind doppelte Ursachen, die zu so-
fortigem Handeln treiben. Und wie man hier ohne diese Hilfe diesen
Winter durchkommen soll, ist mir Nacht, ein Bauen ist für diese Leute
ja auch in Zukunft ausgeschlossen. Wo sollen sie hin? Ich entschuldige
mich für diese Erklärungen, Sie wissen dort ja manches, doch lange
nicht alles; ich selbst kenne die nackte Wirklichkeit zu wenig. . . .

Und nun lasst Euch erbitten, meine Lieben! Machts denen, die da
gehen und denen die da bleiben leichter! Und wenn ich Ihnen erkläre,
dass es notwendig ist sofort zu handeln, wenn überhaupt, dann glauben
Sie mirs

Also, es wird mit Schmerzen gewartet! . . .

Gruss
B. B. Janz

No. 13

Abdruck in der Presse oder sonst Verbreitung strenge verboten.

Am 31. Dez. 1922 und I. Jan. 1923.

An die leitenden Brüder der Konferenzen und Organisationen
der Mennoniten in Amerika.

Teure Brüder.

Gott zum Gruss und unsern Herrn Jesum Christum zum Trost an
der Schwelle des neuen Jahres.

Heute geht das alte schwere, vielbewegte Jahr 1922 zur Ruh. So
mancher der Unsern hat sich nach mühevollem Ringen im Laufe des
Jahres ebenfalls zur Ruh legen müssen. Und so Vieles und Manches ist
uns ausser dem Tode der Lieben begegnet—Jammer und Not und Herze-

leid. Dazwischen viele warme lichte Sonnenstrahlen von den lieben Brüdern und Schwestern in Amerika und Europa. Daher sind unsere Gemeinden, abgesehen von einzelnen Personen oder engern Kreisen, nicht verzagt: es ist die Hoffnung geblieben. Das Brot für den Hungernden, das Kleid für den Nackenden, die tätige Bereitwilligkeit, den Heimatlosen eine neue Heimat zu geben, haben uns laut bezeugt, dass Gott noch Gnade für uns hat.

Wie weit der Ernst Gottes mit uns in die Tiefe ging, haben wir erfahren; er dauert auch noch an und führt einige Kreise noch tiefer in diesem Winter. Wie weit die Gnade Gottes entweder direkt, oder weiter indirekt durch Vermittelung der Brücke uns hinaus aus der Tiefe führen kann—Gott weiss es. Es ist aber unmöglich, in so unbestimmter Lage zu schweben, und unmöglich können die Gemeinden drüben forttragen an der schweren Last der russischen Not in die unbestimmte Zukunft, ohne ein Ende abzusehen. Es möchte sonst das Seil der Liebe abreissen, und die Müdigkeit vermöchte es kaum, es neu zu knüpfen. Und dann?

Was wird uns 1923 bringen?

Jedenfalls wird 1923 in mancher Beziehung entscheidend werden für die Weiterentwickelung unseres Volkes in Russland. Doch die bange Frage ist: Gehts aufwärts zum Heil für uns u. unsere Kinder, für Gemeinde, Schule und Haus? oder noch weiter niederwärts in die Nacht der Verzweiflung, der Verirrung, der Sünde, des Elendes und Todes?

Ich weiss, liebe Brüder, Ihr könnt nicht recht glücklich sein, wenn wirs nicht auch werden. Das macht den Menschen glücklich, wenn er andere glücklich macht. Wie habt Ihr gesorgt and gebangt, als es immer nicht möglich war uns zu erreichen mit Eurer werten Hilfe.

Ihr habt mithin schon damals von Herzen mitgetragen an der grossen Not, wo es noch nicht möglich war, ihr nahe zu treten.

Ach könnte ich noch einmal glücklich sein mit meinem Volke!

Wie habe ich gehadert mit Ihm nach dem Blumenorter Blutbad und -brand. Wie unbegreiflich bis zum Irrewerden (bis zum Aergern an Ihm—Mtt. 11, 6) waren mir seine Wege, nicht in meinem persönlichen Erleben in erster Linie, sondern in dem Dahingeben in grausame Not und Tod so mancher teuren, von Herzen gottergebenen, hochgeschätzten Bruders, die Erschiessung von J. Sudermann in Halbstadt, von P. Schmidt, J. Sudermann, Teichgröb, Friesen—Blumenort; von David Dicks, Apanlee, usw. usw. Ja, wenns eine Glaubensverfolgung gewesen wäre—damals, dann hätte ich eine zum Teil befriedigende Erklärung. Von dem Verlust an Hab und Gut wollen wir nicht reden. Ich breche ab, denn es wallet ein Sturm herauf und stelle das Verständnis der unbegreiflichen Wege Gottes ab bis zu seiner Stunde,—wohl erst droben daher.

Aber nur wir, die wir noch leben?

Sollten wir etwa von der Kugel, dem Feuer und Schwert übergeblieben sein, um im Hungerelend zu verderben, mehr noch, in die Macht des Atheismus, des Sozialismus, des europäischen Heidentums zu versinken?

Wir sind zu schwach uns selbst zu helfen.

Wir haben gesündigt und Er hat unsere Sünde gesucht und gefunden und heimgesucht. Schwer heimgesucht bis auf diese Stunde. Wir sehen unser doppeltes Elend. Wir haben den ernsten Willen, dass es besser werde mit uns: mit unsern Kindern ein fröhliches, friedliches glückliches Leben in seinen Wegen.

Es fehlt noch viel. Man mag dort sagen oder schreiben, wie schlecht die russ. Mennoniten hier u. da gewesen sind. Ihr Lieben, wir haben wirklich viel auf dem Kerbholz, mehr als Ihr wisst; so viel, dass es gar nicht anders ging, als dass Christus für sie sterben musste, dass es nicht anders geht, dass Christus jeden persönlich zu neuem Leben erwecken muss, dass es nicht anders ist, als dass jeder der droben eingeht, aus Gnaden selig wird.

Wir sind ernstlich krank. Und im Laufe der letzten 7 Jahre hat sich der Zustand erschreckend verschlimmert. Wir erkennen uns selbst nicht wieder u. entsetzen uns über Manches. Aber zieht bitte in Betracht, dass man im schweren Krankheitsstadium sich selbst vielfach nicht Rechenschaft geben kann über seine Handlungen. Fragt uns auch mit dem grossen Meister: willst du gesund werden?

Was sind auch für Stürme von Versuchung entfesselt worden, jeder Kerker auf, Sünde, Schande und Gewalttat obenauf; Tag für Tag, Monat für Monat, Jahr für Jahr; Man hat gestrauchelt, ja.

Wer sich dünken lässt, er stehe, mag wohl zusehen, dass er nicht falle.

Wenn es einerseits nach Gottes Zulassung Menschenhände waren, die uns in bodenloses Elend hinabstürzen, richtiger hinabziehen durften, so dürfen es andererseits auch wieder liebe Menschen sein, die da *selbst* pflegen und zahlen und sagen: "Pflege sein (Du, C.P.R.), und so du mehr bedarfst, will ich zahlen, wenn ich wiederkomme." Und wenns im Evangelium ein Wildfremder war, wie viel lieber denn die Brüder und Schwestern, die alle ihre Hand an das Seil der Liebe gelegt, ziehen ohne Ermüden bis auf den heutigen Tag und heissen dem Br. Miller samt allen den andern Gesellen resp. Gesandten: Pfleget ihrer—bis sie kommen (statt: bis wir wiederkommen)!

Und wenn der liebe Gott ihrer vielen ins Herz gelegt hat, wirklich zu kommen—nach Amerika, wer wollte wohl im Ernste dagegen sein, oder mit der Schulter zucken: Es geht mich nichts an?—Sind *Sie dort* nicht sämtliche Kinder derer, die einem innern Zuge folgend kamen? Ausser einigen, die als Emigranten selbst gingen und noch heute leben: Alle guten Mennoniten drüben, die sich frei in Kirche Schule und Haus bewegen, ihrem Gott dienen nach Wissen und Gewissen und sicher wohnen unter ihrem Weinstocke und Feigen—, meinetwegen auch Pappelbaum sind ein beredtes Zeugnis, eine wandelnde Reklame für die Emigration.

Wir erwägen diese ernste Sache immer wieder, zumal die eingetretene Verzögerung uns besonders Zeit und Gelegenheit dazu gibt.

In dem Wirken für die Auswanderung ist vordem kein Hindernis gewesen, immer offene Türen. Und auch diese scheinbare Widerwärtigkeit dient dazu, um die Sache auf solidere Basis zu bringen, damit unterwegs katastrophische Zwischenfälle ausgeschlossen seien; zudem fallen die Einschränkungen weg, sogar die jungen dienstpflichtigen Leute werden entlassen. Gott sei Dank!

Und, Gott sei Dank! Schallts wohl auch von dort herüber. Denn es ist ein Wunder vor unsern Augen. Nicht wahr, man konnte auf eine freie Regierungserlaubnis nie rechnen. Alles andere eher. Sie wäre auch nicht gekommen, wenn nicht eine so grosse Not als zwingender Faktor da wäre. Das ist Glück im Unglück. Man soll damit rechnen, dass mit dem Schwinden der Not auch die Schanzen für den freien Abzug kleiner werden. Darum ist jetzt unsere Zeit, die nicht unbenutzt bleiben darf.

Ob die Emigration auch ein historischer Fehler werden dürfte? wird gefragt. Bei der Beweisführung dagegen wird argumentiert, dass es in R. noch einmal wirtschaftliche Möglichkeiten geben wird, hoffentlich grosse Möglichkeiten, besonders in Handel und Industrie. Hoffentlich. Es soll nicht in Abrede gestellt werden. Aber wie? wann?

Mich über die Gründe für die Em. nach allen Seiten hin schriftlich ausbreiten, halte ich für sehr gewagt (zum mindesten: man darf nicht alles sagen; die Worte sind oft geflügelt und richten Elend an. . . . Solange man nach der Einwanderung in Russl. die Mennoniten als Kulturelement brauchte, hat man sie geschätzt und gewähren lassen. Das war die erste Periode. Nachdem in den siebziger Jahren wohl ein Drittel nach A. auswanderte, setzte allmählich die Russificierung ein. Es ist dann ein langer schwerer Kampf gewesen zur Selbsterhaltung und Selbstbehauptung auf verschiedenen Gebieten, besonders Schule. Die Mittel waren nicht immer einwandfrei. Wir haben immer die Männer gehabt, die Interessen der M. zu vertreten. Und das Geld!

Die alte zaristische Reg. schuf das Liquidationsgesetz, demzufolge wir die Kolonien zu räumen hatten. Das war die Krone des alten Prinzips. Die neue Reg.—die zeitweilige hob dieses Liquid.-Gesetz nicht auf. Da sahen wir, was wir wert waren.

Die Dritte: die heutige liquidiert durch die unaussprechliche Landverteilung, durch die Vermischungspläne tatsächlich die Kolonien. Auf meine wiederholten Vorstellungen da und dort, sagte mir endlich einer der vornehmsten, ein sonst sehr vernünftiger Mann, der mir nie unschicklich begegnet ist: "Wir gehen nicht gegen die Massen, sondern mit den Massen, dieselben sind gegen Euch. Wir wollen Ruhe. Wenn wir euch das Land geben (d.h. das schon 130 Jahre bewirtschaftete Dorfland, von den Gütern gar nicht zu reden) und die umliegenden Russen mal wieder ein Dorf abschlachten, was wollen wir dann dabei tun? Also wir können euch da nicht helfen. Wir müssen mit den Massen rechnen."

Die Masse hat mit Feuer und Schwert manche der schönsten Ansiedlungen vernichtet und nie werden Mennoniten sie wieder bauen. Die Ausdrängung der Fremdstämmigen dauert an und wird bei erster Gelegenheit eines Rummels aktiv sein, da wo sie heute in der Landverteilung ihre Stellung zeichnet. Ruhe wird sein, wenn wir das geworden sind, was sie sind, wenn wir besitzen in dem Masse wie sie.

Wenn aber auch nicht diese Reg. wäre, sondern irgend eine andere, so würde das Bild nicht viel anders sein. Und jede folgende, gesetzten Falls, würde durchaus nationalistisch, slavisch sein und wir blieben immer die Stiefkinder, die Fremden. Schauen Sie um sich. Nun nach dem Weltkriege grenzen sich überhaupt alle Völker sehr radikal von einander ab: die Deutschen sind scharf deutsch, jene mehr Franzosen, Italiener, Ungarn, etc.

Und wenns den Russen mal in R. gut gehen wird, ists doch eine sehr ernste Frage, obs uns dann auch gut gehen mag.

Das arme, arme Land. In jeder Beziehung. Eine Anleihe geben die Mächte nicht. Und wenn sies täten, es muss ja immer bezahlt werden— durch Steuern. Der ganze Staat muss leben—von Steuern. Ihr liebe Brüder, habt im Frühjahr schon geholfen samt den Holländern. Von den holl. Bohnen usw. die den Hungernden zugeteilt wurden, hat man, da man sonst nichts hatte, Steuer gezahlt um nicht ins Gefängnis zu kommen. Jetzt im Herbst hat man vielerorts das Letzte genommen und Ihr habt nun soviel mehr Hungernde in der Küche. Als das System vor einem Jahr so furchtbar durchgeführt wurde, dachten wir als Entschuldigung: man wisse es oben nur nicht, die würdens nicht zulassen, die würden auf jeden Fall den Landwirt mit seinem Minimum leben lassen. Törichter Gedanke! Ich habs der Regierung schwarz auf weiss gesagt, sie hat von oben ihre Vertreter gesandt, man hat im Centralamt Sitzung gehalten und—den kommunistischen Regierungsvertretern am Orte alles geglaubt—und nicht einen Finger gerührt, um die verschiedenen Sachen zu ordnen. Der hohe Beamte sagte mehrmals: Nenne mir Sachen, die in den Augen der Räte-Regierung Verbrechen sind, nicht dieses und jenes usw. usw. Es waren auch solche. Dass die schwere Naturalsteuer nun in diesem Herbste zwei neue Ansiedlungen an den Hungerstab bringt, die Menn. bei Aulieta Turkestan, die Ohrloffer Wollost in Sibirien und die frühern Gebiete Chortitza und Molotschna wieder aussaugt, während die Hungerhilfe von Am. & Holl. dort speist, lässt mich nicht im mindesten im Zweifel. In einigen Bezirken hat man eine sehr leichte Naturalsteuer genommen: Dawlekanowo, Samara, Orenburg; es war nach dem Hungerjahr nur ein kleiner Procentsatz der vollen Steuer aufgelegt worden. Das war gut. Allein nun fürchten sie schon jetzt die volle Steuer für nächstes Jahr.

Sollte ich noch ein Wort über den Beamtenapprais sagen? Wills lieber nicht tun.

Manche hoffen auf eine Aenderung der Verfassung. Darüber zu sprechen ist gefährlich. Doch darauf sollte man nicht rechnen. Die Organisation des Staates ist sehr gründlich und präcise durchgeführt, man sieht alles, hört alles, weiss alles. Rein ausgeschlossen, dass von innen heraus sich etwas bilden könne. Es gäbe nur ein fürchterliches Blutver-giessen. Von aussen wird auch niemand sich mit R. befassen, was hätte er dabei. Alle solche Gedanken muss man fahren lassen und mit dem Sovjetstand rechnen.

Und sollte wider alles Erwarten der Staat zusammenbrechen (was ich aber durchaus nicht annehme), so wäre die nächste Zeit darnach eine entsetzliche—das Chaos. Das wildeste Durcheinander. Jetzt ist in mancher Beziehung doch Ordnung. Dann wäre keine Gewalt da, die Ordnung auf-recht zu erhalten und bis sich eine allmählich bildete und durchsetzte— was müsste da alles geschehen. Dann tauchten auch all die andern politischen Parteien auf und jede will Russland mit ihrem System be-glücken und meint die andere ausrotten zu müssen . . . usw. Wo findet die Seele die Heimat die Ruh? Nein, nein. *Hier* ist sie nicht. . . .

Es sieht für die Kolonisten überhaupt das Jahr 1923 sehr ernst, sehr schwer. Billigt unsere Emigration vollständig, zumal wir als Mennoniten in dem englisch-sprechenden Staate uns leichter finden. Wenn wir nur die rechten treuen Männer an der Leitung haben.—Also Brüder, ich will nicht agitieren (noch nicht), aber *alle, deren Herz Gott erweckt zu gehen,* nehmt herzlich auf, wer da weiss wie uns zu Mute ist. Das binde ich Euch auf die Seele.

B. B. Janz

No. 14

22. Januar, 1923

An die *Mennonite Colonization Association of North America, Limited,* Rosthern, Sask., Canada und
Mennonite Executive Committee of Colonization

Teure Brüder im Vorstande!

. . . Es ist dunkel. Nichts zu sehen, nichts zu fühlen, nichts zu berechnen, keine Stütze, keine Basis, keine Zukunft; das was man sieht und hört, erkennt und berechnet, ist alles faktisches Material für negative Schlüsse, für Verneinung. Nun schon Jahr und Tag gearbeitet, gehofft, gerungen,—mit einem Worte *geglaubt* und alle ernsten Seelen in den Gemeinden sind dabei, haben mitgerungen bis auf den heutigen Tag. Der kleine Kasten mit unserm bischen Hoffen und Glauben schwimmt als letztes Wrack auf den Wogen der russ. Sündflut, scheint darin versinken zu sollen, zu müssen. Wenns nicht bald in den Beziehungen anders wird, muss Janz samt den 7.000 (darf ich so sagen?) kapitulieren, zur Seite treten: Die Idee des Glaubens und Vertrauens mag für die Kirche sein, fürs Leben muss was anderes als Durchschlagskraft sein!

Und ein anderes Princip muss auftreten?—

Hältst Du noch fest—?

Siehst Du nicht, wie schmählich der Glaube durchkommt? Solltest Du nicht den Kurs ändern?

"Bist Du, der da kommen soll, oder sollen wir eines andern warten?" Lass ich Jesum fahren? um die Situation zu retten?

Und wenn ich mit dem Glauben an die Vatertreue, an die heilsame Gnade zu Grunde gehen werde, muss; und wenn nun mit mir zu Schanden werden, die auf seinen Namen bauten;—und wenn nun wirklich das gläubige Princip abwirtschaftet im XX Jahrhundert, dem Wendepunkt der neuen Aufklärung, wegen seines ungeschickten Vertreters an der Spitze und die schwachen Gehilfen im Volke—hier stehe ich—ich kann nicht anders!

Die ganze Lage, alle Umstände treiben zum Ende: da nun das Gewässer kam und die Winde weheten und stiessen an das Haus, da fiel es und tat einen grossen Fall: es war nämlich auch mit Gott kein Ausweg, kein Durchkommen! Den Eindruck machts. Komme ich um, so komme ich um!

Ich kann nicht nein sagen. Ob ich mit dem unbegrenzten Vertrauen auf Ihn sterben werde können, will ich mich nicht vermessen zu behaupten, aber ohne das Prinzip kann ich nicht leben.

Ach in dieses Ringen hineingeraten zu sein, an die Spitze des Volkes gekommen zu sein! Janz mit seinem einfältigen Glauben vor allen Leuten so bloss zu stellen, ihn und das Wohl und Wehe eines ganzen Volkes auf die Spitze zu treiben! Nicht ich bin es eigentlich; mit "ich" kommen hier alle drein aus den sämtlichen Richtungen der Gemeinden, die von IHM alles Heil, alle Hilfe in der Not für unser Volk erwarten.

No. 15

29. März, 1923

Liebe Brüder.

. . . Es wird demnächst ein Jahr, seit die Auswanderung erlaubt wurde und man in grossem Jubel hoffte, in kurzer Zeit neue freie Menschen zu sein in einem freien Lande. Die so schwierigen Fragen hier sind immer wieder gelöst worden. Zur Zeit lautet die Entscheidung des Moskauer G.P.U., dass man den Emigranten der bereits sanktionierten Listen (18) privilegierte Ausreise gebe, . . . Und nun? An meinem Gott bin ich nicht zu Schanden geworden, die Russ. Regierung hat über Erwarten getan, die unglücklichen Brüder hier hoffen von einem Tag, Monat, Jahr zum andern, soll man nun drüben an unsern Brüdern zu Schanden werden. Ich habe meinen Leuten immer wieder absolutes Vertrauen eingeflösst, habe ich geirrt? Bruder, auf wen soll man sich verlassen, welchen Weg gehen? . . .

B. Janz

No. 16

The first emigrant group of 726 had just crossed the border when Janz faced an array of difficult problems. Prospects for a large exodus in 1923 appeared very dim; most Mennonite teachers were forced to resign from their professions; the nonresistance question still faced many obstacles; Janz's friend and colleague, Philipp Cornies, was under arrest. The burden of responsibility weighed heavily on Janz.

Moskau 1.-4. Juli, 1923

Werte Mitarbeiter.

Mehr denn je sind wir gegenseitig hüben und drüben auf die Berichte gespannt, die wir einander zusenden: die Zeit ist aktuell. Sie hat mich derart seit stark einem Monat mitgenommen, in Anspruch gehalten, dass ich Euch nicht in der üblichen ausführlichen Weise habe schreiben können. Könnte man doch die Tätigkeit, das ganze Amtsleben skizzieren; es gäbe später ein durchaus reichhaltiges Material. Doch einmal kann ichs faktisch nicht und dann darf ich nicht—es könnte zu irgend einer Stunde für mich, für die Sache hier verhängnisvoll werden. Also tun wir, was für heute möglich ist. Doch wo fange ich an? Es ist heute alles so sehr in den Brennpunkt der Entscheidung gerückt. Vor allen Dingen—die Auswanderung. Sie ist ja eben die Ursache, dass ich wieder seit gestern in Moskau bin. . . .

Werde mich wohl darauf gefasst machen müssen, der bestgehasste Mann zu werden, weil man nicht allen Wünschen, die nun so sehr stark werden, entsprechen kann. Das ist eine schwere Last, Brüder. Einen Teil davon habt Ihr bereits auch weggekriegt. Man muss wirklich je länger desto mehr—klar und fest das Ziel im Auge behalten, von den tausenden

Stimmen nur soweit Gebrauch machen, als sie auf dieser Linie laufen; alle lieb haben und allen dienen, ohne vom Ziele abzuweichen, u.s.w. Und wer ist hierzu tüchtig? Zu dieser Last kommen aber noch manche, manche dazu, an denen man noch schwerer trägt. Brüder, ich schweige davon und will mit festem Herzen tragen—noch dies Jahr, so Gott will. Wie ers endlich hinausführen wird ist mir Nacht, zu sehen ists nicht. Die Verhältnisse hier verknoten sich immer noch—wie ein Gordischer Knoten —eine Lösung nicht abzusehen. Doch das Einzige—man muss dem bang hoffenden Herzen das „Glaube-nur!" zurufen, wieder und wieder, fest. Die Nacht ist so lang und kalt. Doch andererseits dürfen wir auch mit der Liebe unserer Brüdern rechnen; da wollen wir uns an dem Guten, das da ist, freuen, umsomehr, da man allgemein und ernstlich Einkehr gehalten. . . .

Das Volk ist müde und sucht Ruhe. Entschuldigt, Brüder, solche Durchbrüche. Wir können nicht mehr—nach allen Seiten. Es langen die geistigen Kräfte, die materiellen Mittel nicht aus, um uns halten zu können. . . .

B. B. Janz

Kann nicht mit dem pessimistischen Tone endigen. Unser Optimismus in der russischen oder socialen Nacht ist der ewige Gott, unser Vater. Er hat uns geschlagen, er wird uns auch wieder heilen. Seine Heilung hat bereits eingesetzt, und zwar wo es am nötigsten war: am Herzen. Nun kommt die Verheissung: so wird Euch solches zufallen. **Wie?**

No. 17

23. Juli, 1923

Teure Brüder.

. . . Vieles von dem hier gesagten ist nicht neu. Es ist ein dringender Appell, den ich im Auftrage unseres Volkes an die Brüder in Amerika richte. Es wird hier jeden Tag sehr gewartet. Heute mehr denn je. Immer wieder habe ich den Unsern das Vertrauen auf den Vater im Himmel und die Brüder drüben empfohlen. Nicht wahr, ich darfs auch weiter?

Mit den herzlichsten Grüssen an alle lieben Mitarbeiter,

Ihr geringer
B. B. Janz

No. 18

6. April 1924

Teure Brüder.

So Gott will und wir leben, haben wir im bevorstehenden Sommer gemeinsam an dem grossen Werk der Emigration unserer schwergeprüften Brüder mitzuwirken. Die Aktion soll demnächst beginnen. Da möchte ich in Folgendem ein klares Bild der gegenwärtigen Lage Ihnen darbieten, damit man mit allen Faktoren bei der Arbeit rechnen kann. Der Schnee ist geschwunden, mit dem erwachenden Frühlinge lebt nun die feste Hoffnung in dem Herzen der Wartenden neu auf, dass ihre Stunde nun gewiss geschlagen hat. - Wir zweifeln auch nicht daran, *dass* es gehen

wird, aber tausende Gemüter bewegt die bange Frage, in welchem Umfange die Bewegung vor sich gehen mag. Und von der Antwort auf diese
Frage hängt bei vielen Vieles - ja A l l e s ab. Die schwerbetroffenen
Gruppen im Süden Russlands haben seit der Entsendung ihrer Delegaten
im Jahre 1919 diesen Gedanken - drüben ihr Stück Brot mit Ruhe und
Frieden, mit der Hoffnung auf eine sichere Existenz für die Zukunft zu
essen - unentwegt bis auf diese Stunde f e s t g e h a l t e n. Und das sind
nun v i e r Jahre. Viele sahen diesen Ausgang jahrelang früher. - Und
nicht nur die südlichen Gruppen, sondern überhaupt alle Kreise in den
weiten Länderstrecken von Hammer und Sichel, die hier für sich keine
Existenz sehen, geben sich der bestimmten Hoffnung hin, dass die Brüder
in Amerika das Menschenmögliche für sie tun werden zu ihrer Errettung.
Und das mit demselben Glauben, der die Tausenden vom Hungertode
rettete. Dass trotz einiger wirtschaftlicher Aufbesserung der Drang hinaus nur noch heftiger wird, findet seine Erklärung in dem traurigen Stande
von Kirche und Schule, von Jugenderziehung im Besonderen, von jeder
öffentlichen gesellschaftlichen Initiative. Dies alles muss Gegenstand eines
besonderen Berichtes sein. Es wird den Gemeinden sehr schwer. . . .

B. B. Janz

No. 19

By June 1924, government pressure aimed at terminating the
emigration became more and more discernible. Since relatively
few emigrants had left at this point, the situation gave much
cause for anxiety.

Moskau, 27. Juni 1924.
An die Brüder B. H. Unruh and A. A. Friesen.
Meine lieben Freunde.

Der heutige Moment ist so bewegt und hat eine so grosse Fülle von
Ereignissen, die ausführlich zu berichten Material für einen umfang-
reichen Aufsatz bietet. Morgen um 2 Uhr nachmittags geht mein Zug
nach Kharkoff. Ich muss in dringlichen Fragen dort sein, wo hier nun das
Wesentlichste eben reguliert worden ist. Auch hierher wurde ich tele-
graphisch von der Ruscapa herausgerufen. In der Tat, die Bewegung war
im Sterben. Die Reg-kreise in Moskau wie auch in Kharkoff sind über
die Massenausreise der Mennoniten höchst beunruhigt. Man wundert
sich, man forscht, entsendet Kommissionen zur Untersuchung, nimmt
gemachte Verfügungen zur freien Ausreise zurück. Die Leute kommen
in die schlimmste Bedrängnis, die sich schon zur Reise rüsteten und
andere in die tiefste Trauer, welche in absehbarer Zeit mit ihrer Liste
hofften dran zu kommen. . . .

B. B. Janz

No. 20

Kharkoff, 31. Oktober, 1924
An den Vorsitzenden der M. C. Association of N. America, Rev.
David Toews, Rosthern, Sask.
Lieber Bruder Toews.

Wir danken Gott und durch Sie den Brüdern in Amerika, dass Sie alle soviel Gutes an unsern Leuten erweisen können, dass viele unserer bangen Sorgen vom Sommer so gut erledigt werden. Das geht über Erwarten. Wir danken Ihnen für jeden Mann, Frau und Kind, für welche Sie zur Kreditierung "ja" gesagt haben. . . .

Man sollte meinen es wäre mal genug. Jedenfalls macht Ihnen die Unterbringung viel Mühe, wo Sie dann wieder und wieder zu dem Gedanken kommen: Es ist genug.

. . . Dass wir in unserer Ukraina nun schon durch den ganzen Sommer ganz besonders schwere Verhältnisse in jeder Beziehung haben, wissen Sie. Infolgedessen wird der Drang zur Ausreise immer schärfer, so elementar, dass er die Schranken durchbricht. Nun stehen wir infolgedessen vor der schweren Entscheidung, von denen, die sich auf alle Fälle zur Ausreise schier gewaltsam rüsteten, einer Gruppe abzulehnen. Wie gross sie sein wird, wird von den Verweigerungen der Pässe abhängen. Dass manchen die Pässe trotz aller Mühe und grosser Kosten abgelehnt werden, scheint mir ohne Zweifel zu sein, doch entzieht es sich bis zum letzten Augenblicke unserer Beurteilung, wer und wieviel es sein mögen. . . .

Schelten Sie mich. Aber helfen Sie uns. Nun schon den ganzen Sommer und Herbst nervieren wir Sie und die ganze Board mit unsern Depeschen und Briefen. Nun noch eine Ergänzung, dann eine Verlängerung, dann noch eine Ergänzung. . . .

Nocheinmal. Wills Gott, komme ich auch bald hinüber, dann tadeln und schelten Sie nach Belieben, wills alles hinnehmen. Aber jetzt, teuerster Br. Toews, lassen Sie mir diese kleine Gruppe nicht sitzen. Ich bitte auch sehr für den Fall, dass auf meine Depesche ein endliches schweres "nein" kommt. Dann soll dieses Schreiben die Frage noch einmal zur Entscheidung stellen. Dann tröstet mein Inneres mich bei dem Gedanken, dass A. A. Friesen bei Ihnen diese Gruppe auch befürworten wird. Ich scheide von dieser Frage mit einem bestimmten Hoffen. . . .

Mit herzlichem Gruss an Sie und alle Mitarbeiter am Werke,

B. B. Janz

No. 21

Zur Zeit M o s k a u, am 21. XII. 1924.

An unsere Vertreter.

Es sei Ihnen ein reich gesegneter Christtag beschert. An der Jahreswende tun wir einen Rückblick und Ausblick zur Existenzfrage unseres Volkes in seinem schweren Ringen ums liebe Stück Brot, das wärmende Kleid und Obdach und seinen Glauben. Die folgenden Zeilen machen keinen Anspruch auf erschöpfende Behandlung der Frage, dazu müsste man mehr Musse und mehr Information haben. Auch kann man unschwer einen gewissen Subjektivismus konstatieren in wieweit man durch Zeit und Erfahrung objektiv urteilt, muss zu gewissem Teil die Zukunft bestätigen.

Dass unser Volk eine unverwüstliche Zähigkeit und Energie betätigt, ist nach der Liquidation des Hungers besonders scharf hervorgetreten. Hätte es nicht für möglich gehalten, dass bei d e m Umfange und d e r Tiefe des Hungerelendes, des Wirtschaftsruins man infolge einer einzigen guten Ernte sich auf der ganzen Linie so sehr herausrappeln könne. Das war die Ernte 1923. Besonders die Monate Februar, März, April 1924 zeigten die steigende wirtschaftliche Konjunktur zur Gesundung. Jedenfalls hat die amerikanische Hungerhilfe in ihrem Teile dazu beigetragen.

Allein mit e i n e r nun folgenden M i s s e r n t e ist auch die ganze Basis angegriffen, das wirtschaftliche Können dahin. Die Dörfer sind mit wenigen Ausnahmen nicht kaufkräftig. Unsere Kooperative (Konsumläden) konstatieren, dass unser Bauer wenig, wenig kauft - kaum das Notwendigste, immer das Billigste. Die nahegelegenen Russen kaufen bedeutend mehr und besser; sie kaufen vorzugsweise in unseren Geschäften, womit das Vertrauen zu denselben ohne Worte ausgedrückt wird, dann aber auch bessere Auswahl, dem Geschmack mitspricht. Auf den Auktionen der Emigranten kaufen wieder meistens die Russen: sie haben Geld. Es ist ein entsetzliches Uebel gewesen, dass man unsere Kolonien so radikal von der Zugkraft, den Pferden losgemacht hat mit allen möglichen Mitteln. Die in dieser Beziehung am meisten pferdelosen Dörfer scheinen sich nicht erholen zu können. Der Bürgerkrieg mit der schrecklichen Machnowschtschina haben uns ganz ausgezogen und die Nachwehen werden dauernd empfunden. Raswjorstka und Hunger taten den letzten Schlag. Sollte es mal wieder einen Rummel geben, wird es mancherorts die Kolonien wieder am ersten treffen. Das bewilligte grössere Landquantum pro Hof; die Abgeschlossenheit, die sich zu einer Assimilation nie hergibt; der frühere Ruf der Behäbigkeit; der Durchbruch des Glaubensprinzips, infolgedessen man gegen einen Teil der Landesbevölkerung (Machn.) mit den Waffen vorging, sind bei dem tieferstehenden Teil der grossen ungebildeten Masse genug Ursache unsere Kolonien entfernen zu wollen. . . .

Dass nun die erneute Missernte m:t einem einzigen Stosse die Stabilität unserer Wirtschaft über den Haufen wirft ist doch sehr bezeichnend für unsere Lage. Dass ferner unsere Wirtschaft noch jahrelang Versuchskaninchen für neue Wirtschaftsprobleme sein wird, ist ja selbstverständlich. . . .

Die schwache Ernte, der grosse Mangel an Geld im Staate schränken die Bedürfnisse auf ein Min:mum ein. Der Bauer kann sich nichts gönnen, zahlt aber auch als Mitgl:ed des Verbandes den Beitrag von nur 0.50 Kop. pro Jahreshälfte sehr schwer, ja wohl in 60 - 70% Fällen unterbleibt es. Das bedeutet für die Zentrale, Taubstummenanstalt etc. die Basis zur Existenz zu verl:eren; damit natürlich fällt der ganze Verein. Wir stehen somit ökonomisch in e:ner ernsten Krisis, von der das Ende nicht abzusehen ist. Freilich können wir uns noch eben halten, wenn auch nur gut die Hälfte einkäme.—D:e Emigration der M. veranlasste in der ukrainischen Zentrale eine gründliche Revision der Mennonitenfrage. Einmal ist uns nun von der Behörde ganz unmissverständlich jede Vertretung der Kolonien und seiner Bevölkerung in Rechtsfragen untersagt worden. Administrative Uebergriffe der Lokalbehörden sollen uns als Vereinszentrum für die Zukunft nichts angehen; die Dienstfrage unserer Jünglinge hat uns sicher auch nichts zu kümmern; die

Emigration in Listen ist verboten, aber es scheint auch mehr gemeint zu sein. . . .

Die Verheissungen von Erweiterung des Landareals für die Kolonien werden nicht Wirklichkeit werden: . . .

Unsere Gesellschaft ist nun aber auch nicht landhungrig. Sie ist nun in ihrer Majorität bereit alles Land abzugeben und zu gehen, voran die stärksten Wirte mancher Bezirke. Es rüsten entschieden zur Auswanderung die allerstärksten Landwirte der Ukraine: . . . Die Lehrerschaft in den meisten Ansiedelungen ist ganz zerschlagen und trostlos; die Forderungen zur antireligiösen Propaganda, zur Heranbildung von "Komsomol" und "Junye Pionery", zum Specialunterricht in den kommun. Fächern werden immer bestimmter und dringender. Ein Ausweichen finden sie nicht mehr möglich. Sie müssen abtreten. Sie sind dann sofort brotlos. Habe ihnen geraten, auf dem Posten zu verharren, ihre Pflicht zu tun, so weit dieselbe mit ihren Ueberzeugungen auszudenken ist und das Weitere abzuwarten, resp. sich hinauswerfen zu lassen. Die gequälten Pädagogen rechnen bestimmt damit, dass dieser Winter der letzte ihrer Schultätigkeit ist. Und dann? Sollte das der Fall sein, liebe Brüder, dann Hilfe für die Entwurzelten, sichere, schnelle Hilfe. . . .

Mit herzlichen Grüssen

Janz

No. 22

Zur Zeit Moskau, am 24. XI. 1925

Teurer Bruder Toews.

Unter dem heutigen Datum sandte ich an Ihre w. Addresse eine längere Depesche, deren Kopie ich hier beifalte, des Inhalts, dass als letzte Gruppe dieses Jahres 1925 nun noch eine kleine Partie von ca 100 Seelen Mennoniten auf Kredit nach Canada befördert werde. Habe mich energisch geweigert ganz America noch einmal mit einer so späten Sendung aufzuregen. Die Pässe sind so spärlich gekommen. Die Leute waren aber schon zu weit vorangegangen, um sich zu lösen. Es gibt für sie nur ein "Vorwärts". Wären die Pässe noch fast gleichzeitig gekommen! Mit Bangen harren, die von unserer rauhen Wirklichkeit so Geprellten, auf den Ausgang. Und dennoch. Wenn Gott im Himmel, die Brüder in Rosthern und Col. Dennis in Montreal auch diesmal noch willig werden, Hilfe in der Not zu bringen, können sämtliche Personen den neuen Lebensanfang machen, ohne für den Winter—oder aber auch für immer ins Bodenlose der Verzweiflung zu stürzen, zu vegetieren. Die lieben Leutchen haben die kargen Mittel ganz aufgebraucht. Dann sind Passbestimmungen neuerdings zu Ungunsten der Emigranten dahin geändert worden, dass jeder Auslandpass im Lande nur drei Monate gültig ist. Reist er in dieser Zeit nicht aus, so kann er die ganze lange Prozedur von unten an bis oben aus zur Erlangung eines neuen Passes von vorne anfangen. Wieder grosse Geldkosten, wer sie dann hat. Und es wird eine Frage sein, ob man dann noch willig sein wird einen zweiten Pass überhaupt auszufertigen. Es sind für nächstes Jahr Passschwierigkeiten zu erwarten, wie sie nie zuvor da waren. Möglich, dass deswegen keine

Bewegung pro 1926 zustande kommen wird.—Daher dieser Notruf. Lieber Bruder Toews und alle Ihr Brüder in der Board, sowie sämtliche unbekannte Brüder, die die Neuankommenden bei Schnee und Frost aufnehmen werden. Tuts noch einmal: Gebt auch diesen Obdachlosen den Anfang zu einem neuen Heim. Es werden Tage kommen, da wird die Bedeutung der Tat ganz anders ins Gewicht fallen. . . .

Weihnachten und Neujahr stehen vor der Tür. An der Jahreswende tun wir einen Rückblick auf unsere Jahresarbeit und einen Ausblick auf die Möglichkeiten pro 1926. Gott sei die Ehre. Die vielgeprüften Gnadenfelder, unser gemeinsames Sorgenkind, sind geborgen, soweit manche der ärmsten von Trachoma etc. nicht aufgehalten worden sind. Unverkennbar ein Stück Riesenarbeit, sowohl die Beschaffung des Kredites für sie dort, als auch ihr Losreissen und Abschieben hier. Und einige hundert andere konnten an den Segnungen teilnehmen. Dann geht eine beträchtliche Gruppe von Kassenpassagieren. Andererseits ist es diese Bewegung, die zum grossen Teil dem Verbande im Süden den Kopf kostet: Wir stehen nämlich vor der Liquidation desselben. Eine Menge Schmähartikel erscheinen in der deutschen Sowjetpresse, deren Zielscheibe die Verwaltung ist. Da muss ich nun grosser Sünder sein. Was nun der kommende Monat der Mennonitenschaft bringt? Der Kongress muss stattfinden, da fallen die letzten Würfel, gewürfelt von der eigenen Hand unseres Volkes, freilich unter starker Beeinflussung. Man steht eben zurück vor einer gewaltsamen Erdrosselung (die es übrigens auch schon bei den jetzigen Massnahmen ist), und versucht die Gesellschaft zu veranlassen, sich auf dem Kongress gegen den Verband, besonders die Verwaltung der Zentrale zu stellen. Diese soll vor allen Dingen liquidiert werden und dann so weiter. Was nun auch passieren möge, sicher ist, dass ich auf dem Posten nicht länger verbleibe und zum andern, dass ich persönlich wohl mit an dem Sarge der teuren Vereinigung aller Mennoniten zu stehen habe, wo ich anno 1921 mit an die Wiege gestellt wurde. Und dann? - Auch Ihnen scheinen dort bei allem besonderen Wohlwollen Ihrer Regierung Störungen nicht erspart geblieben zu sein, wo es nun leider Gottes noch Leute aus unserm Volkstume sind, die nicht wissen, was sie tun.

Bei dem Ausblick auf die neuen Aufgaben muss ich zuerst bemerken, dass es mir dunkel wie die Nacht ist, welchen Weg ich zu gehen, wovon ich mit der Familie zu leben, welch ein Werk ich künftig zu tun haben mag. Menschlich besehen, ist ein Leidensweg das Nächstliegende; aber "Er kann helfen" und es herrlich hinausführen. Wir wollen nicht das Vertrauen wegwerfen. Also liebe Brüder, wenn wir nun jahrelang von hüben und drüben an einem grossen Werk gestanden und Gottes reichen Segen dazu bekommen haben, muss ich hier ganz aus dem Dienste ausscheiden. Sie möchten vielleicht vorschlagen, dass Sie mit dem alten Vertrauen an demselben Werke mit mir weiterarbeiten möchten auch ohne meine offic. Legitimation. Allein man wird mich als Privatmann augenblicklich angreifen und in Nummero "Sicher" bringen, sobald ich in der Em.-sache irgend aktiv werde. Jetzt ist der Titel des Vorsitzenden und vor allem das grosse Vertrauen der Massen mein Talisman, mein Schutzengel gewesen, nicht zu vergessen, dass der höchste Schutz der erste in der Sache war. . . .

Mit den obigen Ausführungen glaube ich das Wesentliche der Sache Ihnen gebracht zu haben. Ob es mir möglich sein wird Ihnen später noch privat zu schreiben, wird von den Umständen abhängen. Doch ist kaum damit zu rechnen. Jedenfalls wird meine Korrespondenz immer noch später sorgfältig zensiert werden. Werde es also vermeiden überhaupt zu schreiben, bitte Sie, mir das Schweigen nicht krumm zu nehmen. Nicht besser wird es stehen, wenn etwa die Post Briefe von Ihnen an mich haben wird. Daher wird es angebracht sein, mich von Ihnen, resp. der Board zu verabschieden. In dem Grossen Ringen um den persönlichen Herzensglauben, um die Prinzipien der Täter, wo "der Väter Glaube" unser Glaube ist und es bleiben soll, dann um das teure Kleinod - die Jugend sind von hüben und drüben grosse Werte hineingelegt worden, ist von beiden Seiten des Ozeans mit der ganzen Inbrunst der Seele nach Möglichkeiten, nach Wegen gesucht worden, das L e b e n zu erhalten und pflegen. Was können wir, die wir mitten drin stehen, zur objektiven Beurteilung sagen? Das werden andere beurteilen, die teilnahmen an den Nöten und Leiden und doch persönlich mehr Beobachter waren und weniger aktive Vorposten. Die mennonitische Seele hat nur zu richtig verstanden, wieviel die Uhr schlägt (in Russland) und hat Ausdauer in dem Ringen; das ist ihr gut zu schreiben. Tausende und Abertausende von Händen der Brüder aus den verschiedensten Richtungen der Mennoniten haben sich ausgestreckt, um den russischen Mennoniten beizustehen in ihrer beispiellosen Not um das Brot des Leibes und der Seele. Es ist uns beiden vorzüglich vergönnt gewesen den warmen Herzschlag zu vernehmen und sein Streben in die Tat umzusetzen zur Rettung Tausender. Dass wir das nun seit drei Jahren mit einander nach dem Willen des Herrn und der Gemeinden haben tun dürfen und dass wir uns verstanden haben, ist mir eine grosse innere Befriedigung. Möge es Ihnen vergönnt sein, das Werk ganz auszuführen, wie Er, der Herr, es lenkt.

B. B. Janz

Chronological Data

August 14-18, 1917 - First General Mennonite Congress in Orloff.

June 30, July 1, 2, 1918 - Mennonite General Conference in Lichtenau at which the nonresistance issue was discussed.

September 19-21, 1918 - Second General Mennonite Congress in Orloff.

December 3, 4, 1918 - Special Mennonite General Conference in Landskrone. Premature termination of the sessions due to civil unrest.

January 4, 1919 - Lenin decrees that the Tolstoyist and other pacifistic Christian groups may form a Council to process individuals desiring exemption from military service.

March 6-10, 1919 - Mennonite *Selbstschutz* makes its last stand against the Makhno and the Bolshevik forces.

September 25, 26, 1919 - Mennonite General Conference held in Rudnerweide. Terminated after one day due to the approach of the Makhno forces.

November 11, 1919 - Bloodbath in Blumenort.

June 13, 1920 - The Study Commission arrives in New York.

November 1, 1920 - B. H. Unruh returns to Germany to begin his work as a member of the Study Commission.

March 4, 1921 - Alexanderwohl Assembly elects B. B. Janz to head the newly formed *VMSR*.

July 22, 1921 - The Paraguayan Congress authorizes Mennonite immigration into that land.

October 22, 1921 - Signing of the American and Dutch Relief Contracts in Kharkov, Ukraine, between Alvin J. Miller and C. G. Rakovsky and B. Yermoshtchenko.

December 17, 1921 - The first Mennonite petition to emigrate was presented to the Ukrainian Central Executive Committee by *VMSR* chairman B. B. Janz.

January 3, 4, 1922 - Margenau Congress of the *VMSR*.

February 7, 1922 - The *VMSR* executive decides to pursue emigration from Russia as an operational principle.

March 11-14, 1922 - AMR shipments arrive in Alexandrovsk and Halbstadt.

April 24, 1922 - The Ukrainian Foreign Commissariat approves the emigration of Mennonite refugees to Paraguay.

April 25, 1922 - The *VMSR* charter is officially sanctioned by the government and its name changed to *VBHH* (*Verband der Bürger Holländischer Herkunft*).

May 29, 31, 1922 - Landskrone Congress of the *VBHH*.

June 2, 1922 - The Liberal government repeals the Order-in-Council barring the entry of Mennonites to Canada.

September 22, 23, 1922 - Osterwick Congress of the *VBHH*.

April 17, 1923 - The German government, the *DMH*, and Study Commission members agree on a plan to house the medically unfit Mennonite emigrants in Lechfeld.

May 16, 1923 - The Presidium of the Central Executive Committee in Moscow sanctions the charter of the *AMLV*.

June 22, 1923 - The first group of 726 emigrants leave Chortitza for Canada.

October 10, 1923 - The first Congress of the *AMLV* is held in Alexandertal, Alt-Samara.

December 23, 1923 - B. B. Janz's first *GPU* hearing.

March 1-4, 1924 - Kalinovo Congress of the *VBHH*.

June 23, 1924 - The first echelon of the 1924 emigration leaves the Lichtenau terminal.

June 27-30, 1924 - The second *AMLV* Congress meets in Davlekanovo.

January 13-18, 1925 - The last All-Russian Mennonite Conference meets in Moscow.

February 26-28, 1925 - Grigoryevka Congress of the *VBHH*.

February 17-19, 1926 - The last Congress of the *VBHH* in Kharkov.

March 6, 1926 - B. B. Janz's second *GPU* hearing in Kharkov.

March 11, 1926 - B. B. Janz officially resigns his duties as chairman of the *VBHH*.

May 13-16, 1926 - The third *AMLV* Congress meets in Moscow.

June 4, 1926 - B. B. Janz crosses into Latvia at Sebezh.

October 5-9, 1926 - Ukrainian Mennonite General Conference held in Melitopol.

BIBLIOGRAPHY

BIBLIOGRAPHY

Stumpp, K., *Das Schrifttum über das Deutschtum in Russland* (Stuttgart, 1958).

PRIMARY SOURCES

Canadian Mennonite Relief and Immigration Council Archive (Canadian Mennonite Bible College, Winnipeg, Man.). Formerly the Canadian Mennonite Board of Colonization.

A. A. Friesen Archive (Bethel College Historical Library, Newton, Kan.).

F. F. Isaak Papers (C. A. DeFehr, Sr., Winnipeg, Man.).

B. B. Janz Archive (Mennonite Brethren College of Arts, Winnipeg, Man.).

C. E. Krehbiel Collection (Bethel College Historical Library, Newton, Kan.).

BOOKS

Adams, A. E., *Bolsheviks in the Ukraine. The Second Campaign 1918-1919* (New Haven and London, 1963).

Arschinoff, P., *Geschichte der Machno-Bewegung (1918-1921)* (Berlin, n.d.).

Carr, E. H., *The Interregnum 1923-1924* (London, 1954).

Dmytryshyn, B., *Moscow and the Ukraine 1918-1953* (New York, 1956).

Dyck, H. L., *Weimar Germany and Soviet Russia 1926-1933* (New York and London, 1966).

Dyck, P. P., *Orenburg am Ural. Die Geschichte einer-mennonitischen Ansiedlung in Russland* (Yarrow, B.C., 1951).

Ehrt, A., *Das Mennonitentum in Russland von seiner Einwanderung bis zur Gegenwart* (Berlin-Leipzig, 1932).

Epp, F. H., *Mennonite Exodus* (Altona, Man., 1962).

Fast, G., *Im Schatten des Todes* (Wernigerode, 1935).

—————, *In den Steppen Sibiriens* (Rosthern, Sask., n.d.).

Fast, M. B., *Geschichtlicher Bericht wie die Mennoniten Nordamerikas ihren armen Glaubensgenossen in Russland geholfen haben* (Reedley, Calif., 1919).

Friesen, A. and Loewen, A., *Die Flucht über den Amur* (Steinbach, 1946).

Görz, A., *Ein Beitrag zur Geschichte des Forstdienstes der Mennoniten in Russland* (Gross-Tokmak, Russia, 1907).

Goerz, H., *Die mennonitischen Siedlungen der Krim* (Winnipeg, Man., 1956).

—————, *Die Molotschnaer Ansiedlung. Entstehung, Entwicklung und Untergang* (Steinbach, Man., 1950/51).

—————, *Memrik; eine mennonitische Kolonie in Russland* (Rosthern, Sask., 1948).

Harder, B. J., *Alexandertal: Die Geschichte der letzten deutschen Stamm-siedlung in Russland* (Berlin-Charlottenburg, n.d.).

Harder, Helene, *Feuerproben. Lebensschicksale eines deutschen Siedlers in Russland* (Wernigerode, 1934).

Heidebrecht, D. P. (ed.) and G. J. Peters (ed.), *"Onsi Tjedils" Ersatz-dienst der Mennoniten in Russland unter den Romanows* (Yarrow, B.C., 1966).

Hildebrand, J., *Sibirien* (Winnipeg, 1952).

Hofer, D. M., *Die Hungersnot in Russland und unsere Reise um die Welt* (Chicago, 1924).

Isaak, J. F., *Aus schwerer Zeit. Aus der russischen Revolution 1917-1920* (Muenster, Sask., 1929).

Klassen, J. P., *Dunkle Tage* (Scottdale, Pa., and Winnipeg, Man., 1923).

————, *Reiseskizzen über die Auswanderung im Jahre 1923* (Scott-dale, Pa., and Winnipeg, Man.).

Kraus, H., *International Relief in Action 1914-1943* (Scottdale, Pa., 1944).

Kroeker, A., *Auf dunklen Pfaden. Aus dem Leben unter Hammer und Sichel in den Jahren 1921 bis 1924* (Striegau in Schlesien, 1933).

————, *Bilder aus Sowjet-Russland* (Striegau in Schlesien, 1930).

————, *Meine Flucht. Erfahrungen unter der Sowjetherrschaft* (Strie-gau i. Schlesien, 1929).

————, *Unsere Brüder in Not. Bilder vom Leidensweg der deutschen Kolonisten in Russland* (Striegau in Schlesien, 1930).

Lehmann, Heinz, *Das Deutschtum in Westkanada* (Berlin, 1939).

Lindemann, K., *Von den deutschen Kolonisten in Russland. Ergebnisse einer Studienreise 1919-1921* (Stuttgart, 1924).

Lohrenz, G., *Sagradowka. Die Geschichte einer mennonitischen Ansied-lung im Süden Russlands* (Rosthern, Sask., 1947).

Neufeld, David, *Russland das "Sowjet-Paradies"?* (Bretten in Baden, 1933).

Neufeld, Dietrich, *Ein Tagebuch aus dem Reiche des Totentanzes* (Em-den, 1921).

————, *Mennonitentum in der Ukraine. Schicksalsgeschichte Sagra-dowkas* (Emden, 1922).

————*Zu Pferd 1000 km durch die Ukraina* (Emden, 1922).

Peters, G. A., *Die Hungersnot in den mennonitischen Kolonien Süd-Russ-lands* (Scottdale, Pa., 1923).

————, *Menschenlos in schwerer Zeit. Aus dem Leben der Mennoniten Süd-Russlands* (Scottdale, Pa., and Winnipeg, Man., n.d.).

Quiring, W., *Russlanddeutsche suchen eine Heimat* (Karlsruhe, 1938).

Reshetar, J. S., *The Ukrainian Revolution 1917-1920* (Princeton, 1952).

Schleuning, J, *Aus Tiefer Not. Schicksale der deutschen Kolonisten in Russland* (Berlin, 1922).

Sullivant, R. S., *Soviet Politics and the Ukraine 1917-1957* (New York, 1962).

Toews, C. P., *Die Tereker Ansiedlung. Mennonitische Kolonie im Vor-derkaukasus. Entstehung, Entwicklung und Untergang* (Rosthern, Sask., 1945).

Toews, Gerhard, *Schönfeld. Werde- und Opfergang einer deutschen Sied-lung in der Ukraine* (Winnipeg, 1939).
————, *Die Heimat in Trümmern. Deutsche Schicksale im Russland der Anarchie* (Steinbach, Man., 1936).
Toews, Heinrich, *Eichenfeld-Dubowka. Ein Tatsachenbericht aus der Tragödie des Deutschtums in der Ukraine* (Karlsruhe i. B., n.d.).
Unruh, B. H., *Fügung und Führung im mennonitischen Welthilfswerk 1920-1933* (Karlsruhe, 1966).
————, *Revolution und Reformation in Russland* (Wernigerode am Harz, 1928).

ANONYMOUS WORKS

Deutsche Mennoniten-Hilfe, ihre Entstehung und Arbeitsgebiete (Ober-ursel, Taunus. 1924).
Die Kubaner Ansiedlung (Steinbach, 1953).
Die Mennoniten-Gemeinden in Russland während der Kriegs- und Revo-lutionsjahre 1914 bis 1920 (Heilbronn a. Neckar, 1921).
Einige Erlebnisse während der Kriegs- und Revolutionszeit in Russland n.p., n.d.).
Vor den Toren Moskaus (Clearbrook, B.C., 1961).

PERIODICALS AND NEWSPAPERS
GENERAL ARTICLES

Epp, D. H., "Zur Geschichte der Bundeskonferenz der russländischen Mennonitengemeinden," *Unser Blatt*, Vol. 2, Nos. 1-4 (Oct. 1926 to Jan. 1927); *Der Bote*, Vol. 3, Nos. 44, 45 (Nov. 3, 1926, Nov. 10, 1926).
Ewert, J. W., "Aus dem Leben der Chortitzer Mennoniten-Gemeinden während der Kriegs- und Revolutionszeit," *Die Mennonitische Rund-schau*, Vol. 43, Nos. 20-22 (May 19, 1920, to June 2, 1920).
Fast, Selinda, "Alexander J. Fast," *Mennonitisches Jahrbuch* (1954), pp. 6-9.
Hiebert, G. G., "Die südrussischen Mennoniten in der Kriegs- und Revo-lutionszeit," *Die Mennonitische Rundschau*, Vol. 43, Nos. 27-29 (July 7, 1920, to July 21, 1920); *Vorwärts*, Vol. 18, Nos. 26, 27 (June 25, 1920, July 2, 1920).
Janzen, J. H., "Die Mennoniten Süd-Russlands," *Die Mennonitische Rund-schau*, Vol. 49, Nos. 41-46 (Oct. 13, 1926, to Nov. 17, 1926).
————, "Erinnerungen an A. A. Friesen und David Toews," *Menno-nitisches Jahrbuch* (1950), pp. 18-24.
Klassen, Cornelius F., "The Mennonites of Russia, 1917-1928," *Mennonite Quarterly Review*, VI, No. 2 (April 1932), pp. 69-80.
Kuhn, Walter, "Die mennonitische Altkolonie Chortitza in der Ukraine," *Deutsche Monatshefte. Zeitschrift für Geschichte und Gegenwart des Ostdeutschtums*, IX (Sept. to Nov. 1942), pp. 1-40.
Latour, K., "Der russische Volkheld Machno," *Vorwärts*, Vol. 18, No. 41 (Oct. 8, 1920), pp. 4, 5.
Lohrenz, G., "Nonresistance Tested," *Mennonite Life*, XVII (April 1962), pp. 66-68.

Miller, A. J., "Clothing the Naked," *Mennonite Life,* XVIII (July 1963), pp. 118-21.

————, "The Beginning of American Mennonite Relief Work," *Mennonite Life,* XVII (April 1962), pp. 71-75.

————, "Relief Work in Revolutionary Russia," *Mennonite Life,* XVII (July 1962), pp, 126-31.

Rempel, David G., "The Expropriation of the German Colonists in South Russia During the Great War," *The Journal of Modern History,* IV, No. 1 (March 1932), pp. 49-67.

Schleuning, Johannes, "Professor Lic. theol. D.h.c. Benjamin Heinrich Unruh zum Gedächtnis," *Heimatbuch der Deutschen aus Russland* (1960), pp. 102-8.

Schnebele, Christian, "Aus Benjamin Unruh's Tätigkeit," *Mennonitisches Jahrbuch* (1952), pp. 45-47.

Unruh, B. H„ "Die Mennoniten in Russland," *Ostdeutsche Monatshefte,* Nr. 12 (März, 1925), pp. 1157 ff.

————, "Die Wehrlosigkeit," *Die Mennonitische Rundschau* Vol. 49, Nos. 27-30 (July 7, 1926, to July 28, 1926).

————, "Tatsachen," *Der Bote,* Vol. 14, Nos. 36-40 (Sept. 8, 1937, to Oct. 6, 1937).

————, "The Background and Causes of the Flight of the Mennonites from Russia in 1929," *Mennonite Quarterly Review,* IV, No. 4 (Oct. 1930), pp. 267-81; V, No. 1 (Jan. 1931), pp. 28-41.

Wall, Peter and Peter J. Braun, "Die Mennoniten in Russland während des Bürgerkrieges (1917-1920)," *Die Mennonitische Rundschau,* Vol. 43, Nos. 46, 47 (Nov. 17, 1920, Nov. 24, 1920); *Vorwärts,* Vol. 18, No. 45 (Nov. 5, 1920), p. 6.

Warkentin, Heinrich, "Zur Zeit des Bürgerkrieges in der Altkolonie," *Die Mennonitische Rundschau,* Vol. 44, Nos. 31-35 (Aug. 3, 1921, to Aug. 31, 1921).

Willms, Johann H., "Ein Beitrag zur Geschichte der Auswanderungsbewegung. Erinnerungen und Eindrücke," *Der Bote,* Vol. 4, Nos. 6-17 (Feb. 9, 1927, to Apr. 17, 1927).

ANONYMOUS ARTICLES

"Die Wehrlosigkeit unter den Mennoniten Russlands," *Mennonitisches Jahrbuch* (1952), pp. 33-41.

"Kurze Leidensgeschichte der Ljwowschen Tereker Ansiedlung," *Die Mennonitische Rundschau,* Vol. 43, Nos. 39-43 (Sept. 29, 1920, to Oct. 27, 1920).

"Zur Geschichte des Verbandes der Bürger holl. Herkunft in der Ukraine," *Der Bote,* Vol. 3, Nos. 19-21 (May 12, 1925, to May 26, 1925).

"Zur religiösen Lage in Russland," *Mennonitisches Jahrbuch* (1950), pp. 27-34.

DENOMINATIONAL PUBLICATIONS

REPORTS AND TRAVEL ACCOUNTS

Allgeyer, J. R., "Zustände in Russland," *Die Mennonitische Rundschau,* Vol. 43, No. 4 (Jan. 28, 1920), p. 10.

Bärg, Gerhard W., "Unsere Reise von Russland nach Canada," *Die Mennonitische Rundschau*, Vol. 48, No. 22 (June 3, 1925), pp. 23, 24.

Bartsch, H., "Zur Lage an der Molotschna, Südrussland (1923)," *Die Mennonitische Rundschau*, Vol. 47, No. 2 (Jan. 8, 1924), pp. 9, 10.

Bender, H. S., "Hilfswerk der amerikanischen Mennoniten in Russland," *Bericht über die Mennonitische Welt-Hilfs-Konferenz vom 3. August bis 3. September 1930 in Danzig*, pp. 59-64.

Block, Th., "Bericht über das Durchgangslager Lechfeld," *Die Mennonitische Rundschau*, Vol. 48, No. 9 (March 4, 1925), p. 11; *Der Bote*, Vol. 2, No. 7 (Feb. 18, 1925), p. 5.

————, "Bericht über das Durchgangslager Lechfeld (April 20, 1925)," *Die Mennonitische Rundschau*, Vol. 48, No. 20 (May 20, 1925), p. 12; *Der Bote*, Vol. 2, No. 19 (May 13, 1925), p. 5.

————, "Bericht über das Durchgangslager Lechfeld," *Der Bote*, Vol. 2, No. 31 (Aug. 5, 1925).

————, "Der Selbstschutz der Kolonisten Tauriens (1919-1920)," *Die Mennonitische Rundschau*, Vol. 44, No. 39 (Sept. 28, 1921), pp. 12-14, 16; *Mennonitische Blätter*, Vol. 68, Nos. 11, 12 (Nov. to Dec. 1921).

————, "Die Flucht der Molotschnaer Kolonien (10./11. März, 1919)," *Mennonitische Blätter*, Vol. 68, No. 10 (Oct. 1921), pp. 76, 77.

————, "Die Mennoniten und die anarchistische Bewegung in Süd-Russland," *Die Mennonitische Rundschau*, Vol. 43, No. 27 (Sept. 15, 1920), pp. 10, 11.

Boldt, P. J., "Von Sibirien nach Canada," *Die Mennonitische Rundschau*, Vol. 47, Nos. 6, 9, 12 (Feb. 11, 1925, to Mar. 25, 1929).

Braun, P., "Zur Auswanderung der Mennoniten aus Russland," *Der Bote*, Vol. II, No. 5 (Feb. 4, 1925), pp. 5, 6.

Classen, P., "Der Terrorismus der Bolschewiki in Russland," *Die Mennonitische Rundschau*, Vol. 44, Nos. 19, 20 (May 11, 1921, to May 18, 1921).

Doerksen, Franz, "Reisebericht," *Die Mennonitische Rundschau*, Vol. 49, Nos. 14-18 (Apr. 7, 1926, to May 5, 1926).

Dürksen, J., "Aus dem Terekgebiet," *Die Mennonitische Rundschau*, Vol. 43, No. 37 (Sept. 15, 1920), p. 16.

Dyck, A., "Unsere Reise nach Sibirien," *Mennonitische Blätter*, Vol. 71, No. 10 (Oct. 1924), pp. 66-68.

Epp, Dietrich, "Die Lage der Chortitzer Wolost im Januar 1922," *Die Mennonitische Rundschau*, Vol. 45, No. 18 (May 3, 1922), pp. 5, 6.

Epp, P., "Ein paar Gedanken zur Geschichte der Mennoniten in Russland in den letzten zehn Jahren," *Die Mennonitische Rundschau*, Vol. 48, No. 40 (Oct. 7, 1925), pp. 3, 4.

Ewert, J. G., "Die neue Leidenszeit in Südrussland," *Die Mennonitische Rundschau*, Vol. 43, No. 18 (May 5, 1920), p. 11.

Friesen, G., "Einige Tagesnotizen aus der Zeit des Krieges zwischen den Bolschewisten und der Armee General Wrangel im Jahre 1920," *Die Mennonitische Rundschau*, Vol. 47, Nos. 5-13 (Jan. 30, 1924, to Mar. 26, 1924).

Gebhardt, J., "Zur Auswanderungsbewegung unter den Mennoniten," *Der Bote*, Vol. I, No. 39 (Oct. 8, 1924), pp. 5, 6.

Hallman, E. S., "Mennoniten-Auswanderung von Russland nach Canada," *Die Mennonitische Rundschau*, Vol. 47, No. 15 (Apr. 9, 1924), pp. 12, 13.

Hiebert, P. C., "Ein Besuch nach Alt-Samara," *Die Mennonitische Rundschau*, Vol. 45, No. 29 (July 19, 1922), pp. 10, 11.

————, "In dem Hafen von Odessa (March 24, 1922)," *Die Mennonitische Rundschau*, Vol. 45, No. 17 (Apr. 26, 1922), pp. 7, 12.

Hildebrand, J. J., "Die Einwanderungsfrage," *Die Mennonitische Rundschau*, Vol. 47, No. 27 (July 2, 1924), pp. 10, 11.

Horch, M., "Bericht über das Werk der Flüchtlings-Fürsorge in Deutschland (October 11, 1921)," *Die Mennonitische Rundschau*, Vol. 44, No. 49 (Dec. 7, 1921), pp. 3-5.

————, "Die Uebersiedlungsmöglichkeit der mennonitischen Flüchtlinge nach Amerika," *Gemeindeblatt der Mennoniten*, Vol. 54, No. 12 (June 15, 1923), pp. 46, 47.

Janz, B. B., H. Bartel, A. Fast, "Bericht," May 27, 1922. *Die Mennonitische Rundschau*, Vol. 45, No. 30 (July 26, 1922), Beilage, pp. 11, 12.

Janz, B. B., "Bericht der Zentralverwaltung des Verbandes der Bürger holl. Herkunft in der Ukraine zum Congress am 17. bis 19. Februar 1926 in Charkoff," *Der Praktische Landwirt*, Vol. 2, Nos. 3, 4 (Mar. to Apr. 1926), pp. 6-8.

————, "Brudernot und Bruderliebe im zwanzigsten Jahrhundert," *Report of the Sixth All-Mennonite Convention held at Hillsboro, Kansas*, Aug. 28-30, 1937 (n.p., n.d.), pp. 54-62.

————, "Die Grundlage der grossen Auswanderung aus Russland in den 20er Jahren," *Die Mennonitische Rundschau*, Vol. 84, Nos. 35 36 (Aug. 30, 1961, to Sept. 6, 1961).

————, "Regeln für private Ausreise von Mennoniten nach Amerika," *Die Mennonitische Rundschau*, Vol. 47, No. 9 (Feb. 27, 1924), pp. 9, 10.

Janzen, J., "Der Herbst 1922," *Die Mennonitische Rundschau*, Vol. 46, Nos. 7, 8 (Feb. 14, 1923, to Feb. 21, 1923).

————, "Der Hunger," *Die Mennonitische Rundschau*, Vol. 45, Nos. 23-26 (June 7, 1922, to June 28, 1922).

————, "Ostern 1922," *Die Mennonitische Rundschau*, Vol. 45, Nos. 31-33 (Aug. 2, 1922, to Aug. 16, 1922).

Janzen, J. H., "Ein Ritt an die Front," *Die Mennonitische Rundschau*, Vol. 49, Nos. 18-26 (May 5, 1926, to June 30, 1926).

Klassen, A., "Ein Ueberblick über die Ereignisse in Süd-Russland," *Vorwärts*, Vol. 18, No. 31 (July 30, 1920), p. 1.

Klassen, C. F., "Die Lage der russischen Gemeinden seit 1920," *Bericht über die Mennonitische Welt-Hilfs-Konferenz vom 31. August bis 3. September 1930 in Danzig*, pp. 49-58.

Krehbiel, C. E., "Relief Work in Russia," *Report of the Sixth All-Mennonite Convention held at Hillsboro, Kansas*, Aug. 28-30, 1927.

Lepp, A., "Das schreckliche Elend in der Alten Kolonie," *Die Mennonit-*

ische Rundschau, Vol. 43, No. 45 (Nov. 10, 1920), pp. 5-7; *Vorwärts*, Vol. 18, No. 43 (Oct. 22, 1920), pp. 1, 5.

————, "Neueste Nachrichten aus der Altkolonie Chortiza, Ukraine," *Mennonitische Blätter*, Vol. 67, No. 11 (Nov. 1920), pp. 85-87.

Lindemann, K., "Meine Reise durch die deutschen Kolonien Süd-Russlands und der Krim in den Jahren 1919-1921," *Hammer und Pflug. Wochenblatt für die deutschen Kolonisten*, Vol. 2, Nos. 24, 25 (May 31, 1922), pp. 10-16.

Loewen, A., Die Vorbereitungen zur Reise und die Reise der Orenburger Gruppe," *Die Mennonitische Rundschau*, Vol. 49, No. 47 (Nov. 24, 1926), p. 10.

Miller, A. J., "Kurzer Ueberlick der Chortitza Gegenden," *Die Mennonitische Rundschau*, Vol. 45, No. 15 (Apr. 12, 1922), p. 5.

Miller, A. J. and P. F. Fröse, "Unsere Reise in den Süden (19. Februar bis 19. März, 1922)," *Die Mennonitische Rundschau*, Vol. 45, Nos. 27-30 (July 5 to July 26, 1922).

Miller, O. O., "Eine Reise durch Krim und Molotschna. Orie O. Millers Tagebuch vom 6. bis 20. Oktober 1920," *Die Mennonitische Rundschau*, Vol. 43, No. 52 (Dec. 29, 1920), p. 5; Vol. 44, Nos. 1-10 (Jan. 5, 1921, to Mar. 9, 1921).

Nansen, Fridjof, "Das Kinderelend in Russland," *Die Mennonitische Rundschau*, Vol. 47, No. 1 (Jan. 2, 1924), p. 11.

Neff, C. and A. Braun, "Einiges über die Lage unserer Glaubensgeschwister in Russland," *Mennonitische Blätter*, Vol. 71, No. 9 (Sept. 1924), pp. 61, 62.

Neufeld, Herman A., "Die Heimsuchung über unsere Gemeinden in Russland," *Die Mennonitische Rundschau*, Vol. 47, No. 9 (Feb. 27, 1924), pp. 3, 4.

————, "Die Mennoniten Gemeinden in Russland," *Die Mennonitische Rundschau*, Vol. 47, No. 15 (Apr. 15, 1925), p. 7.

Neufeld, J., "Die Schreckenstage in Blumenort, Halbstädter Wollost," *Mennonitische Blätter*, Vol. 67, No. 5 (May 1920), pp. 38, 39.

Neufeld, N. J., "Wanderungen, Atlantic Park," *Unser Blatt*, Vol. 2, No. 10, (July 1927), pp. 305-6.

Peters, J., "Im Jahre 1919," *Die Mennonitische Rundschau*, Vol. 50, No. 35 (Aug. 31, 1927), pp. 8, 9.

Quiring, D. A., "Die Schreckenszeit in dem Dorfe Eichenfeld, Süd-Russland im Oktober 1919," *Die Mennonitische Rundschau*, Vol. 49, Nos. 34-42 (Aug. 25, 1926, to Oct. 20, 1926).

Quiring, Jacob, "Die Mennoniten im Gouvernement Orenburg, Ost-Russland, von Januar bis August 1921," *Die Mennonitische Rundschau*, Vol. 44, Nos. 50-52 (Dec. 14, 1921, to Dec. 28, 1921); Vol. 45, No. 2 (Jan. 11, 1922), pp. 7, 11.

Peters, G. A., "Mennoniten-Wanderungen," *Die Mennonitische Rundschau*, Vol. 49, Nos. 11-14 (Mar. 17, 1926, to Apr. 7, 1926).

Reimer, Aron, "Bericht über Sibirien (May, 1924)," *Die Mennonitische Rundschau*, Vol. 47, Nos. 39-41 (Sept. 24, 1924, to Oct. 8, 1924).

Reimer, H., "Auswanderung und Einwanderung," *Die Mennonitische*

Rundschau, Vol. 49, No. 9 (Mar. 3, 1926), p. 5; No. 10 (Mar. 10, 1926), p. 5.

Reimer, K., "Kurzer Ueberblick über die Tätigkeit der American Mennonite Relief in S.S.S.R.," *Der Praktische Landwirt*, Vol. 1, No. 6 (Nov. 1, 1925), pp. 7-9.

Reimer, Peter, "Die Lage der Zurückgestellten in Southampton, England," *Die Mennonitische Rundschau*, Vol. 49, No. 45 (Nov. 10, 1926), p. 10.

Rempel, A., "Die erste Immigrantengruppe in 1925," *Die Mennonitische Rundschau*, Vol. 48, No. 22 (June 3, 1925), pp. 21, 22.

Rempel, G., "Unsere Reise," *Die Mennonitische Rundschau*, Vol. 47, No. 48 (Nov. 26, 1924) pp. 17-20.

Rempel P., "Ein Ueberblick über die Siedlungsmöglichkeiten für die neu eingewanderten Mennoniten aus Russland," *Die Mennonitische Rundschau*, Vol. 47, No. 5 (Jan. 30, 1924), pp. 10, 11.

Schroeder, G., "Etliches aus der Zeit der Hungersnot 1921-22," *Die Mennonitische Rundschau*, Vol. 46, Nos. 48-52 (Nov. 28, 1923, to Dec. 26, 1923).

Smucker, V., "Hilfswerk-Notizen," *Die Mennonitische Rundschau*, Vol. 45, No. 29 (July 19, 1922), pp. 7, 8.

Teichröb, A. H., "Notizen von unserer Reise aus Russland nach Canada," *Die Mennonitische Rundschau*, Vol. 49, Nos. 28, 29 (July 14 to July 21, 1926).

Thiessen, J., "Warum muss die Auswanderung der Mennoniten fortgesetzt werden?" *Die Mennonitische Rundschau*, Vol. 47, Nos. 9, 11, 12 (Feb. 27, 1924, to Mar. 19, 1924).

————, "Schwalben aus Südrussland," *Die Mennonitische Rundschau*, Vol. 46, No. 17 (Apr. 25, 1923), pp. 8, 9.

Toews, David, "Die Auswanderung aus Russland bis Herbst 1928," *Bericht über die Mennonitische Welt-Hilfs-Konferenz vom 31. August bis 3. September 1930 in Danzig*, pp. 73-79.

————, "Die Auswanderung aus Russland in der Vergangenheit und in der Zukunft," *Der Bote*, Vol. 3, Nos. 46-52 (Nov. 17, 1926, to Dec. 29, 1926); Vol. 4, No. 2 (Jan. 12, 1927).

————, "Ueber die Einwanderungssache," *Die Mennonitische Rundschau*, Vol. 47, No. 2, (Jan. 9, 1924), pp. 6, 7.

————, "Kurzer Reisebericht," *Die Mennonitische Rundschau*, Vol. 49, Nos. 19, 20 (May 12 to May 19, 1926).

————, "Probleme und Bedürfnisse in unserer Immigrationsarbeit," *Die Mennonitische Rundschau*, Vol. 50, No. 34 (Aug. 24, 1927), p. 4.

Unger, H., "Ein paar Worte über die Emigration der ukrainer Mennoniten nach Amerika," *Der Bote*, Vol. 1, Nos. 3, 4, 10 (Jan. 30, 1924, to Feb. 6, 1924, Mar. 19, 1924).

Unruh, B. H., "Abram A. Friesen," *Der Bote*, Vol. 25, Nos. 46, 47 (Nov. 17, 1948, to Nov. 24, 1948).

————, "Die Massenflucht der deutschen Bauern aus der Sowjetunion, ihre Gründe, ihre Auswirkungen in Russland und ihre Folgen für das Hilfswerk im Ausland," *Bericht über die Mennonitische Welt-*

Hilfs-Konferenz vom 31. August bis 3. September 1930 in Danzig, pp. 79-88.

————, "Atlantic Park," *Die Mennonitische Rundschau,* Vol. 50, No. 43 (Oct. 26, 1927), p. 3.

————, "Atlantic Park," *Die Mennonitische Rundschau,* Vol. 50, No. 21 (May 25, 1927), pp. 3, 11.

Wittenberg, J. A., "Ein Situationsgemälde aus dem Territorium des Sibiria District der A.M.R.," *Die Mennontische Rundschau,* Vol. 47, No. 11 (Mar. 12, 1924), pp. 11, 12.

Yoder, H. C., "Allgemeiner Bericht über das amerikanisch-mennonitische Hilfswerk in der Ukraine (August 1, 1923, to July 1, 1924)," *Die Mennonitische Rundschau,* Vol. 47, No. 44 (Oct. 29, 1924), pp. 18-20.

ANONYMOUS REPORTS AND TRAVEL ACCOUNTS

"Aus dem Leben der Chortitzer Mennonitengemeinden während der Kriegszeit," *Mennonitische Blätter,* Vol. 65, No. 7 (July 1918), pp. 50-53.

"Aus der alten Heimat (August 10, 1925)," *Die Mennonitische Rundschau,* Vol. 48, No. 43 (Oct. 28, 1925), pp. 3, 10.

"Auswanderung aus Orenburg," *Der Bote,* Vol. 4, No. 10 (Mar. 9, 1927), pp. 4, 5.

"Benjamin H. Unruh," *Der Bote,* Vol. 28, Nos. 35-38 (Sept. 5, 1951, to Sept. 26, 1951).

"Bericht der Kommission für Kirchenangelegenheiten vom 6. Februar bis zum 20. März 1925," *Der Bote,* Vol. II, No. 26 (July 1, 1925), pp. 5, 6.

"Bericht der KfK vom 21. März bis zum 1. Juni 1925," *Der Bote,* Vol. 2, No. 30 (July 29, 1925), p. 6.

"Bericht der KfK für den Zeitraum vom 1. Juni bis 1. August 1925," *Der Bote,* Vol. II, No. 41 (Oct. 14, 1925), p. 6.

"Bericht der KfK vom 1. August bis 10. Oktober 1925," *Der Bote,* Vol. 2, No. 52 (Dec. 30, 1925), p. 5.

"Bericht der KfK der Mennonitengemeinden SSSR vom 10. Oktober 1925 bis zum 20. Januar 1926," *Der Bote,* Vol. 3, No. 13 (Mar. 31, 1926), p. 6.

"Bericht der KfK von der Altukrainischen Konferenz in Melitopol im Oktober 1926 bis zum 1. März, 1927," *Der Bote,* Vol. 4, No. 18 (May 4, 1927), p. 3.

"Die Einwanderung im Jahre 1925," *Die Mennonitische Rundschau,* Vol. 49, No. 32 (Aug. 11, 1926), p. 10.

"Die Hungersnot in der alten Chortitzer Kolonie nach der Missernte im Jahre 1921," *Die Mennonitische Rundschau,* Vol. 49, Nos. 39, 40, 42 (Sept. 29, 1926, to Oct. 20, 1926).

"Die Leiden unserer Brüder in der Ukraine unter den Bolschewiken," *Mennonitische Blätter,* Vol. 65, No. 6 (June 1918), pp. 44-47.

"Die Mennonitischen Ansiedlungen in Sibirien," *Der Bote,* Vol. I, No. 44 (Nov. 12, 1924), pp. 4, 5.

"Die Mennoniten in der Ukraine nach dem Abzug der deutschen Truppen bis jetzt," *Mennonitische Blätter,* Vol. 67, No. 7 (July 1920), pp. 51-54.

"Die Schreckenstage in Blumenort," *Vorwärts,* Vol. 18, Nos. 30, 31 (July 23, 1920, July 30, 1920).

"Die Schreckenszeit in Chortitza 1919-20," *Die Mennonitische Rundschau,* Vol. 45, No. 15 (Apr. 12, 1922), pp. 6, 7, 12.

"Die Schreckenstage in der Ukraine," *Mennonitische Blätter,* Vol. 65, No. 10 (Oct. 1918), pp. 77, 78.

"Ein Durcheinander vom Atlantic Park," *Der Bote,* Vol. 4, Nos. 15, 16 (Apr. 13 to Apr. 20, 1927).

"Ein Memorandum," *Der Bote,* Vol. 1, No. 2 (Jan. 23, 1924), pp. 3, 4.

"Etwas über die Auswanderungsbewegung in Russland," *Der Bote,* Vol. I, No. 19 (May 21, 1924), p. 4.

"Können die Mennoniten in Russland noch eine freundliche Zukunft erwarten?" *Der Bote,* Vol. 2, Nos. 7-9 (Feb. 18, 1925, to Mar. 25, 1925).

"Liste der am 20. November bis 1. Dezember, 1919 auf Sagradowka, Gouv. Cherson, durch anarchistische Banden Ermordeten," *Vorwärts,* Vol. 18, No. 42 (Oct. 15, 1920), p. 6.

"Neue Hiobsposten aus dem Terekgebiet," *Die Mennonitische Rundschau,* Vol. 43, No. 37 (Sept. 15, 1920), pp. 14, 16.

"Warum wollten und wollen wir auswandern?" *Die Mennonitische Rundschau,* Vol. 47, No. 2 (Jan. 9, 1924), pp. 7, 8.

"Wie die Kolonisten aus der Molotschna nach der Krim flüchteten," *Die Mennonitische Rundschau,* Vol. 43, No. 29 (July 21, 1920), pp. 7, 10.

"Wird es in Russland besser?" *Die Mennonitische Rundschau,* Vol. 49, No. 46 (Nov. 17, 1926), pp. 3, 4.

"Zu dem Aufsatz 'Atlantic Park,'" *Die Mennonitische Rundschau,* Vol. 50, No. 13 (Mar. 30, 1927), p. 4.

"Zur Auswanderungsbewegung in der Ukraine," *Der Bote,* Vol. 3, No. 18 (May 5, 1925), p. 6.

"Zur Aus- und Einwanderung," *Der Bote,* Vol. 1, Nos. 37, 38 (Sept. 24, 1924, Oct. 1, 1924).

"Zur Einwanderung 1927," *Die Mennonitische Rundschau,* Vol. 50, No. 5 (Feb. 2, 1927), p. 7.

"Zur Zeit des Bürgerkrieges in der Altkolonie Chortitza," *Mennonitische Blätter,* Vol. 68, No. 7 (July 1921), pp. 54-56; No. 8 (Aug. 1921), pp. 61-64.

"Zustände in Sibirien," *Mennonitische Blätter,* Vol. 65, No. 7 (July 1918), pp. 53-55.

PRINTED MINUTES

"Beschlüsse der sibirischen Mennoniten vom 12. Juli 1920," *Die Mennonitische Rundschau,* Vol. 44, No. 29 (July 20, 1921), p. 12; *Mennonitischer Blätter,* Vol. 68, No. 6 (June 1921), pp. 45, 46.

"Der Congress der Bürger holl. Herkunft in der Ukraine, Grigorjewka vom 25.-28. Februar, 1925," *Der Bote,* Vol 2, Nos. 21-24 (May 27 to June 17, 1925).

"Protokoll der Allukrainischen Konferenz der Vertreter der Mennoniten-gemeinden in der USSR in Melitopol vom 5.-9. Oktober 1926," *Unser Blatt,* Vol. 2, No. 2 (Nov. 1926), pp. 47-51.
"Protokoll der Bundeskonferenz der Mennonitengemeinden Russlands vom 13.-18. Januar 1925 in Moskau," *Die Mennonitische Rund-schau,* Vol. 48, No. 13 (Apr. 1, 1925), pp. 5, 8, 9; *Gemeindeblatt der Mennoniten,* Vol. 56, No. 6 (Mar. 1925), pp. 35, 36.
"Protokoll des Allukrainischen Kongresses des Verbandes der Bürger holländischer Herkunft in der Ukraine vom 17. bis 20. Februar 1926 in Charkoff," *Der Praktische Landwirt,* Vol. 2, Nos. 3, 4 (Mar. to Apr. 1926), pp, 8-16.

ENCYCLOPEDIA ARTICLES

Froese, P. F., "Allrussischer Mennonitischer Landwirtschaftlicher Verein," *Mennonite Encyclopedia* (Hillsboro, Newton, Scottdale, 1955), Vol. I, pp. 62, 63.
Hiebert, P. C., "Mennonite Central Committee," *Mennonitisches Lexikon,* Vol. III (Frankfurt a. M., 1939), pp. 97-99.

UNPUBLISHED DISSERTATIONS

Friesen, A., "Emigration in Mennonite History," unpublished MA thesis, University of Manitoba.
Rempel, David G., "The Mennonite Colonies in New Russia. A Study of the Settlement and Economic Development from 1789 to 1914," unpublished doctoral thesis, Stanford University, 1933.

PAMPHLETS

Peters, G. A., "Wehrlos?" (Scottdale, Pa., and Winnipeg, Man., n.d.).
Woelinga, D., "Nood van en hulp aan de Mennisten van Rusland 1920-1921." Reprint from the Doopsgezind Jaarboekje 1922 (Assen, L. Hansma, 1922).

UNPUBLISHED MANUSCRIPTS
GENERAL
Dyck, J. J., Aufzeichnungen über die mennonitische Ansiedlung "Am Trakt" Gouvernement Samara, später "Republick der Wolga-deutschen" von 1914-1929. Fost Koepental, Russland (ms. in Bethel College Historical Library).
Miller, O. O., Personal Diary of Orie O. Miller covering his trip into the Mennonite communities of South Russia, Oct. 6-20, 1920 (ms. in Bethel College Historical Library).
Neufeld, Jacob, Erinnerungen eines Beteiligten des "Verbandes der Bürger Holländischer Herkunft in der Ukraine" (ms. in Bethel College Historical Library, Newton, Kan.).
Unruh, B. H., Zum Verständnis der Russischen Revolution: Ein Beitrag zur Klärung des Auswanderungsproblems (ms. in Bethel College Historical Library).
Willms, J. H., Politisches Geschehen an der Molotschna von Februar 1917 an. (ms. in possession of the author).

SIGNIFICANT MATERIAL IN COLLECTIONS

1. C. E. KREHBIEL ARCHIV (Bethel College Historical Library, Newton, Kan.)
"Bericht der Nicopoler Mennoniten an die Vertretung der AMR in Alexandrovsk," Dec. 13, 1922. (File 46)
Slagel A. W., "Bericht über die Arbeit der amerikanischen mennonitischen Hilfe in der Ukraine im Jahre 1922." (File 46)
Bärg, P., to B. B. Janz, "Chortitza," July 19, 1922. (File 47)
2. B. B. JANZ ARCHIVE (Mennonite Brethren College of Arts, Winnipeg)
"Die Gründung des Verbandes in Alexanderwohl." (I,c)
"Die Wehrlosigkeit der Mennoniten in Russland nach dem ersten Weltkriege." (I,c)
Froese, P. F., "Wie entstand der Allrussische Mennonitische Landwirtschaftliche Verein?"
B. B. Janz Memoirs,
  "Das Statut."
  "Die Reise nach Moskau."
  "Die Rückreise von Moskau."
  "Eine Mai-Feier im Sovietlande."
  "Soldaten und Kassenpassagiere."
  "Wieder das Statut."
  "Zeit-Tafel für die Zeit des ersten Weltkrieges 1914 bis 1926."
  "Zweite Reise nach Moscow."
  "Zweite Reise nach Moskau."
3. A. A. FRIESEN ARCHIVE (Bethel College Historical Library, Newton, Kan.)
"Bittgesuche an das All-Ukrainische Zentrale Executiv-Komitee. December 17, 1921."
Ens, H., J. Klassen, and others, "Denkschrift zur Frage über die Auswanderung der russländischen Mennoniten." Chortitza, July 1922.
Friesen, A. A., Betrachtungen über die gegenwärtige Lage der Mennoniten in Russland und die Aussichten für eine Auswanderung, June 25, 1921.
Froese, P. F., "Durch die mennonitischen Dörfer in Sibirien." Moscow, Aug. 1924.
Janz, H., "Warum ich auswandere." Halbstadt, June 21, 1922.
Janzen, J., "Meine principielle Stellung zur Auswanderungsfrage." Tiege, June 22, 1922.
Klassen, C. F., F. Isaak, and P. F. Froese, "Bericht über die Entstehung des Allrussischen Mennonitischen Landwirtschaftlichen Verbandes." May 21, 1923.
"Schematischer Ueberblick über den wirtschaftlichen Niedergang der mennonitischen Kolonien des Chortitzer Gebiets."
"Statuten des Verbandes der Bürger holländischer Herkunft in der Ukraine."
Wiens, K., "Zur Auswanderungsfrage der Mennoniten." Neu-Halbstadt, June 20, 1922.
4. CMRIC ARCHIVE (Canadian Mennonite Bible College, Winnipeg, Man.)

Klassen, J. P., "So kam es zur Auswanderung."

Rempel, J. G., "Die Auswanderung 1923."

Unruh, B. H., "Fügung und Führung im Mennonitischen Welt-Hilfs-
werk, 1920-23: Streiflichter in persönlicher und dienstlicher
Rückschau."

5. F. F. ISAAK PAPERS (C. A. DeFehr, Sr., Winnipeg, Man.)

Fast, A. J., "Denkschrift zum Wiederaufbau der mennonitischen Kolonien in Russland." Berlin-Lichterfelde, Jan. 22, 1923.

RUSSIAN NEWSPAPER ARTICLES (TITLES TRANSLATED)

"A Good Lesson," *The Red Star*. Ekaterinoslav (Nov. 16, 1924).

Mossenko, F., "Hollanders," *Visti*. Kharkov, No. 182 (Aug. 12, 1925).

Petrovski, G., "Mennonites in the Ukraine," *Communist*. Kharkov, No. 141
(June 22, 1924).

"Toward Improving the Lot of the Colonists in the Ukraine," *Die Arbeit*.
Moscow, No. 18 (Aug. 15, 1924).

Unger, H., "A Few Words About the Emigration of the Ukrainian Mennonites to America," *Die Arbeit*. Moscow, No. 20 (Sept. 15, 1923).

"Who Are the Mennonites?" *Communist*, Kharkov (July 22, 1922).

INDEX